THE ETERNAL FOUNTAIN of YOUTH

(Youth's Revolution)

by
Thomas Peace

First published by Dog Ear Publishing
4010 W. 86th Street, Ste H
Indianapolis, IN 46268
www.dogearpublishing.net

dog ear PUBLISHING

ISBN: 978-1-4575-1264-3

This book is printed on acid-free paper.

Printed in the United States of America

This book is dedicated to Gerald; he will be my friend for eternity. It is also dedicated to my wonderful wife, who puts up with all the critters and my late night writing.

Mortality is fatal, –
Gentility is fine,
Rascality, heroic,
Insolvency, sublime!

(Excerpt from Emily Dickinson)

Brief Introductory Comment:

The author of this book would like to indicate here that the poems and works by others, within this book, were selected by him (i.e., by this author himself) and may have no correlation or connection with the author's views whatsoever, (other than the author himself having an affinity for them as a possible aid for explaining).

The poet Wallace Stevens once stated: "...Things that have their origin in the imagination or in the emotions very often take on a form that is ambiguous or uncertain. It is not possible to attach a single, rational meaning to such things without destroying the imaginative or emotional ambiguity or uncertainty that is inherent in them and that is why poets do not like to explain. That the meanings given by others are sometimes meanings not intended by the poet or that were never present in his mind does not impair them as meanings."

Replacement Poem
for P. 116:

from Emily Dickinson:

On this wondrous sea
Sailing silently,
Ho! Pilot, ho!

Knowest thou the shore
Where no breakers roar—
Where the storm is o'er?

In the peaceful west
Many the sails at rest—
The anchors fast—
Thither I pilot thee—
Land Ho! Eternity!
Ashore at last!

Preface

Most of us are used to (i.e., accustomed to) existing with what is "possible," and, for most of us, what is possible is rather ordinary and mundane. Is it possible, or impossible, for a mere book to provide an irrefutable mystery, a mystery that boldly presents eternity to humanity?

"Creating a mystery out of nothing would be a most blackguardly thing to do because that would be exploiting people and ruthless—that's a dirty trick. Either one creates a mystery when there isn't one, or there is a mystery which you have to approach with extraordinary delicacy and hesitancy, and, you know, tentativeness." — (excerpt from J. Krishnamurti)

Anyone who reads *The Eternal Fountain of Youth — (Youth's Revolution),* with an open mind, is bound to get a substantial glimpse of the profound mystery that it emanates. The legendary fountain of youth is a spring that reputedly restores the youth of whoever drinks from its waters. If you objectively read the book from beginning to end, you definitely will get a taste of mystery and a taste of what supersedes death and ending. (In an indirect way, it may be like drinking directly from the Grail cup itself.)

We need to change the world for the better. It is a profound responsibility that each one of us shares. *Changing for the better* may not involve wallowing in the same-old, worn-out traditions that we have stagnated in before. At first, the book will seem rather deep and a bit difficult, but keep diligently reading; then, a profound metamorphosis will occur. Throughout the first half of the book, a certain degree of necessary repetitiveness is utilized, to remind the superficial layers of the mind about how extensively restricted and reactionary they are and how one must look with what perceives much deeper. If you are afraid to look at life, consciousness, religion, society, and time in wholly new ways, then do not read the book. (If you do not cherish the essence of life as it is, please do not read the book.) The book involves real and profound change. What real change entails may be a tremendous shock to our systems. However, we cannot go on as we have in the barbaric past; to do so would be terminal.

——Thank you, Thomas Peace

Chapter 1

If it is not the riddle and the untying of the riddle, then it is nothing.

This book is for the youth of the world. It has been written with college, high school, grade school, and chronologically younger individuals in mind, although anyone with a healthy, youthful oriented mind may indeed benefit from it immensely. This book is about breaking all the rules. It is not about breaking all the rules in a manner involving conflict, violence, physical destruction, retributive riots, and such. Conflict, violence, and physical destruction are the "old fashioned," worn-out, adult, *dead* ways of doing things; such actions are antiquated, primitive, and barbaric.

This book promotes real change. It is not merely what alters and redirects the old, adult, antiquated patterns that are already out there. So, if you are not merely a complacent coward, afraid of new things and of change, fasten your seat-belt and read on. It is not going to be what you expect at all. Most likely, the reader would probably like to know the age of the author of this zestful book regarding "youthful revolution." The author of this book is 60 years old and is retired from being a teacher for the multiply handicapped. Do not let my age fool you, however. There is a very good chance that my mind has remained young and bubbling with spirited life, though the body has aged. Most assuredly, I am not one of the regular adults by any means whatsoever. My mind is not merely as theirs is. The author's mind is not something that merely contains the old, worn-out ideas of former elderly authorities. The author learned, early on, to keep his cup empty, not to let it be filled with the stale, archaic ideas and limited perspectives of others. Once one is blessed by what is not merely the small and limited, one does not easily succumb to the chains of control and the obstruction that comes with shallow and superficial mental frameworks.

When I was very young, I looked for the wise, splendid, sagacious entity who would tell me the secrets of life, who would explain life's deep mysteries. There wasn't anyone. There was no wise man to guide me and to help me along the way. I had the misfortune — which was truly fortunate in the long run — of having parents who were both very unstable and unbalanced. They would fight a lot (often chronically swearing at each other and at myself with words of hatred and deep scorn). Unfortunately, they would do innumerable other crazy things, including (my father) severely beating me and psychologically torturing my mother (for instance, often calling her a "whore"), and (my mother) frequently and repeatedly asking me (as a child) to talk her out of committing suicide. I had observed my father starting my mother's hair on fire; hair burns rapidly, I unfortunately found out. Additionally, while in grade school, a fair number of the teachers that I had were rather "off the beam" and were unstable and rather neurotic themselves; the nuns within the parochial school, where I grew up, would severely strike us with rulers and yardsticks, in quite cruel ways. (They were like the nuns in the Blues Brothers' movie, only they were much crueler.) So, early on, I became very independent and autonomous. I eventually realized that adults got most everything wrong; they (the adults) had accepted basic tenets and principles about life that were, in actuality, probably erroneous and dead (i.e., un-alive).

Many of us, as youth, have relatively stable parents, and these parents (and teachers), for the most part, are usually accepted as being good authority and dependable guidance. We then absorb what they provide and end up mimicking them and emulating them. Of course, in later youth, we often go through a stage of rebelling, wherein we try to become more independent and mature without them. However, for the most part, we have absorbed all the basic values from them, and most of us end up being essentially just like them. We grow out of childhood… and end up becoming primarily what they are, though we think that we are quite independent and unique. To be truly independent and unique is an arduous thing; but it can be effortless once significant things about life are realized. Merely absorbing the old-fashioned forms and patterns of others may not be, in actuality, truly what living is. Most people assume that they, themselves, are living; they may not be. Merely being one series of reactions after another may not truly be "living"; being residual after-effects (i.e., reactions) may not be what profound living is whatsoever. Many are, unfortunately, dead-from-the-neck-up, and they are not anywhere near being six feet under.

When I was a teacher for the multiply handicapped, I had, as one of my students, a fellow who happened to be quadriplegic; he, very unfortunately, could not control his arms or legs. He was unable to talk or eat; he received his nutrition via a gastrostomy tube, which entered into his stomach area. (My wife currently uses a gastrostomy tube for much of her nutrition, by the way, because she had intensive neck surgery with many, very unfortunate complications; she has been using a gastrostomy tube for quite some time now. She, unlike most of us, has a very heavy cross to bear regarding serious health issues.) The student, whom I am referring to, went by the name of Gerald. Gerald, unlike the other individuals within my classroom, was not significantly mentally handicapped. Gerald was extremely intelligent in many ways. Gerald would easily communicate, by smiling for "yes" and by shaking his head back and forth for "no." Gerald would often remain (or "hang out") with me, after class, and we would have some excellent discussions concerning truth, self-understanding, and perception. Though limited in his ability to communicate, Gerald would readily indicate his deep understanding and keen insight. He was extremely happy most all the time, and I would see ordinary, bourgeois businesspersons with sad, sullen looks on their faces, walking in town with their briefcases; unlike them, Gerald had a glowing smile and a keen, perceptive mind. Gerald taught me as much as I taught him. His joy with life was contagious. He lived simply, without many complicated desires. He, much like my amazing wife, never wasted time expressing pity for his condition involving suffering. He was too busy enjoying each precious moment. His passionate nature (i.e., he loved people) and glowing smiles were, indeed, blessedly infectious. If he can do it, most all of us can. We can all learn a lot from people like Gerald; he will be greatly missed.

Gerald has passed away. However, he and I shared some penetrating insights concerning the nature of life and eternity. There is a very good chance that Gerald had more penetrating insights and deeper joy than did many so-called normal individuals. I am so very glad that we shared some special time and some special secrets together.

As I had done with Gerald, I would very much enjoy sharing some of these secrets with you. Please do not misuse them; they are so very easily misused and abused by those without a lot of heart. Like with Gerald, I am not merely your teacher. What I share with you is just the tip of the iceberg. There is a lot more to learn (if you can perceive with profound depth); that will be up to you… and you alone. No one can take you there. True wisdom (which profoundly contains love) cannot merely be given by way of teaching or other processes. This book is about thinking and existing for yourself as a child of wisdom, away from the corruption and lack of understanding that most adults have provided by way of their teachings, which have often been harmful. This book is about looking at everything with fresh eyes, away from the merely calculating influence of elders who were themselves programmed to think and act in certain robotic, mechanical, specific, (and often selfish) ways. If one is content merely to grow up to become another puppet on a string — doing what you (like a robot) were programmed to do — then this book is not for you. If one wants a mind that is composed of "their" thoughts, of "their" patterns of looking at things, of "their" way of reacting to things, then this book may not be for you. It is easy merely to do as you are told.

It is easy merely to become what you were programmed to become. Most adults are calculating; they want you to become what they have decided you should become... which, interestingly and unfortunately enough, is often not so separate from what their so-called teachers and elders decided they should become. It may be a vicious circle; it may be very easy and comfortable merely to stay within the boundaries of that circle. This book, however, is not for those youth who would prefer just to fit into the prefabricated mold that was prepared for them. This book is for those who dare to go beyond the confines of the well-established "known"; it is for those who dare to venture out into (and "as") the *unknown*. The *unknown* is beautiful; it is not (as you were taught) something to be frightened of. However, do not be misled into thinking that this book is merely a revolt against authority. To merely revolt against authority may be to create more friction, more ignorance, more hatred, more uncaring turmoil, and more of the same garbage of before, which would, in reality, just be the continuation of the same-old ways of before. No, this book is for those who care (and dare) to die (mentally, not physically) to all of that trash. Life is not a lot of stale ideas; it is what nature's harmony and what vibrant blossoming exists as. One may, in one day, learn more by silently sitting in one's living, sun-lit back-yard, or by placidly sitting in one's local natural park or forest preserve, than by sitting in a confining classroom with a stale, conditioned, dead-from-the-neck-up, so-called instructor. When I was physically young, I spent a great deal of time outdoors. I still spend a lot of time outdoors with mother-earth and with all the splendid creatures that are her children. (By the way, we are not advocating dropping out of school; dropping out of school would be foolish!)

from Walt Whitman:

Now I see the secret of the making of the best persons,
It is to grow in the open air and to eat and sleep with the earth.
Here a great personal deed has room,
(Such a deed seizes upon the hearts of the whole race of men,
Its effusion of strength and will overwhelms law and mocks all
authority and all argument against it.)
Here is the test of wisdom,
Wisdom is not finally tested in schools,
Wisdom cannot be pass'd from one having it to another not
having it,
Wisdom is of the soul, is not susceptible of proof, is its own
proof,
Applies to all stages and objects and qualities and is content,
Is the certainty of the reality and immortality of things, and
the excellence of things;
Something there is in the float of the sight of things that
provokes it out of the soul.
Now I re-examine philosophies and religions,
They may prove well in lecture-rooms, yet not prove at all
under the spacious clouds and along the
landscape and flowing currents.
Here is realization,
Here is a man tallied—he realizes here what he has in him,
The past, the future, majesty, love—if they are vacant of you,
you are vacant of them.

One of the easiest things to do, as a human being, is to imitate others: to do just as they do. It is very good to imitate and to learn certain things — this helps us to function better — but it may be that most of us tend to overdo the imitating, letting it interfere with the way we act and perceive. Therefore, instead of acting directly, many of us are just reacting. We are merely like *machines*; we respond in pre-programmed, pre-arranged ways, just becoming the results expected. Alternatively, if we rebel, our rebellion is merely an over-reaction in the opposite direction, which may just be an extension of what we were programmed to be, but in a somewhat different pattern considered unacceptable, (but still really the same-old thing). Such a rebellion may not truly be much of a rebellion at all! Actually, to be truly revolutionary, one may need a free, non-tethered mind that understands when authority sneaks into the mind, masquerading as one's own supposedly free decisions. [The famous poet, E. E. Cummings, once had written (and I quote, just as he had written it): "when Americans stop being themselves they start behaving each other."] (One can wisely suspect that what Cummings might really be saying is "When Americans stop being themselves, they start behaving like each other.")

It is very easy merely to belong to a group and to follow someone else. That seems like a safe way to exist. Many elderly people, indeed, do have helpful things to teach us concerning how to do things to survive more safely and healthfully. However, their teachings and suggestions about surviving (in life)... may extend much too far. In trying to get their children to be successful, they may be (like their parents before them) teaching things to youth that are not at all true. They may be providing things that are designed to make youth turn into something that they (the elders) were taught to be, maybe even to be something *that succeeds apart from "others,"* or even (perhaps) at the *expense of so-called "others."* It may be that to merely become what one was taught to become makes one become much like a ball in a pool (billiards) game or pinball game; the ball is basically pushed around and reacts in a second-hand way and is not calling the shots at all. Unfortunately, all too often, many people, especially adults, think that they are independently "calling the shots" and making, on their own, important decisions on things — while all the while they are merely doing what they were taught or instructed to do — which is mechanically reacting in programmed ways that are, in reality, second-hand. Second-hand clothes may be, in actuality, very nice. However, a second-hand consciousness, that is full of mere reactions that were implanted in it, may not at all be very wonderful.

from Stephen Crane:

A learned man came to me once.
He said, "I know the way, —come."
And I was overjoyed at this;

Together we hastened.
Soon, too soon, were we
Where my eyes were useless,
And I knew not the ways of my feet.
I clung to the hand of my friend;
But at last he cried, "I am lost."

Be very careful; it is very easy to come to conclusions and to sully the mind with all kinds of preconceptions. It may be very easy to look at life through a screen (in the mind) that filters out much of what is really there and, instead, lets us see what we were merely taught and programmed to see. Perhaps that is why many people, especially older people, live in such sorrow; they merely look from the "dead known" at the "living now." They, therefore, never actually perceive the "living *now*." They cling to and radiate from dead ideas, of the past, that are not dynamically alive in the "here and now." Their ideas are from and of the past... and, with these worn out, rather shoddy, cobweb ideas, they try to look at life. However, such a "looking" may not be looking at life, because it may be that life cannot be seen by dead, worn-out images from (and of) the past.

This may be why people who easily come to conclusions, about everything all of the time, are often very sorrowful, sad people. They are full of old, worn-out images that are mostly just symbols. How can mere symbols be what is truly happy? Not being intrinsically happy, they easily project their sorrow, by "picking on" and belittling others. Therefore, it may be wise to continually examine and enjoy life without merely coming to conclusions all the time, without merely labeling everything with dead, symbolic words and images. A truly happy individual may exist without always trying to accumulate. A truly happy individual may exist without always trying to categorize everything to fit into neat little caverns of knowledge and thought. The map is not the reality. Thoughts are symbols, and symbols are not what reality is. The word "horse" is not a real, warm-blooded mammal that you can hug.

It is easy to take symbolic representations (which are what "thoughts" actually are) and accept them wholeheartedly as being realities. However, symbols (via the "thinking" process) are always rather dead tokens of what the true, living cosmos consists of. These representative images, usually occurring either in a pictorial or auditory form, are fabricated by the mind to *stand for things* that we can use to *function better*. However, are we *functioning better* if we forget that our symbolic representations are not the reality? They are merely *symbols* that we correctly or incorrectly fabricate about what the reality may consist of; and we are often merely "taught" what that reality consists of. However, most of us dwell mentally as these symbols most of the time, rarely, if ever, going beyond them. Are we substituting a *learned and provided fiction* for a *much deeper reality*?

Therefore, be very careful. It may be best to question everything wisely and to look at life, not from dead conclusions, not from the way others have instructed us to look, not look, perhaps, from mere words and separating images, but in a totally new, fresh way! Please, be very careful: because we can think that we are looking in a fresh and new way… when, in reality, we are not.

from Stephen Crane:

The wayfarer,
Perceiving the pathway to truth,
Was struck with astonishment.
It was thickly grown with weeds.
"Ha," he said,
"I see that none has passed here
"In a long time."
Later he saw that each weed
Was a singular knife.
"Well," he mumbled at last,
"Doubtless there are other roads."

If one merely grasps at the things in life that one was taught to grasp at, it may very well be that one will be groping for very superficial, rather meaningless things and possessions that, in the end, do not make one whole and happy. Unfortunately, it may be that most of those who were teaching us were, themselves, taught wrongly. They, in themselves, may not at all be truly happy in the deepest sense; however, they teach us in exactly the same ways in which they were taught. They do not invite us to question everything with deep passion. They do not ask us to find out for ourselves anew. They do not tell us not to follow anyone. They do not suggest that we need not belong to separative groups, countries, establishments, sects, and institutions, which merely divide people from each other, which merely add to the conflict and separation of people. They do, however, teach us to grope after specialized positions in life... so that we can succeed in what they consider important. They do invite us to merely grasp after ordinary detailed possessions (i.e., plentiful monetary rewards), which are supposedly going to keep us happy. Money is important; but it is not what is most important.

Very few of them suggest to us that it is a petty, little mind that merely depends upon experience for its happiness. Very few of them suggest that merely existing within (and as) the realm of "thinking" may cause us to merely look at life with what may be equivalent to mere shadows within *a deeper reality that is beyond a mere shadow-like existence.* Very few of them suggest that we can go beyond mere "representational, mental symbol forming." Very few of them suggest that we are not separate from the whole of the universe. Very few of them suggest that we can thoughtfully help others who are not separate from us, just as the right hand is not separate from the left arm. Very few of them suggest that there is a place for thought and thinking, (and a place for when thought and thinking need not take place at all). Very few of them suggest that we can be most joyous without ruthless competition, without clinging to endless awards, without merely existing as a bunch of pre-programmed thoughts (as reactions to things).

from Walt Whitman:

Thought

Of persons arrived at high positions, ceremonies, wealth,
scholarships, and the like;
(To me all that those persons have arrived at sinks away from
them, except as it results to their bodies and
souls,
So that often to me they appear gaunt and naked,
And often to me each one mocks the others, and mocks
himself or herself,
And of each one the core of life, namely happiness, is full of
the rotten excrement of maggots,
And often to me those men and women pass unwittingly the
true realities of life, and go toward false
realities,
And often to me they are alive after what custom has served
them, but nothing more,
And often to me they are sad, hasty, unwaked somnambules
walking the dusk.)

The wisest thing — without merely being influenced by others — that a male or a female can do, may be to understand the instrument of the whole mind. The mind, which can deeply understand, is not at all separate from what the true order of the universe (i.e., cosmos) consists of. Such a mind may be what exists in deep harmony and deep order; therefore, it would not easily consist of sorrow or remorse; therefore, it would not merely be, in ignorance, destroying many things. Such a mind would be straight and not crooked. It would not be fooled by absurd traditions, beliefs, customs, and practices handed down to it from the primitive past. Such a mind would stand alone and would be free of much of the disharmony that most people partake in and become.

People who merely follow others — who merely go to institutions to become what they are molded to become — often turn out to be like collective *leaves* blown by the wind. When the wind stops, they tumble down and have no movement of their own. So do not depend on anyone or anything, including this book, to find out what the truth is. One must look deep within, without being deeply influenced, and one may find that the self that one looks into... is vastly composed of what others have made it to be; so it is the product of the others. It, in fact, may be the very movement of the others. Therefore, let it stop, in silence, and function without merely being what was fabricated and constructed by others. In deep stillness, which is not what is merely constructed by any special technique or method, the pure *bliss* of deep insight and the secret wisdom of eternity may occur to the mind that is truly blessed.

from Walt Whitman:

Have you reckon'd a thousand acres much? Have you reckon'd the earth much? Have you practis'd so long to learn to read? Have you felt so proud to get at the meaning of poems?

Stop this day and night with me and you shall possess the origin of all poems, You shall possess the good of the earth and sun, (there are millions of suns left,) You shall no longer take things at second or third hand, nor look through the eyes of the dead, nor feed on the spectres in books,

You shall not look through my eyes either, nor take things from me,

You shall listen to all sides and filter them from your self.

How does one look at things? Need one always look with a separation between the so-called *perceiver* and *what is perceived*? If the perception of a beautiful sunset helps constitute what my mind consists of, then are the perceptions of such a sunset really all that separate from what I am? (Are such perceptions separate from what the mind actually is?) Not to say that when one looks toward the sun... one, as a person, is actually made up of solar flares. However, when one does look at something, doesn't the image (or the attributes, which make up that thing) help to compose what consciousness actually is? When a red rose is being looked at, for example, is not the mind made up of the color red? Do not the shapes of the petals and the surrounding scenery, etc., help make up one's inner mental visual patterns and mental framework? Without things to perceive, what would the mind be? Could the mind exist without being full of images that it perceives, and could it exist without things to think about? Does the mind necessarily need to be thinking ideas in order to exist as it is? Can the mind let go of images, patterns to analyze, things to consider, and symbols (called words) to spin around within (or "as") itself? Moreover, can the mind just exist without mentally engaging in the "juggling of things around" all of the time? Actually, who is the juggler? Is he truly so very separate or different from *the juggled*?

Probably most people would laugh and call me a fool, if I told them that I truly feel that I am the images of the things around me, which are perceived; I am not some entity apart from the images. The images, which are perceived, make up my consciousness. My consciousness is what I am; it (i.e., consciousness) is what the brain consists of. Those who believe in lies seldom have an opportunity to see the truth behind everything. Most people, unfortunately, remain apart from the truth. It may be that, unfortunately, most people do not even realize that what they *perceive* is not so very separate from what they *are*. When a woman sees and likes a certain kind of horse-drawn carriage, is not her mind constituted and made-up of images of that carriage? We were taught that we are so very separate from the things and patterns that we see; but the patterns and images that we see actually help to make and shape the minds of the persons seeing them and taking them in. Actually, one is not so very separate from that which one sees. One is not so very separate from the ideas and images in one's head. When one looks at something with distance between the "looker" and the "thing looked at," the very distance that is perceived is part of the mind that perceives it. Therefore, the distance actually helps compose and make up what the mind is, and the distance does not merely function to keep one truly separate from what is perceived. Therefore, it may very well be that the *image* of what *is perceived* is what consciousness is. Thus, a boy, who is looking at trees, has (and "is") a consciousness (i.e., a mind) that consists of the patterns and colors of branches and leaves.

from Walt Whitman:

There Was A Child Went Forth

There was a child went forth every day;
And the first object he look'd upon, that object he became;
And that object became part of him for the day, or a certain part of
the day, or for many years, or stretching cycles of years.

The early lilacs became part of this child,
And grass, and white and red morning-glories, and white and red clover, and the song of the phoebe-bird,

And the Third-month lambs, and the sow's pink-faint litter, and the mare's foal, and the cow's calf,
And the noisy brood of the barn-yard, or by the mire of the pond-side,
And the fish suspending themselves so curiously below there—and the beautiful curious liquid,
And the water-plants with their graceful flat heads—all became part of him.

The field-sprouts of Fourth-month and Fifth-month became part of him;
Winter-grain sprouts, and those of the light-yellow corn, and the esculent roots of the garden,
And the apple-trees cover'd with blossoms, and the fruit afterward,
and wood-berries, and the commonest weeds by the road;
And the old drunkard staggering home from the out-house of the tavern, whence he had lately risen,
And the school-mistress that pass'd on her way to the school,

And the friendly boys that pass'd — and the quarrelsome boys,
And the tidy and fresh-cheek'd girls — and the barefoot negro boy and girl,
And all the changes of city and country, wherever he went.

His own parents,
He that had father'd him, and she that had conceiv'd him in her womb, and birth'd him,

They gave this child more of themselves than that;
They gave him afterward every day—they became part of him.

The mother at home, quietly placing the dishes on the supper-table;
The mother with mild words—clean her cap and gown, a wholesome odor
falling off her person and clothes as she walks by;
The father, strong, self-sufficient, manly, mean, anger'd, unjust;
The blow, the quick loud word, the tight bargain, the crafty lure,
The family usages, the language, the company, the furniture—the yearning and swelling heart,
Affection that will not be gainsay'd—the sense of what is real—the thought if, after all, it should prove unreal,
The doubts of day-time and the doubts of night-time—the curious whether and how,
Whether that which appears so is so, or is it all flashes and specks?
Men and women crowding fast in the streets—if they are not flashes and specks, what are they?
The streets themselves, and the façades of houses, and goods in the windows,

Vehicles, teams, the heavy-plank'd wharves—the huge crossing at the ferries,

The village on the highland, seen from afar at sunset—the river between,

Shadows, aureola and mist, the light falling on roofs and gables of white or brown, three miles off,

The schooner nearby, sleepily dropping down the tide—the little boat slack-tow'd astern,

The hurrying tumbling waves, quick-broken crests, slapping,

The strata of color'd clouds, the long bar of maroon-tint, away

solitary by itself—the spread of purity it lies motionless in,

The horizon's edge, the flying sea-crow, the fragrance of salt marsh and shore mud;

These became part of that child who went forth every day, and who now goes, and will always go forth every day.

Chapter 2

It may be that a mind that is twisted and crooked will inevitably have to look at things through a screen of distortion. Such a mind is incapable of seeing the wholeness of everything; such a mind is not likely to see the truth. Not only will a twisted and crooked mind cause much suffering in others, but also such a twisted mind is, in itself, suffering. A twisted, distorted mind is not of a stable and free happiness. A twisted and crooked mind is, unfortunately, not blissful; a twisted and distorted mind needs unceasing forms of stimulation. It is a distorted mind that craves for an excess of ordinary things that appear to it at a distance; so it constantly needs many things that it thinks are "out there," away from "itself." However, the *images* within it, which constitute the things that it craves, are not truly separate from what it is. So it may enthusiastically crave for many unnecessary things, which are fabricated as desirable; and *things desired* constitute what it actually is composed of. Its barren, symbolic thoughts (about things wanted) are not merely what it creates... but, instead, they are what it actually is. Moreover, it is afraid to go to where thought and thinking do not exist. It is the "learned known" that is afraid (like an overly frightened rabbit) of the "unknown." It cannot look without thought... because "thought and thinking" is practically the entire *essence* of what it is composed of; and it wants sluggishly to remain in the norm or in the stratagem of normalcy, where it lazily will not have to understand about how to be truly revolutionary in the deepest sense. It is afraid to psychologically die to *barren thinking*, and it is simultaneously afraid to exist as what are not mere reactions, symbols, images, patterns, and residual sequences. As a fragmentary, isolated mind, it tends to remain with what is partial, separated, incomplete, and merely symbolic; it clings to "what it was taught," almost as dried paint clings to the unwashed brush that once directed it. It sees through pre-programmed mental frameworks of distortion; it lives a life of distortion.

Excerpt from Walt Whitman:

I swear the earth shall surely be complete to him or her who shall be complete,
The earth remains jagged and broken only to him or her who remains jagged and broken.
I swear there is no greatness or power that does not emulate those of the earth,
There can be no theory of any account unless it corroborate the theory of the earth,
No politics, song, religion, behavior, or what not, is of account,
unless it compare with the amplitude of the earth,
Unless it face the exactness, vitality, impartiality, rectitude of the earth.
I swear I begin to see love with sweeter spasms than that which responds love,
It is that which contains itself, which never invites and never refuses.
I swear I begin to see little or nothing in audible words,
All merges toward the presentation of the unspoken meanings of the earth,
Toward him who sings the songs of the body and of the truths of the earth,
Toward him who makes the dictionaries of words that print cannot touch.

Though one can be appreciative of each country and each religion of the world (especially those that happen, by chance, to be given to you as your own), the wisest, the most prudent thing to do may be to go beyond all separative governments, countries, and religions. Separate countries and separate religions are one of the major factors that contribute to war between human beings. All countries that seem to be separate from each other… are the result of thoughts and are the result of the thinking process. Poland seems (to many) to be separate from Germany, but is it? Is there really such a thing as Poland, or is it a manmade thing (resultant from thought)? Like islands that appear to be separate regions in a vast ocean, thought tends to divide things; however, if one looks deeply, with perceptive depth, one sees that each island extends down under the waters (as all the islands extend down), and they (i.e., the islands) are thus connected to each other as one vast unit or whole. They are like fingers of a hand that seem separate, but really are not. They are like mountains, of a region, that happen to have flooded water around them, but they are still together as one; the great flood of water really cannot truly separate them. Thought and the process of thinking often separate and act in fragmentary ways. Such fragmentation is often ignorance and foolishness. It may be far wiser to exist as a global individual who is free of separating beliefs and perspectives; separating beliefs and perspectives lead to (and directly contribute to) conflict and war.

One can live mostly free of conflict. The true art of wisdom and the deepest spirituality may involve being free of separative beliefs and separative countries. Religions, through their leaders, tell you that you will gain something in the future if you believe in them and follow their path. They often promise people a future heaven, or a future ecstasy, or future bliss of some sort. Countries, through their leaders, tell you much the same thing; they tell you that you will gain something in the future if you believe in them and follow their path. Just like religions, countries, with their leaders, often promise some sort of a future heaven, or a future ecstasy, or upcoming bliss of some sort. All these big-shots, all these so-called leaders, with their fancy robes, fancy clothes and titles, promise you all kinds of things. If you are wise, however, you immediately realize that your true value as a true human being is not what exists in the conceptual, projected future, but is what exists "now." Wisdom and compassion (united) is what takes place in the *present*, if one has understanding, (and understanding is not what big-shots can give to you in the future). You, in wisdom, have to understand things as they occur in the *present* and, concomitantly, go beyond what mere words and symbols are. (The political and so-called religious leaders are very good at, with fabricated words, promising you a future heaven that you can wait for.) Words and symbols were what was given to you in the past, and the *past* is old and dead; do not merely cling to the dead *past*. Words and symbols often help to divide people. People cling to beliefs, which are composed of words and symbols; they cling to images of countries and to separative religions, which are composed of words and symbols; then they often fight (even to the death, in wars) over these multitudinous words and symbols (and systems) that have been implanted within them. To be a global citizen beyond merely being filled with words and symbols… is not the same as being shackled and tethered down to mere separative concepts, which lead to friction and war. Being free of separative patterns is not another separative pattern. (Drink up the water that divides us, like the great oceans, and do not spit it out!)

Interestingly, some of the lyrics from the excellent musical group *Rush* may be helpful here, such as "Like a teardrop in the ocean, a diamond in the waste, some world-views are spacious — and some are merely spaced."

from Walt Whitman (from Passage to India):

After the seas are all cross'd, (as they seem already cross'd,)
After the great captains and engineers have accomplish'd their work,
After the noble inventors, after the scientists, the chemist, the geologist, ethnologist,
Finally shall come the poet worthy of that name,
The true son of God shall come singing his songs.
Then not your deeds only O voyagers, O scientists and inventors, shall be justified,
All these hearts as of fretted children shall be sooth'd,
All affection shall be fully responded to, the secret shall be told,
All these separations and gaps shall be taken up and hook'd and link'd together,
The whole earth, this cold, impassive, voiceless earth, shall be completely Justified,
Trinitas divine shall be gloriously accomplish'd and compacted by the true son of God, the poet,
(He shall indeed pass the straits and conquer the mountains,
He shall double the cape of Good Hope to some purpose,)

Nature and Man shall be disjoin'd and diffused no more,
The true son of God shall absolutely fuse them.
Year at whose wide-flung door I sing!
Year of the purpose accomplish'd!
Year of the marriage of continents, climates and oceans!
(No mere doge of Venice now wedding the Adriatic,)
I see O year in you the vast terraqueous globe given and giving all,
Europe to Asia, Africa join'd, and they to the New World,
The lands, geographies, dancing before you, holding a festival garland,
As brides and bridegrooms hand in hand.

In terms of separate countries, for instance, it is easy to go along with the crowd, to belong to groups and organizations that make things easier once we fit into them, once we become a member no longer alone. In such groups, we feel sheltered and protected; furthermore, it is far easier to be told what to do, rather than to learn for oneself. It is very comfortable to belong to a large group of people; when one does so belong, one often (with them) looks down on others who "do not belong." They are over "there," away from "our" group. They are not as fortunate as "we" are.

The whole idea and phenomenon of supposedly separate "countries" may very well be an extension and subsequent movement from primitive, tribal, territorial fighting and group-selfishness. It may be that people who believe in "their country above all others," are rather simple-minded and ignorant of the fact that the idea of a country is merely a manmade thing that (all too often) causes people to fight and feel superior to others whom they view from a separative distance. Religions additionally cause many people to act in opposition to others, or cause many people to feel superior to those who do not belong to "their" organization. Thousands of religious wars have taken place upon this earth, all dealing with one group against another. People fight and kill each other very easily over beliefs and traditions. Very few people go beyond groups, traditions, beliefs, gangs, and systems, to where there is no reason to fight, to where there is no feeling of separation or superiority. Not belonging to a religion is not another religion.

from Stephen Crane:

"Think as I think," said a man,
"Or you are abominably wicked;
You are a toad."

And after I had thought of it,
I said: "I will, then, be a toad."

Most everyone belongs to something or other that can, and often does, lead to friction due to leaders who exploit others for various reasons. People often "belong" to groups and "follow" leaders in life, without ever really thinking or pondering for themselves; this is because it is much easier for a lazy mind to follow others and to conform to worn-out traditions, rather than to actively question everything with a supple mind that is not a mere shadow. It is comfortable to "fit in" with the way that others have planned for us. However, a second-hand life may be no life at all. Such a second-hand life may create much sorrow for others (even though it may not perceive how it contributes, either directly or indirectly, to such sorrow). For example, someone might be prejudiced (either mildly or strongly) against a certain race, all the while not realizing that he and his immediate ancestors have many strong genetic ties to, and involving, the very race that he despises; Hitler was a good ("un-good") example of this. (We are, all of us, branches of the same tree. Some of the branches may have yellow, white, red, or brown leaves in different sections, or these leaves may change in the same section via extended time; to let that bother you is ludicrous.) Additionally, for instance, merely revolting violently against perceived authority may often be a waste of time, causing needless friction, conflict, suffering and turmoil for man, (while other, more peaceable, options may concomitantly exist).

from Stephen Crane:

Once there came a man
Who said:
"Range me all men of the world in rows."
And instantly
There was terrific clamor among the people

Against being ranged in rows.
There was a loud quarrel, world-wide.
It endured for ages;
And blood was shed
By those who would not stand in rows,
And by those who pined to stand in rows.
Eventually, the man went to death, weeping.
And those who stayed in the bloody scuffle
Knew not the great simplicity.

Most people, after they've "grown up," after they've become *programmed* to perceive things in certain ways, become rather jaded, faded, and poisoned by old, cob-web ideas and dust-laden perspectives of authority. Such people, then, actually look at the world... not with an uncontaminated vision that is truly fresh, but rather with a canned, mapped-out prearrangement that sees things through a screen that was designed by *scheming and maneuvering "others."* After being programmed with rather second-hand, calculated blueprints, no wonder such people easily feel frustrated, bored, depressed, and rather "un-alive." It is easy to go into an abysmal descent when one is overburdened by titanic amounts of unfeeling rigidities; then, no wonder one feels cumbersome, ordinary, heavy, gross, bored, and unwieldy. A mind so burdened often does not have full freedom; often then, unfortunately, inelasticity with its inertia must inevitably develop into over-indulgence, haphazard sensuality, and uncaring debauchery. Such a poverty-stricken mind would likely not really see just how terribly impoverished it is. Such a mind might wallow in contentment, happy to put up with a psychologically imprisoned existence that is incapable of seeing its own lackadaisical insensitivity, its own crude, coarse, uncaring pseudo-existence. Merely rebelling against authority, by accusing authoritarian structures of stifling one's intrinsic right to freedom, may likely be just a purported change away from authoritarian ways; in reality, it likely would be a fallacious attempt to move from the very authoritarian precepts (that it continues to maintain while erroneously "thinking" that fundamental change has taken place). Merely substituting "inner" authority, for the uncomfortable edicts of a supposed "outer" authority, still coddles the puppeteer-like mentality involving strings of suppression, subjugation, with the ensuing tension that renders life full of needless suffering.

It would be palatable to the minds of many if it were an intention here merely to posit a reactionary revolution against all forms of authority. Revolutions or insurrections that are merely reactionary revulsions against authority are, however, often merely a continuation of the same-old game; the players may be disguised in different appearing uniforms with different purposes in mind, but such mutiny may be fundamentally not so very different from what went on previously. Unfortunately, it is easy to get lost in the puppet show while thinking that one is not a puppet, while not seeing or caring to see the strings, while being dominated by one's attachments, while erroneously thinking that one is a puppeteer who dominates thoughts and dominates other creatures.

Power is relished here (in life, unfortunately). Those who supposedly pull the most strings (or the biggest cords or the most massive strings) are often respected and worshiped above all others. There is much more to life, however, than being a mere puppeteer. In fact, interestingly enough, the puppeteer and the puppet may be one in the same. Most of us like to put on a show for others, unrolling and unveiling our achievements, suspending them for others to admire. We shift our components for exhibition while we each have a "me" or an "I" who purportedly pulls the right (or wrong) strings in this sometimes unyielding dance that we call life. Puppets, in a marionette show, rely heavily on dependability; without the puppeteer, they are merely inanimate dolls with no real life of their own. However, a puppeteer — who is immersed in a dependency of his own, based on fear, ambition, exploitation, comparison, and mechanical reactions — who manipulates people as if they are merely pawns, may be tethered, in life, to cord-like restraints that render him rather like a cadaverous, plastic mannequin suspended from strings. It is comfortable and easy to remain suspended from strings; it is easy to remain mediocre and to let society dictate how we react. The thought of an "I" or a "Me" that is a separate entity that is controlling "thoughts at a distance"... may be erroneous, for example. In actuality, the "I" or the "Me" may be just another set of thoughts in a series of thoughts; it may be another puppet masquerading to be a free-moving puppeteer.

Oftentimes, either we want to pull the strings, in life, or we want to languidly sit back and let others make the decisions for us; or a convenient combination of the two aforementioned situations might be in order. Life, however, real life, might be beyond this manipulating puppet-like play that we have come to accept as the norm (of how things are). Life may be of a joyous, *sacred* wholeness that cannot merely be described in terms of symbolic words suspended upon a page for a series of reactions to hang on to; life and real ecstasy may be much deeper than what reacting words and thoughts can manipulate in (or "as") the mind. The clatter and clangor of symbolic thoughts can never equal what is beyond mere representative modes. Thoughts, being representations, may be second-hand shadows that are not the actualities that they represent. One cannot really get wet in any sea of thought, no matter how deep it is; but most of us exist almost exclusively in thoughts, perpetually thinking and cogitating "about" things, but rarely (or never) joyously just "being." Through eons, thinking evolved as a means, as a tool, for protecting the movement of the organism, such as to help avoid dangerous circumstances and precarious situations; however, instead of using thinking as a helpful tool or helpful process, which it is, we have turned and twisted *thinking* to become the actual *essence* of the organism. We made the *tool* "all important." We love getting lost in our tools; look at how some people cannot function away from their computers. Computers have their place and can be very useful; however, it is easy to lose sight of reality and get lost in a virtual pseudo-world. Similarly, we have placed all of our eggs into the basket of "thinking" or, rather, "mental calculation"; and we remain lost in this virtual dimension, this virtual world that *thinking* consists of. Pseudo-naturally, many of us would suggest that it would be absurd to consider sometimes existing outside of the limited dimension which symbolic calculation consists of. Unfortunately, too many of us merely live in the shallow dimensions of *thought* and *thinking*, and too many are afraid to venture out of the "known" into the "unknown." Too many are unconcerned about living in the true beauty of silence.

from Walt Whitman:

When I heard the learn'd astronomer,
When the proofs, the figures, were ranged in columns before
me,
When I was shown the charts and diagrams, to add, divide,
and measure them,
When I sitting heard the astronomer where he lectured with
much applause in the lecture-room,
How soon unaccountable I became tired and sick,
Till rising and gliding out I wander'd off by myself,
In the mystical moist night-air, and from time to time,
Look'd up in perfect silence at the stars.

How does *thinking* take place? What is the form, or what are the attributes, of *thinking*? Some of us often think in pictorial terms — that is, seeing *visual images* that the mind fabricates. Many of us often think in auditory terms — that is, we *hear* (in a sense) *thoughts* as the mind *talks internally to itself.* Just because the mind talks to "itself," however, does not necessarily mean that a legitimate, central "self" exists which is independent of thought. When "thinking" takes place, it is often in a virtual form of what the actual, physically constructed, vocal "voice" consists of. Mental pictures, of course, are not the realities that they envision; for instance, a good piece by Picasso, envisioned in one's head, certainly is not something that can be sold as a Picasso painting! Therefore, it may be that mental, pictorial images are essentially *virtual* phenomena. This is also applicable to the *auditory rambling* which occurs in (and "as") the mind. If "thinking" occurs in terms (or with some characteristics) of what the actual physical voice sounds like — it is really not an *actual* voice that one hears — it is, rather, a type of *virtual voice.* So *thinking* is imitative and tends to make *impressions* of (or about) things. These *impressions* are, however, always partial and incomplete, because thinking is limited, as computers are, by how many calculations per second (or moment) can be ciphered or processed. We tend to worship "thinking." We associate complex and intricate thinking with success and power; interestingly, to be sure, individuals who can think with complexity tend to have better positions, more secure positions in life. We often give more respect to the man who "knows" a lot and who has interesting things to say, while we often tend to bypass or overlook the simple man who speaks slowly about relatively rudimentary things; this human bias is almost universal. With thoughts, we can acquire things; memory storage, in and of itself, is an accumulative process. Many of us have very hungry appetites for accumulating things. We are gluttons for more knowledge, ingesting more and more information with insatiable appetites. It is good, and it is necessary, to eat, and it is good, and it is necessary, to think. However, one can go overboard within the realms of eating and thinking. Unfortunately, some people do not sensibly stop eating; neither do they understand when to stop thinking; (not that the termination of thinking is something that one can "know" how to do via a thought process nor via any other "learned" process). It may be that only when one goes beyond mere (symbolic representations, which are what thoughts are), that there is a possibility of merging into the wholeness and beauty of a true *sacredness* and the insights that go along with it.

from Walt Whitman:

A Clear Midnight

This is thy hour O Soul, thy free flight into the wordless,
Away from books, away from art, the day erased, the lessons done,
Thee fully forth emerging, silent, gazing, pondering the themes thou lovest best,
Night, sleep, death and the stars.

There is an extremely interesting story, in *Plato's Republic*, which is about education and ignorance; it relates about how people who live in an underground cave exclusively see, throughout their lives, the shadows of puppets. (The light from a fire behind the crowd helped to create these shadows.) The people would always take the shadows to be reality. Each person has been there, in the cave, from childhood, and each one cannot turn around due to having his or her neck and legs tied down by rather rigid fetters. In fact, they would name the various types of shadows, count them, and give each other splendid prizes for who could best remember which came before, which came between, and which came after. When they named the shadows that they saw passing, they sincerely believed that they were naming legitimate (separate) things. In the story about the cave, it was conjectured that if someone should release and then drag one of the cave dwellers back toward the fire or light source, such an individual could then be forced or compelled to look toward the more real light. It would cause his eyes to be painful, it is said, and he might escape by turning them away to the shadowy things that he was more accustomed to perceive; amazingly, these shadows he might believe to be clearer and more understandable than what was being shown to him.

Then, it is suggested, if a *higher power* should drag the individual passionately by force, far up the difficult ascent, the incredibly steep way up, and never stop until he could drag him out into the light of the sun, would not the individual (initially) be disturbed and highly distressed about being dragged? When the individual would come into the sunlight, would not the brilliance fill his eyes and wouldn't it be difficult to see even one of the (things that are now called real when in sunlight)? However, after the individual's eyes would become adjusted to the real light and the more real objects, would he not feel immense pity for the poor people dwelling within the cave? These cave dwellers would give each other prizes for who could best predict which shadow-constructed objects were going to come, in sequence. Would the freed individual, after seeing the light of the sun and a deeper reality, set his desire again on those shadowy, detailed things? Would he envy those living in the cave who were honored men or pundits/scholars among the rest? Would he not feel as Homer relates and fervently desire rather to be a slave of some poverty-stricken man on earth and endure many hardships, rather than to misconstrue and think as they did in the cave, and live accordingly?

If the individual took pity upon those dwelling in the cave and would go back to help them, may it be that, upon returning into the cave, those there might laugh at the individual for going up there, saying that he might have spoiled his eyesight and mind by venturing there. Furthermore, might also they say that it was not at all beneficial to try to go up to the place of light? Wouldn't many of them laugh at him, for being a fool, and call him "insane"?

The aforementioned story may teach us something about conforming to patterns set by authority. It is fine to follow an authority or follow the accepted, common techniques when an individual needs to, for instance, "grow edible plants, or live cooperatively in society, or help heal people medically, or fix something like a bicycle." However, in the realm of understanding all about reality, spirituality, and life, it may be absurd and be a very precarious situation if one merely follows the crowd. There are few people, at the present time, who really go beyond what second-hand knowledge provides, regarding what the truth may actually be. This is very unfortunate, and it should be pointed out here that shadows, in and of themselves, are very much *second-hand* in their essence and behavior. To be a mind that merely clings to dead words, and to merely cling to rather barren symbols and to virtual images of what is really out there, unfortunately, is not a very "living" way to exist. Life is much more dynamic and passionate than what mere words, mental symbols, and concocted patterns can manifest as; a mind that does not go beyond such fabrications... may not at all be truly living. One may be full of all kinds of fancy theories and beliefs about how things are and about how things "should be"; but if one does not often live in the "here and now," beyond the tools of "thought," one is likely to merely be a rather dead, second-hand replica of what life really is. "Thinking," since it is from the memory bank, is always a manifestation of the "past"; it is always something rather old and second-hand. It is very necessary and useful to think, but it is something that is very limited. The "here and now," *without always merely thinking*, may be what *living deeply* truly consists of. As with the people in the cave, do psychological fetters tie down most of us? Aren't all of us tied down by the powerful psychological fetters of conditioning and opportunistic programming (that elder "authorities" have instilled around and within us)?

Thinking is very important, and it is essential that thinking take place with great precision and great performance (as part of what one is). For instance: helping people or animals medically, helping to heal them, or helping them to eat in a more organic, healthy way, or helping them to exercise better to physically improve, or helping them to live in a greener environment... may be some of the wisest, most passionate things that a person (a true human being) can do. However, "thinking," in and of itself, may only be a tool; it may not at all be the *true essence* of what someone should be. Therefore, if you look through the patterns of mere cogitation, you may be looking exclusively "as thought," and if you are merely functioning from thought, you may be of a rather barren, shadow-like personality. Reality is better than just a collection of mere shadows, mere dark impressions. Is it wise to merely accept living in (and "as") darkness? E.E. Cummings has a poem, by the way, that starts out by stating "unlove's the heavenless hell and homeless home of knowledgeable shadows." (Please read the poem sometime, when you get a chance.)

from Stephen Crane:

Behold, from the land of the farther suns
I returned.
And I was in a reptile-swarming place,
Peopled, otherwise, with grimaces,
Shrouded above in black impenetrableness,
I shrank, loathing,
Sick with it.
And I said to him:
"What is this?"
He made answer slowly:
"Spirit, this is a world;
This was your home."

Most likely, most everyone who has ever taught you has tried to get you to think that you are in control of your thoughts and actions. Are you? Even the first sentence of this paragraph is designed, in its very nature and essence, to subtly help convince you that "you" are in charge of what is thought of and done. Are you? Will you find out? Will you inquire into it? Will intelligence find out?

It may very well be that deep intelligence is constituted of what can happily exist without the need of a central "I" or "Me" that seems to be in control of the other thoughts. Such a central "I," that most people cherish, may be merely nothing but another thought or series of thoughts. Unlike such a temporary thing, as a mere thought or series of thoughts, deep intelligence is of a living energy that is profoundly eternal; and this eternity does not separate itself via superficial space (between itself and so-called others). This deep intelligence may "livingly" permeate everything, as silence and true space do. It may be beyond all sequential patterns, such as those that *thoughts* are fabricated of. This intelligence would not be merely of a *center* with a limited circumference all around it; it would not merely have (or be) a limited space from "here" to "there," but would, instead, be wise enough to look without the space between "one that perceives" and "that which is perceived." It, in its profound eternity, would be dynamic enough to care deeply for all living things. It would go beyond small areas of limitation into the unlimited, and it would do so without mere time and space interfering. It would not be unintelligent enough to belong to separative and limited governments, religions, sects, creeds, nationalities, gangs, and families that separate themselves from so-called "others," while causing hate and division by doing so. (We are not suggesting that you "leave your family"; we are suggesting that your family is much larger than you had ever thought.) An intelligent mind would not belong to a limited "I" that, as just another thought, thinks of itself as being better and separate from the rest of life. It would not merely be a virtual, conceived image; it would not be a mere limited pattern or sequence (which is what "time" is). It would not be just what society teaches one to be. It would be beyond all teachings. It would not be what one could merely practice attaining. It would be beyond all methods of practice, beyond all mechanical techniques and formulas. No mere ladder of practice or methodology could reach to it. It is a divine *bliss* beyond all patterns, beyond all cravings, beyond the hatred and divisions of man. A truly living human, deeply aware of all, may be lucky enough to actually be visited (and touched) by it without deception. It may be a living and *dynamic truth and beauty* beyond mere patterns of static thought, beyond the mere known. The person visited (and touched) by it is, in the very deepest sense, truly blessed, and so then the whole world is blessed eternally, because such a person is not merely something separate from the world.

from Walt Whitman:

It is time to explain myself — let us stand up.
What is known I strip away.
I launch all men and women forward with me into the Unknown.
The clock indicates the moment—but what does eternity indicate?

It is imperative that one remain exactly within the mold that society's elders have formulated for one to remain in. Never question anything to any substantial degree, with the exception, of course, of trivial details that enable one to continue to feel in control via manipulative means toward various ends attained through sequential patterns. Always perceive with a separative distance between the "perceiver" and the "images that are perceived." Relish the limited. Unhesitatingly tread along the same road that generation upon generation has trodden upon. Never go against the grain. Keep comparing oneself with those deemed rich in the things in life that can be accumulated by cunning manipulation. Unfalteringly do as you were taught to do. Never look behind any curtain that a dog named Toto stands adjacent to. Always remain within the realm and safety of limited thoughts; continue to perceive through the screen of conditioned reactions. Let auditory-oriented thinking be a virtual pseudo-copy of the actual physical voice of the organism and insist that it is "you" separate from all others. Envy those who win prizes for naming the types and characteristics of shadows best. Think that fear and yourself are two different things. Think that fear is something that you have, rather than something that you are. Think that the envy concerning the things that your neighbor has (and that the image of your neighbor) are separate from what you actually are. Always do as you are told. Let cruel and sadistic people harm the handicapped near to you while, physically, you do nothing whatsoever about it. Function only as a limited network of thoughts, and be sure to have one thought think that it definitely is in control of the "other" thoughts. Cherish what is second-hand without question. Function merely as thought; react merely from thought; desire endlessly from thought; feel exclusively from thought; hate passionately from thought; obey fearfully from thought; perceive exclusively through the screen of thought. Keep all of your eggs in one basket. Stay in line and be cold and callous toward others. Be representative, residual, symbolic patterns that categorize and classify, that divide life up into neat little patterns. Cling exclusively from one experience to another in order to be happy. Grope for deep happiness as if it can really be acquired by what is void of happiness. Never transcend the barbarism of reaching for things and places. Be sure to continue as if under the presumption that a mind that functions within the common norms of society is not one of the most cadaverous, un-alive, stagnant things out there. Continue to look at things through an ordinary perspective, and continue to fight for "your" country and "your" religion (which is better than "their" country and "their" religion). Again, as we suggested, act as if "being normal" — like the masses are — is not one of the most tragic things in occurrence. Let others walk all over you, while you do nothing and remain indifferent and passive. Remain comfortable in thoughts that you think are *yours* but which really are *theirs*. Harm little animals because you have so much more power (and so much more importance) than they do. Be a shadow of mimicry. Incessantly communicate with others via electronic media, and everlastingly maintain the fear of being alone. Think that you are entirely *in control*. Do selfish things and make lame excuses for why you had to do them. Worry endlessly about details and fragments, but never deeply ponder about the whole meaning and eternal essence of real life. Never wet your pants. Remain in that which has sorrow as its essence. Do as they do. Always merely use the energy that cannot be created or destroyed, but never actually become "one with the energy"; never deeply consider being in a true communion with what eternity (i.e., energy, not just ideological symbols about it) is. Never fundamentally change, lest you become a threat to the well-established order. Sleep tight; don't let the bedbugs bite.

The musical group Rush has a song entitled "Subdivisions" that may be relevant here.

from Walt Whitman:

Transpositons

Let the reformers descend from the stands where they are forever
bawling—let an idiot or insane person appear on each of the stands;

Let judges and criminals be transposed—let the prison-keepers be
put in prison—let those that were prisoners take the keys;
Let them that distrust birth and death lead the rest.

We are saying that those who remain with old mental frameworks are each constituted of a consciousness that is incapable of easily existing as the fresh, new, and insightful. What is "old" is entrenched in worn-out patterns and perceives through screens and mental filters, which were positioned by bygone and antiquated beliefs and conditionings. Unless such "elderly" constituents psychologically die to their archaic thoughts and images, they will continue dwelling as what is not youthful, whole, and dynamic. For this transformation from the "old ways," an internal, dynamic revolution is needed; it involves the internal thoughts ending, in a kind of *psychological dying*. No one can do this for you, only yourself. It is internal, but it is not merely an internal struggle, for strenuous effort and friction are not what it involves. When one engages with it, with wide-open and fresh eyes, one may even understand what "ending" and what "eternity" is; they are not two separate things. As the following poem by the gracious Emily Dickinson may suggest, consciousness *must* discover something immense about *ending* within itself, and *must* partake in something: (a *tremendous*, new *experiment* for *humankind*) that is extremely *profound*.

This Consciousness that is aware
Of Neighbors and the Sun
Will be the one aware of Death
And that itself alone

Is traversing the interval
Experience between
And most profound experiment
Appointed unto Men —

How adequate unto itself
Its properties shall be
Itself unto itself and none
Shall make discovery.

Adventure most unto itself
The Soul condemned to be —
Attended by a single Hound
Its own identity.

Will one be afraid to see the truth, rather than what the elders of society have spoon-fed to us? Will we have the courage to die to our old values, images, and patterns of "how things are," to perceive holistically with fresh eyes, not contaminated by primitive fears, erroneous fabrications, and aged beliefs? To die to their "dead patterns," their "dead ways" of seeing things, may only be done by standing alone (away from what millions accepted before).

From Stephen Crane:

There were many who went in huddled procession,
They knew not whither;
But, at any rate, success or calamity,
Would attend all in equality.

There was one who sought a new road,
He went to direful thickets,
And ultimately he died thus, alone;
But they said he had courage.

It may indeed be best to, at first, learn things in a certain sequence, and later (when one is more safely beyond the clutches of their superficial, old-fangled beliefs and structures) there is a possibility of perceiving the deeper, more profound things (that occur beyond the illusions which selfish, egocentric limitations manifest as). As one blossoms in life without restrictive authority to block one's growth — and this does not mean that one reacts against all rules and regulations, but is, rather, intelligent enough to not merely need them — as one truly investigates with love and a deep feeling for every living thing, one may discover the essence of what real eternity is. When one fully discovers it, without merely knowing about something told intellectually, one is immensely immersed in the joy of it, because one may then be united with the *sacred benediction* of *eternal life*. Such an understanding would come to a mind that exists in a vast quietude that exists beyond the confines and limitations of symbolic (shadowy) thoughts; and such a mind would not have "made" itself quiet, for such a "made quietness" would merely then be an artificial construction fabricated by the mind. It would have come to it (i.e., come to the silence) naturally, without the effort of mere greed and active grasping. It would have come as the outcome of a life of deep care and passion for all. Such a life would live in the *present*, in the "*now*," (not merely with, or "as," ideas of the past). Such a mind would not be foolish enough to merely brag about eternity, or foolish enough to merely peddle crude concepts about that eternity which is, when all else is said and done, too dynamic to be pigeonholed and merely categorized by minds which are exclusively functioning in thoughts.

A mind that has come upon what the "*eternal benediction*" really is, is a lucky mind that is "one" with the whole energy of the cosmos. Such a living mind is of that energy which, as Einstein alluded to, has no beginning and no end. Such a mind that is truly with such a living (not conceived) eternity is with a very *sacred, spiritual benediction*, and needs no false images of gods or masters. Such a mind does not have innumerable fears that are the result of delusions and conflicting misconceptions; and such a mind does not cling to the limitations that are the result of being "mis-taught" and "mis-educated" by overpowering authorities. Such an eternal mind would be a light in all the darkness of uncaring humanity. Such a mind would really be joyous and whole. It would be a mind that would care for plants and animals. It would be a mind that would care very deeply for humans too. It would be a mind that would learn from suffering and that would transcend all suffering. It would be a mind that would often be beyond merely being offended by shallow, shadow-like words. It would be a mind that would not be afraid to stand alone. It would be a mind that would do things to educate people about overpopulation, about alternative energy sources, global warming, helping endangered species, and about natural living. It would be a mind that would be intelligent enough to care about eating pure foods that help the body and mind to be wise and whole. It would not be a mind that is merely the result of some blueprint or technique. A mind that is merely the result of some formulated systems is most likely a very dead, mechanical, "un-alive" type of mind. E. E. Cummings once wrote (and I quote it just as he had written it): "false is alike. False teeth".

Therefore, the aforementioned sentences allude to why the real feeling of *profound eternity* cannot merely be told to others; but it can possibly become manifest when individuals look deeply, with insight and care, into what constitutes life. Then, if they live with real seriousness and without merely jumping from one self-oriented experience to another, they will come upon that which is beyond time, beyond suffering, and beyond the mere symbolic confines of sequential thinking. *All sequential thinking* must exist as *time.* If a *true eternal energy* would come, to be in a communion with very open minded humans, it would be the touch of a most profound, deep, *timeless*, and intelligent bliss and would communicate the essence of all life. Those that may be visited by it would truly be *deeply blessed.* Being visited by the most *sacred*, even if for just a few minutes (time-wise) — and even if it were to occur at the end of a long existence full of rather tiring, somewhat mundane experiences — would be a *benediction* that would render typical experiences, in time, as being quite shallow and superficial. However, merely craving for it is but a crude part of the sequence of desires that greedy thought manifests as. One must not merely crave for it. Then it may come (perhaps even finally toward the end of one's life when one is old, yet having a youthful mind). Those who are truly touched by the *sacred...* are whole, blissful, wise entities (and are not merely foolish dreamers claiming to be something important). What is truly *sacred* cannot be found by what shadowy, rather lifeless, symbols and second-hand thoughts consist of. When visited by this *sacredness*, it may be (though words cannot describe it) like being a trillion times more alive than one has ever been. Though words can never describe it, it may be like being visited and blessed, all at once, by all of the vast energy that makes up the multiverse (i.e., the complex of universes). When it occurs — and the word "when" is not truly functional here — a "*timelessness*" manifests which nullifies "sequential thinking," allowing it (i.e., thought in time) to disappear (with the superficiality that it is). Neither can methods, calculated practices, systems, nor drugs induce it or bring it about. Sequential methodologies can never bring it about; (please remember that all thoughts are sequential and thus are dependent upon time). Only in an organic, holistic, innocent mind may it take place. Blessed are those who are visited by it.

from Walt Whitman:

Has never come to thee an hour,

A sudden gleam divine, precipitating, bursting all these bubbles, fashions, wealth?

These eager business aims—books, politics, art, amours,
To utter nothingness?

Chapter 3

Most people are perfectly afraid of being alone. They need someone around them most all of the time, or else they become very frightened, very bored. Being a social animal, it is good for man to be in the company of others; but it may also be good to frequently be alone, at times, without merely being lonely. Even when someone is by himself or herself, he or she usually has many thoughts churning away within (and "as") the brain. These thoughts are often actually the thoughts from others, churning within, keeping one company, keeping one amused. However, it may only be a rather shallow mind, a rather broken mind, that constantly needs amusement and the entertainment of others to keep happy. It may only be a rather shallow mind, a rather disorderly mind, that constantly needs music, cell phones, computers (which are the products and patterns of others), and other socially oriented electronic devices, in order to keep happy. True wisdom may include a mind that often exists without inner noise, without the inner commotion of thoughts, without inner turmoil and confusion, without the constant need of one stimulus after another. Such a mind may be of a silence that is beyond the old memory bank (full of cobweb thoughts) of the past; such a mind may exist in (and "as") the new and young "*now*," which is totally free of the old "past." Its silence might be what is beyond the limited. (Moreover, all thoughts are limited, in that they can only represent something symbolically, to a very confined extent.) The silence of a wise mind might be beyond forms and patterns of movement; hence, such silence would be beyond the aspect of time. It would not be a stagnant mind; it would be of a living stillness that does not depend on sensation after sensation in order to be joyous (although it would go through many sensations with joy).

Thought — if its nature is rather second-hand, if its essence consists of being symbolic representations that are merely residual images — is a very barren, very empty state of affairs. Therefore, anyone merely remaining in the realm of thought must, by natural law, be what suffering consists of. However, struggling and using effort to get away from thought may, in reality, just be a continuation of the sequence of thought (contending against itself). Real silence may not at all be the result of any system, or method, or desire; it may not at all be what any effort (including the effort of thought) can come upon or attain. Shadows, when they "try" to leave themselves, only propagate themselves. Shadows, when they feel sorry for themselves, only add more suffering. To die, not physically, but psychologically, to this inner turmoil of thinking, may be the only way to really live. (Moreover, by "way to really live," we are not implying that it is a way to live by some type of practice or methodology; living merely by way of systems is not truly living at all.)

Most of us like to fall into the rut and into the routine of a system or method of living. We let others tell us how to live; we become full of the thoughts of others, thinking that such thoughts are truly our own. We become languid and dull, get bored easily because of having minds that are essentially second-hand, and then we wonder what next friend or what next amusement might come along that will pull us out of our depression. Something might pull you out temporarily; but even an exciting experience cannot put a dull, superficial mind far out from its depression. Sorrow can try to escape from itself by all kinds of tricks, but it can only go so far, and it is never far enough. A mind that can be truly alone (even though it is in the middle of a crowd, or in a house by itself) — without always merely depending on thoughts, experiences, amusements, and entertainment to escape from boredom — is the intelligence that does not depend on sensation after sensation in order to be happy. Such an alone mind is a light unto the whole. It may be beyond cause and effect; furthermore, being beyond cause and effect (and this may sound silly, but it is not), it may be beyond time. Understand yourself, but not by any method or formula, and you will have gone beyond what crude suffering consists of. (Do not force yourself into silence; let it come naturally, just a little here and there every day.) Effortlessly let there be a little pause between thoughts now and then; that is enough. It may be the only way to truly transcend suffering, and it occurs not by cunning calculation or by practicing some methodology. Not going by (i.e., not using) any system or method... is truly standing alone; the masses of people indoctrinated by the elderly will not subscribe to this. Not blindly following tradition… is truly standing alone. Observing things simply — without artificially created separation and conflict — is truly standing alone.

from Stephen Crane:

Tell me not in joyous numbers
We can make our lives sublime
By—well, at least, not by
Dabbling much in rhyme.

At the time of the writing of this book, the news on television has been indicating that many youth, in schools, are engaged in acts involving cruel bullying and harsh, direct belittling of others. How can this book maintain that youth are of the fresh, new, beautiful, and innocent, if such activity is taking place (at the time of this writing) within the schools? Well, the sad fact is that such so-called "youth" are not, in reality, "youthful"; they are, rather, indoctrinated by the "old" and are (polluted by the "old" and by the "contaminated.") Violent and corrupt television, crude video games, primitive mannerisms by their parents, fear of being "lower" in some kind of childish "hierarchy," have all contributed to their having lost their youth, unfortunately, very early on. Their defiance, their exercises of power and domination are merely extensions of what "old" minds have filtered into them as. They have embraced and have become the "old" and "corrupt." They want to safely "fit in" within their cliquish groups and gangs as, all the while, they react insensitively apart from the whole of life. What kind of "fitting in" is that? They have become empty reactions, which merely continue reacting (rather mechanically). As E. E. Cummings once said, "Hatred bounces."

One can be very knowledgeable, but if one does not know oneself, one is a very ignorant person, utterly lacking in true treasure. Life is not this shallow business that we were taught; instead, it is something full of deep mystery, deep mystery that can be discovered with (and "as") profound insight. If one merely clings to the apron strings of knowledge and to the symbolic images of thought, then what one experiences must, inevitably, often be rather boring, second-hand, mundane, and shallow. However, if one uses thinking as the wonderful tool that it is, but is not trapped only within that particular instrument of being, then one is free; then one can perceive beyond limitation and sorrow; then one can function with real care and precision, without regrets.

Exploring the mind, with care and keen insight, may be much more rewarding and much more worthwhile than going to some far-away planet, to some very distant planetary moon or deep ocean. Understanding the mind may be nobler, more exciting, and much more profound than treading into the far recesses of the earth, into dense jungles or underwater ravines.

No one can take you deeply there except you, yourself. However, you cannot go very far if you want to carry all the burdens of memory, all the weight of tradition, all the sorrow of having a brain that functions from a narrow, little point out of fear. You cannot go very far if you are afraid to crash through all the absurdities that have been programmed into you. You cannot go very far if you are laden with heavy, hard armor that is there to protect your ego and precious self-esteem. Truly, whoever tries to save his own life will lose it. Moreover, this does not mean that one should jump off cliffs or take chances with one's body; it does mean that one can go beyond the fallacious aspect of the central "I" or ego. It means that insight can transcend the small limitation that exists as a selfish, central point involving a distance to what it thinks is "not itself." Such a limited distance is a like a cheap lie. Why be satisfied with a little distance that is the result of an illusion, when all the while one can go into the illimitable? Would you rather be in a little box, or in the whole sky?

Understanding of the self, for oneself, may be the wisest endeavor that a human being can undertake, and it is something that is truly never-ending. It is something that is not merely the result of desire and greed. It is something that is not just a struggle. One does not partake in it if one is manifesting as a sequential set of patterns that are always striving to attain something. A mind that is always groping for stimuli… may be like a tricked jack-ass that is eternally reaching for the suspended carrot that hangs down from the extended pole attached to the donkey's saddle. Additionally, a mind that is actively always trying to avoid stimuli... may be equally asinine. A balanced mind that functions when necessary, but which naturally becomes quiet at other times, may be of a true blessing that acts with great insight and that perceives with the deepest wisdom. Such a mind exists beyond cruelty, for it sees the mysterious whole and is naturally compassionate for what it sees as what is not separate from itself.

from Stephen Crane:

Unwind my riddle.
Cruel as hawks the hours fly;
Wounded men seldom come home to die;
The hard waves see an arm flung high;
Scorn hits strong because of a lie…
Yet there exists a mystic tie.
Unwind my riddle.

If one functions from an illusory, distorted, little mind that seems to operate from a specific point, one functions from a limited ego, or concept of "I," or "Me," that happens to be very narrow (and narrow minded). From that illusory point to what is considered to be "other" separate things or beings... exists as what the mind sees as space, (as limited space). Without a limited space, a limited ego could not exist. Without distortion, a limited ego could not exist. Without miscalculation, friction, and wastage of energy, a limited ego could not exist. To be a limited, little ego takes time, a limited amount of time. (It may very well be that a truly intelligent mind functions beyond the limited web or framework of time; without limited space, there is no limited time.)

To conceive of a *dominating entity* that is in charge of "thoughts," the network of thoughts must think of a thought of "Me" or "I." To think of itself, the mind must fabricate itself through thought. In order to reflect on oneself as a central controlling entity or "I," one must create (through thinking) a controlling self, or entity, or "I" to reflect on. In order to have fear and in order to try to avoid being fearful, one must be what considers itself as being apart (or separate) from fear (and apart from other phenomena). In order to be the same "I" that one was before, one must remain stagnant, and to do so, a certain kind of repetition of thinking must occur. To remain deeply repetitive and stagnant, one must remain rather "un-alive." Not to go in (and "as") the flow of things, one must exist as a separate "I" or "Me." In order never to truly partake of the *sacred benediction*, one must exist as a separate "I" or "Me." In order to possess something, there must be a possessor; in order to hate something, there must be a hater.

One cannot merely get rid of the "I" or "Me" (i.e., the ego) by effort; the sweeper may be the swept. The swept may be the sweeper. To try to get rid of the ego (or "Me") may just reinforce and support another version or aspect of the ego (or another aspect of "Me.") Before taking a swipe at the ego, consider who is doing the swiping. However, without effort, without sequential methods that occur in time or that take time, the ego can be transcended (by a mind that naturally perishes, psychologically, to all kinds of friction and chaos); this *dying*, to ignorance and friction, is the highest form of *real living*. A mind that exists in (that functions "as") this way of *living*, is free of the limited space of a narrow-minded ego. Such a mind does not trick itself into chasing itself away; such a mind does not think that "it" reigns supreme over other domains; such a mind does not think that "it" reigns supreme over all the other thoughts or over some of the other individuals in its environment. Such a divine mind may be with what is *truly sacred*, in the deepest sense.

A limited ego (i.e., a limited concept of a "central" self that thinks that it dominates and controls the "other thoughts") is, by natural law, something that creates its own circumference; it is in the "center," and everything else is around it (for "it" to control or manipulate). There is nothing frightening about understanding this. It may only be frightening to a consciousness that wants to continue deluding itself with falsities. What "thinks" that it is a "controller," or "thinks" that it is a "Me" in charge of the other thoughts, is, in itself, just another one of the thoughts. Thought may be a conglomeration of many reactions, but there is nothing that is independently controlling them. This does not mean that one can have excuses to "go out of control because there is no central entity that is truly in charge." No, we still have responsibility and the possibility of intelligence and freedom. Each one of us is responsible for action, which is wisdom and intelligence manifesting as excellence and order. Like a monkey tethered to a limited string, the space that a limited ego manifests as: is bounded and small.

While in college, I read some articles about how scientists severed the "corpus callosum." The brain, in reality, is like two halves of the nutty, internal sections of a walnut; the human brain actually looks a lot like the two sections of the inside of a walnut; the corpus callosum is an important section that connects the two halves in the brain. Scientists and doctors have discovered this, regarding the brain. A walnut also has a small, internal structure that connects its two main sections. When the corpus callosum must be cut and severed (by surgical operation), such as in extreme cases involving epilepsy, the split-brain patient then has the equivalent of two minds. Following the operation, what the left-brain perceives, learns, and thinks, is unknown to the right-brain, and vice versa. In other words, after the operation, there exists two fields of awareness, two fields of consciousness. Experiments have shown that there are significant differences between the two separate sections of the brain, once the corpus callosum is severed. It has been demonstrated that the left hemisphere can be revealed to be more logical, analytic, quantitative, rational, and verbal, whereas the right hemisphere has been shown to be more conceptual, holistic, intuitive, imaginative, and non-verbal. Therefore, we have to look at consciousness in different ways. The process of thought, in and of itself, is often very fragmentary and rather mechanical in its performance; it is often just symbolic parts of the total reality. Furthermore, if we look in ways that are very fragmented, in other words, in ways that are distorted and not straight and direct, we will be going around in circles.

excerpt of a poem by Wallace Stevens, entitled Six Significant Landscapes:

Not all the knives of the lamp-posts,
Nor the chisels of the long streets,
Nor the mallets of the domes
And high towers,
Can carve
What one star can carve,
Shining through the grape-leaves.

Rationalists, wearing square hats,
Think, in square rooms,
Looking at the floor,
Looking at the ceiling.
They confine themselves
To right-angled triangles.
If they tried rhomboids,
Cones, waving lines, ellipses —
As, for example, the ellipse of the half-moon —
Rationalists would wear sombreros.

Growing and blossoming beyond the limitations that everyone offers... may be true wisdom. Blossoming beyond self-centered superficiality may be what being "deeply alive" is all about. Even Walt Whitman, whose works are presented as part of this book, may have had some ideas that were limiting and somewhat in error. However, for the most part, Whitman may have been full of deep insight and deep perception, such that, for instance, he could sense the real presence of other worlds and of multiple universes. He loved America; but too many people end up loving one country over another, one family or group above all others. When that happens, it invites a feeling of superiority, a feeling of distance and separation; (not that Whitman really had feelings of distance and separation from any others; Whitman's love of the people of his area included all so-called distant areas).

Very concrete feelings of distance and separation from "others" allows one to let those so-called "others" go "down the drain," without one deeply being concerned for what is happening to them. If one's left hand is being damaged, one acts immediately with quick care and deep concern; however, "they" seem to be not of one's constitution, so one lets "them" suffer without much concern. It is as if the left hand thinks that the right hand is something so distant from itself... that there isn't any real concern or love for the right hand whatsoever. As was suggested before, many islands may seem to be very separate, at a great distance from each other. However, if one looks with more depth, one can see that all the islands connect under the oceans to each other; they are all really just parts of the same thing; they are not at all so separate, as many foolish people erroneously think. We are "one" globe, one world, not truly separate countries, not truly separate families. Separation is fiction.

Find out, discover for yourself all about real relationship and real goodness. Do not let the shallow ideas of others turn you into what is also superficial. Look deep into yourself, deep into life, deep into the water, deep into the cosmos. In one's journey through life, if one finds out about the nature of eternity, if one finds out about the way that the whole cosmos (and all so-called parts of it) operate, it might be best not to merely directly divulge much of this (and all that one has learned) to others who are callous, indifferent, and cruel. It may be best if they would find out for themselves and not merely be told. As Lao Tzu said, in the ancient *Tao Te Ching,* "He who knows, does not say; he who says, does not know." To really understand the cosmos, or the whole, requires much more than words and mental patterns anyway; so informing others by way of the symbolic patterns of words is a very limited process, for sure. One may think that one understands how the cosmos works (by means of consciousness, internal words, and patterns/ideas). However, the whole of the cosmos functions far deeper than what mere mental images can conjure up (as mere patterns). Life and true energy may be far deeper than what the superficiality of symbolic patterns of thought can reach. It may even be that thoughts are the vapid holes in the cosmos where true energy does not function. Like phantom-oriented holes in Swiss cheese, these areas (where energy is not) may be representations, words, signs, or symbols *about* the energy, but they may not at all actually *be* the energy.

It may not be wise merely to be satisfied with ideas about energy, with symbols about what energy is; they (the ideas and images of the mind) may be essentially nothing. They may be less than holes, in that they are virtual patterns (of thought), and are not even constituted of true space. True space is a vast plenum full of beautiful potential and amazing, active energy; but since most people are afraid of actually having a truly empty mind, they never commune with the energy. True emptiness is beautiful; it is true order and freedom. Innocence may truly commune with universal energy and true order; an innocent mind is an open, untethered freedom. Such freedom is not afraid of emptiness. True energy is life, and life is far beyond merely being a lot of fancy, symbolic images and representational patterns. True energy is real living. A dead, uncaring mind cannot, unfortunately, be of such vital energy. True energy cannot be contained within the limited walls and the limited space of barren ideas and cannot be contained in the limited recesses of narrow thoughts within a merely self-centered, superficial brain. Such vibrant energy is of a vast space; it is not a limited, shallow, little space that the fragmentary mind can fabricate (and occupy). It is beyond what the limited, little mind can grasp; nevertheless, it is possible for the mind, if it is lucky, to be visited by it. The following consists of some limited words about the cosmos... trying, in their own somewhat feeble but passionate way, to express the unlimited.

from Walt Whitman:

Kosmos

Who includes diversity and is Nature,
Who is the amplitude of the earth, and the coarseness and sexuality of
the earth, and the great charity of the earth, and the equilibrium also,
Who has not look'd forth from the windows the eyes for nothing,
or whose brain held audience with messengers for nothing,
Who contains believers and disbelievers, who is the most majestic lover,
Who holds duly his or her triune proportion of realism,
spiritualism, and of the aesthetic or intellectual,
Who having consider'd the body finds all its organs and parts good,

Who, out of the theory of the earth and of his or her body understands by subtle analogies all other theories,
The theory of a city, a poem, and of the large politics of these States;
Who believes not only in our globe with its sun and moon, but in other globes with their suns and moons,
Who, constructing the house of himself or herself, not for a day but for all time, sees races, eras, dates, generations,
The past, the future, dwelling there, like space, inseparable together.

Many priests, gurus, rabbis, ministers, atheists, and various types of religious leaders attempt to get people to adhere to various doctrines, beliefs, and suppositions about what they consider God to be or not be. They try to get people convinced that their way to approach God is the best (or the only) way to go. Many religious leaders have profited tremendously by monetary and environmentally comforting rewards that were a direct result of their having peddled ideas about how they are middlemen between people and God. Presenting themselves as "middlemen," who dwell between people and what is considered sacred, has been very profitable for them. At the end of all this "following of leaders," either religiously or politically, is often what takes place as a phenomenon called: war. Separation and division, from so-called others, is a necessity, in order for war to take place. There have been thousands of religious and political wars. People kill themselves over their beliefs, over their ideas about how things "should be." Their ideas, their beliefs, and thoughts of how things "should be," actually take precedence over their value of human life (or life in general). Beliefs and ideas are mental patterns. Mental patterns are sequential representations; sequential representations may never be the deepest truth, may never be the holistic, majestic energy.

Not belonging to any religion is not another religion. Not belonging to any country does not give substantiality to the fallacious notions about the reality of countries. A mind that tears all beliefs to pieces — beliefs that have previously constituted its foundation — no longer supports what really separates and divides people. A mind — that no longer looks through the screen of separation that religions, countries, beliefs, prejudices, and second-hand values have provided —may actually be capable of looking at nature without a separative wall between "itself" and pure life. Such a mind may be able to perceive the real beauty of life directly, without conflict.

Such a mind would possibly be intelligent enough to understand the conflict that is existent throughout much of nature; however, it would be capable of going beyond that conflict, to perceive the real beauty, harmony, and deep cooperation within nature. Such a mind might, perhaps, even be capable of going beyond nature... into an *eternal* field of *sacred benediction* — where time and space are not limitations — where conflict and disorder are nonexistent.

It may be that an intelligent mind that goes beyond words, that goes beyond the domain of thought and thinking, is capable of existing where mere sequential, symbolic patterns need not exist (except when necessary). Being beyond dead symbols of the past, such a mind may actually be what is *truly living* in the deepest sense. No longer would it be a puppet on a string. No longer would it lick the boots of death out of fear; nor would it cling to mere road signs along the way. Being free of false values, it would not have a shroud of barren images to cloud its perceptions. It would depend on no one to find the truth, for the truth, for it, would not exist at any distance needing traveling to. It would not be afraid to be immensely compassionate in front of those who see compassion as something to laugh at. It would see the laughter of those who exist with separative values as being issued forth from phantom-like shadows, from sleep-like dreams.

Could it be that adults, out of greed and the desire to control, domineer, use, exploit, and guide others, have given us religions based on permanent middlemen and spiritual merchants? Many powerful adults have kept us at each other's throats with politics (stemming from ancient tribalism), politics based on separative factions, leagues, federations, and governments, thus encouraging wars, even in this day and age.

Considering the lyrics of the John Lennon song entitled "Imagine" may be appropriate here. Additionally, "living is easy with eyes closed... misunderstanding all you see..."

From Stephen Crane:

A little ink more or less!
It surely can't matter?
Even the sky and the opulent sea,
The plains and the hills, aloof,
Hear the uproar of all these books.
But is only a little ink more or less.

What?
You define me God with these trinkets?
Can my misery meal on an ordered walking
Of surpliced numbskulls?
And a fanfare of lights?
Or even upon the measured pulpiting
Of the familiar false and true?
Is this God?
Where, then, is hell?
Show me some bastard mushroom
Sprung from a pollution of blood.
It is better.

Where is God?

At the precise moment of wanting something, so that one will (in the future) be happy, one is not what happiness is. Unhappiness, expending energy in order to become happy, may be like darkness trying to capture the light. The wise man, instead of always attempting to escape from unhappiness, instead of trying to run away from unhappiness, may look deep into not only *unhappiness*, but also deep into the way the mind *perceives* in the first place. A truly whole, joyous, healthy mind may not need to do (or get) a great deal of things in order to be truly happy and joyous. True light may not need to go far to get more light. (This is not to say that one "should not" collect things or seek after things, as with, for example, a simple hobby; I find and collect fossils locally, and purchase fossils; it is interesting, educational, and a lot of fun!) Things can be done with balance, integral proportion, and within reason. Endlessly sitting around without doing things or investigating things is as equally dead as being caught in the endless pursuit of things; there has to be a balance. A mind that functions with deep self-knowledge is aware of all the pitfalls of functioning with the ignorance that emerges as avarice, conflict, and friction; such a mind is beyond the internal and external manifestations that result in suffering, wastage of energy, and indifference.

When "desire" or "craving" takes place, there is often a gap in the mind, (involving distance between "what is" and what one "wants.") Fear, also, involves distance and space. When fear takes place, does one, if one is wise, try to escape from or run from that fear? Does one try to create a distance between that fear and what one considers oneself to be? A wise person, truly interested in deeply learning about life, instead of trying to get rid of the fear, perceives that he is not different from what the fear is. Similarly, a man who hates someone, for something or other, may look at that hatred not as being something that he *has*, but rather as something that he *is*; and he may see that the *mental image* of the one that is hated is also a part of what he *is*. Trying to get rid of the hatred may not curtail much hatred in the long run; for hatred is conflict, and a mind that has much conflict within (and "as") itself is bound to often project hatred. Hatred is born of conflict. A mind that knows and understands itself, that goes beyond the conflicts within itself, may have the key for going beyond conflicts in society.

A mind that is full of inner conflicts... is a mind that tricks itself numerous times. It is like a dog that chases its own tail as something separate but can never catch what it is after. Deep happiness eludes such a mind, because it is perpetually wasting its own energy. A mind, that has conflict as an essence of what it is, is bound to create conflict and turmoil in society. Furthermore, no matter what such a mind does, it can never be truly happy. Only if it transforms itself, and not according to anyone else's patterns of "how things should be," can it leave the hole that it has dug for itself. Real transformation, not according to any pattern, may not be a matter of time. "Delaying transformation and delaying true learning about oneself" is a matter of time. *Dying* (psychologically) to one's stupidities does not, whatsoever, take time. In such "*dying*" may exist the ecstasy of life; in such *dying* may be *eternal wisdom* free from the rigid patterns that others have imposed. It is a mental dying, not a physical dying.

Of course, this writer may be terribly wrong. It may be that we should encourage the rigid elders in society to help us to cling to the old systems and help us to be the good, little followers whom they want us to be, (while we are happily willing to dangle from the puppet strings).

[Gracie H.: "The author of "The Eternal Fountain of Youth — Youth's Revolution" is clearly against established authority because of suffering from a continuing, chronic dilemma related to severe, childhood trauma due to a psychologically unhealthy, unstable, and substandard home life. Therefore, let's laugh at his very foolish efforts and forget his absurd proposals."

Ernest H.: "That's a splendid idea! You are always so right, Mom! Bring me another brandy, would ya, Mom?"]

Alternatively, regarding labels about you, it may be that your name represents more than what is a mere set of symbolic representations. It may be that you have the beginnings of profound understanding and can see that you are here because of divine, natural laws that provide for what is cherished, valuable, and significant. If you will be essential for helping others to see the far-reaching significance of being here on this planet, will you merely function as what depends on past, old-fashioned ideas? Will you merely be another reacting-domino-piece in a sequence involving "copying what 'they, (the elderly authorities)' do"? Will you be what depends upon high-ranking authorities (at a distance) for your own true understanding and serenity?

from Walt Whitman:

Whoever you are! motion and reflection are especially for
you,
The divine ship sails the divine sea for you.
Whoever you are! you are he or she for whom the earth is
solid and liquid,
You are he or she for whom the sun and moon hang in the sky,
For none more than you are the present and the past,
For none more than you is immortality.
Each man to himself and each woman to herself, is the word
of the past and present, and the true word of immortality;
No one can acquire for another - not one,
Not one can grow for another - not one.

In "Song of Myself," where Whitman writes of "creeds and schools in abeyance," is he possibly suggesting that in order to really find out about what the truth is, one must put aside all that one has learned and all that one has been told about the way things are? Is he suggesting that everyone must find out for himself or herself, away from what their elders have spoon-fed to them, and away from what the experts have carefully provided? Walt Whitman was not a man who was afraid of standing alone. He did not merely cling to the edicts and patterns that others laid out to follow. Perhaps this "standing alone" was what enabled him to see with sagacious foresight and keen insight into the whole of the cosmos. He, during the 1800s, far ahead of his time, wrote in his poems of a multiplex of universes, and he wrote in such a way, far ahead of when most scientists even recognized that the cosmos consists of many universes. (They hardly see the existence of a multitude of universes at the time of this writing!) In Whitman's poem, entitled "On the Beach at Night Alone," he writes of "the clef of the universes," and he writes of the future… (a time when the majority of scientists will recognize that a multiplicity of universes exists). In "Song of Myself," Whitman gives advice to any man or any woman to "let your soul stand cool and composed before a million universes." Whitman was a man, I think, who saw the love and divine order within (and "as") the energy of the whole of everything; amazingly, he observed all of this with great clarity.

Whitman may have been a direct reflection of much of this love within the whole of everything. Within "Song of Myself," Whitman states: "Mine is no callous shell," about himself. Indeed, one can see the soft warmth of his caring character as one contemplates about how he selflessly helped the wounded throughout much of the Civil war era. He even contracted tuberculosis during the days spent holding-dear and caring for war-torn soldiers who were riddled with countless stress-related diseases. Not only was he compassionate, but he wished for others to have the opportunity to operate through compassion as he had, for he sagaciously realized that operating without compassion was a most cadaverous, dead way to exist. In "Song of Myself," for example, he mentions that "whoever walks a furlong without sympathy walks to his own funeral dressed in his shroud." His love was not merely a love that was shallow, such as the love of money, for example. In "Song of Myself," he writes that "I or you pocketless of a dime may purchase the pick of the earth." He enjoyed going for long walks alone, or with others, outdoors, observing nature's plants and animals with deep affection; such things cannot be calculated easily in terms of any monetary value or rule of measure.

When I was very young, one of my teachers, probably the best teacher I ever had, gave us, as a few of our assignments, instructions to read poems by a man whose first name was Walt. She gave me something eternally precious. She was not one of those ordinary teachers. Back then, I was not as appreciative of him (i.e., Walt) as I am now, but perhaps reading him back then was very beneficial, nonetheless. In "Song of Myself," Whitman writes that "You will hardly know who I am or what I mean, but I shall be good health to you, nevertheless, and filter and fibre your blood."

from Walt Whitman:

Excerpt from Song of Myself:

I have said that the soul is not more than the body,
And I have said that the body is not more than the soul,
And nothing, not God, is greater to one than one's self is,

And whoever walks a furlong without sympathy walks to his own funeral drest in his shroud,
And I or you pocketless of a dime may purchase the pick of the earth,
And to glance with an eye or show a bean in its pod confounds the learning of all times,
And there is no trade or employment but the young man following it may become a hero,
And there is no object so soft but it makes a hub for the wheel'd universe,
And I say to any man or woman, Let your soul stand cool and composed before a million universes.

What does it mean to be fully alive and deeply aware, as a human being? Would a fully alive and deeply aware human being go through life in a superficial manner, just casually looking at things in an ordinary way? May it be that a human being, who is truly alive and deeply aware, would look at things with a profound appreciation, with an ever renewing, immense freshness that would be a flow in miracles of wonderment and joy? Such a mind might look at everything with eyes that are not contaminated with the old, worn-out images and patterns of the dead past. In such ever-renewing originality, it would be untouched by the boring mediocrity of seeing the same-old thing, time and time again. It would look at things anew, as if for the first time, and it would not operate through a mental screen of "what it was taught to see." Being free of the screen of memory and stored images, it would even be capable of going beyond the need of experiencing things at all. It would frequently be experiencing joyfully, but its inherent brightness and inner stability would put it beyond the bourgeois need to always be "experiencing" in order to survive blissfully.

Being a light to itself, it would not need to be constantly groping for things via endless experiences. It would be beyond experiences. However, in experiencing, it would be in wonderment and awe, for it would be appreciative of all the unending miracles of life. Being a blessing, it would be appreciative of blessings, blessings not very separate from what it is; these blessings would be of it and with it — with humility and respect — regardless, for the most part, of what misfortunes would befall it. It would learn, in its shining, about the value of giving rather than merely taking, and its outpouring would often not want anything in return. It would move through life not questioning life's value, not questioning life's meaning; for it would be, itself, life's value, life's meaning. It would operate in (and "as") humility, for it would not see itself as being superior or at a higher level than others, for it would psychologically die to all lies that were directed to it, and it would actually not be separate from those "others." It would walk fit and lean, and not stuffed, of the things of life. It would be consumed, consumed by that intelligence which leaves no real barriers, no real authorities who are superior. It would not look down upon others as if it were something better or something very separate from them.

Would it dive deep for the real questions? Would it dive deep for the real answers? Alternatively, would it remain superficial, ordinary, uncaring, frightened, unconcerned, indifferent, bored, agitated, frustrated, cold, blind, sullen, sluggish, wasteful, and narrow-mindedly selfish? If it were intelligent, would it not change from the limited, dead-end track that it was on? It may very well be true that what goes beyond the barriers of words and symbols is capable of also going beyond the barriers of indifference, hatred, and beyond the mediocrity which separative countries and separative religions are involved in. Furthermore, it may be that: that which goes beyond the barriers of words and symbols… may be what is capable of going beyond the barriers of time and space, in a most profound way. The beauty of it is that no technique, that takes up time and that involves space, can take one there, to what is *timeless* and free of circumstance. *Bliss* is not attainable via any mechanical methods or systems that produce results after doing things in space or after practicing things in time; for deep truth may be beyond the parameters of, and beyond the groping of, time and space. We can function with dignity in space and in time and, if we are pure enough, we can function with much dignity beyond the confines of limited perspectives. Hate and indifference are limited perspectives. Doing drugs, while being unconcerned about the effects those drugs have on so-called others, are limited perspectives. True bliss and real wisdom, fortunately, are not at all confined to the realm of limited perspectives. There is real beauty in life. Real beauty is not confined to the limited.

Although he (i.e., Lennon) did drugs for quite a while, and had related problems, he managed to evolve and create some very meaningful lyrics that can be beneficial. Please obtain and listen to the song by him, entitled *Mind Games*, in which he sings: "We all been playing those mind games forever — Some kinda druid dudes lifting the veil — Doin' the mind guerilla — Some call it magic, the search for the Grail…"

We all sometimes seek amusement in various ways. Some of the ways that we seek amusement are harmful to the beautiful creatures of this earth, and some of the ways we seek amusement are not very harmful. Pleasure and pain are very interrelated; one with the other inevitably occurs in most lives. Pleasure and pain are like two sides of the same coin; joy is of wisdom, and is beyond both sides of the coin. A few minutes before writing this, one was engaging in the act of playing a 3D computer-oriented pinball game. Engaging in such games is probably all right to an extent; we need to do many down-to-earth things throughout the day also, such as taking walks and such as sitting in a park, observing the birds and wildlife. We can engage in computer-oriented activities and games now and then, as long as we get enough physical exercise throughout the day and do other, more reality-oriented things; we walked the dogs quite a distance, shortly before one began playing the pinball game; I exercised on an indoor bicycle after the 3D game. Technology is oftentimes quite cool, to say the least; but one is wise not to get carried away with it by neglecting nature, by not spending much time outdoors, and by forgetting about such things as physical exercise.

The body and the mind are very interrelated. If one is stagnant and lethargic, there is a good chance that the other will be additionally. Most people do not listen to their bodies as they could. They do not have that intrinsic, natural, holistic, organic intelligence any longer. They neglect or do not read what the body is telling them, and they neglect much of other important things that life is telling them. A sensitive mind that listens to life is one that listens to what the body is telling it. A sensitive mind listens to life and does not neglect life or act indifferent towards it, for a sensitive mind is life, not something apart from it. A sensitive mind may engage in amusements now and then, but it does not get forever lost in them. Therefore, it does not merely go from one amusement to the next, without ever going beyond amusements intelligently. A truly sensitive mind is not foolish enough to be merely the immaturity of being stuck in one amusement after another. A truly sensitive mind may be the intelligence that does not merely depend on all of the relatively petty amusements that people normally partake in frequently. A mind such as this, having gone beyond "dependence," does not merely constantly require outside stimulation to keep it being happy. Its happiness is not merely a result; its happiness is not merely an effect brought about by some arranged cause. Its happiness was not sought, for a happiness that is sought and found may be merely a temporary effect in a time-sequential sequence of causes and effects. Just as the wind cannot be put in a jar, so this happiness cannot be obtained by one who is still corrupt and limited; it cannot be found by one who is groping and stealing, by one who is craving and taking. Interestingly, that is the beauty of this true happiness; that is the secret of this true joy. It is not for sale, and it cannot be bought. Anyone trying to fill his or her emptiness cannot be of true joy, for it is beyond grasping. The very groping for it is the denying of it. One cannot attain the unattainable.

Last night, while watching a rerun of the classic comedy, entitled "The Honeymooners," Art Carney, within the show, provided an unparalleled poem that he had learned from his co-workers while working with them down in the sewers. The epic poetry he recited was: "When the tides of life turn against you, and the current upsets your boat, don't waste those tears on 'what might have been,' ... just 'lay' on your back and float!" (Indeed, such a timeless poem belongs within this book!) Unfortunately, most people are constantly groping, constantly reaching for happiness. Instead of *being*, they are forever trying to *become something* or *get something*. They have even made God out to be something (or someone) that can be obtained through effort, as if God could be some sort of effect in a time-sequential paradigm. Merely seeking God within time — as if God can come about as an effect, as a result of some calculated cause — may be very erroneous. Corruption often does erroneous things. Instability is what endlessly gropes for happiness through time, and instability is what exists in time, as a lack of joy and inner peace. Instability is a waste of energy, and unfortunately, many people are wasting their energy; many people are, unfortunately, unstable. Unfortunately, very stable, magnificently poised, immense minds are as rare as huge, lofty boulders that are perfectly balanced while resting upon the peaks of high mountains. Merely seeking happiness exclusively in time, as if true happiness can be captured as an effect that is resultant from some cause, may be very erroneous. Such happiness, found as a result of some superficial cause, likely may be just a temporary sort of happiness that exists as a small part of time, as any temporary effect from any temporary cause soon flies away. True happiness, that manifests not merely as a result of some effort in time, may be the deep joy that eludes most individuals.

from Stephen Crane:

There was, before me,
Mile upon mile
Of snow, ice, burning sand.
And yet I could look beyond all this,
To a place of infinite beauty;
And I could see the loveliness of her
Who walked in the shade of the trees.

When I gazed,
All was lost
But this place of beauty and her.
When I gazed,
And in my gazing, desired,
Then came again
Mile upon mile,
Of snow, ice, burning sand.

The poet Wallace Stevens once wrote: "The poet makes silk dresses out of worms." He also once wrote, "Perhaps there is a degree of perception at which what is real and what is imagined are one: a state of clairvoyant observation, accessible or possibly accessible to the poet or, say, the acutest poet."

from William Blake:

Eternity

He who binds to himself a joy
Does the winged life destroy;
But he who kisses the joy as it flies
Lives in eternity's sun rise.

People place so much emphasis on the intellect; they tend to worship thought and thinking, and tend (as we have mentioned previously) to look down on those that seem to be less intelligent. People often laugh at those who forget things; they often laugh at those who do not know many things; they often laugh at those who are not good at manipulating things. We are deeply prejudiced against those whom we consider very intellectually inferior to "us." We are, if we are at all honest with ourselves, very *afraid* to make *stupid mistakes* in front of "others." We want to become noticed by others for being unusually clever, and we connive various ways to become (and appear to be) very cunning and clever.

Adults encourage children, and encourage themselves, to be ever acquiring more and more knowledge; this is because, to us, knowledge and clever manipulation of thought represent success in the future, represent attainment of security and wealth. But life is meant to be lived, and a mind that is always merely groping for success via thinking and thought processes... may be a mind that remains empty of the deepest joys of living and love. If one is constantly groping for success in the future, via thoughts, one may not be fully living in the "now," in the "present." "Being," not "becoming," exists in the *living present.* If one is merely always trying to "become" something, then one is groping for, and grappling with, the future (while not living fully in the *present*). To really be in direct contact with life, one cannot merely look at it through the screen of thought and memory that society has provided for one. That screen involves time and distance; it involves separation and accumulation. That screen mostly involves "becoming"; "becoming" takes time, incidentally. That screen, unfortunately, keeps one from truly being in direct contact with the whole of life. That screen may be necessary, at times, for one to function; but to be exclusively looking through that screen: may be cheating oneself of what "truth" and "direct contact" really are. One cannot live fully in the present if the mind is constantly chattering with echoes from the *past* that occur as memory, knowledge, and *past* learned events that are rearranging themselves as if they are something new. They may be rearranging themselves as if they are something new, but thoughts, no matter how *new* they may seem, are merely the accumulated symbols of the stored *past.* They are stored symbols rearranging themselves in ways that may be relatively "new," but which are, to a great degree (nevertheless), old and worn out patterns that society has ingrained into one (for one to exist as). Exercising thought and using thought with precision and expertise is important; with it, one can help people and animals in medical and life-saving ways. However, we cannot repeat it enough, thought (i.e., the thinking process) is merely a tool; and over-identifying with what is merely a tool (or a network of tools) is unhealthy and leads to a rather shallow, sorrowful life.

Thought is constantly measuring and categorizing things; often, it is worrying and projecting fear about things. It is necessary and good for thought and thinking to function in such things as medicine, health care, using green-energy, and in science that is beneficial to life. However, is it necessary for thought to exist as fears about what others may think or say about one? Is it necessary to be functioning as thought (i.e., as the thinking process) all the time? Can we function in different ways? We have placed all of our eggs in one basket: the basket of "thought." We are always thinking "about things," with the mind existing as little else, if anything. That basket, that we have placed pretty much "all of our eggs in," is limited; it is very limited and circumscribed. Merely to live that way may not be "living" at all. Merely to live that way may be the equivalent of clutching and clinging to what, in essence, is sorrow. No wonder why so many of us are "real basket-cases." Why cling to the superficial light of the little candle of thought and imagination when instead one can, with keen awareness that transcends thought and thinking, have the sun?

from Wallace Stevens:

Valley Candle

My candle burned alone in an immense valley.
Beams of the huge night converged upon it.
Until the wind blew.
Then beams of the huge night
Converged upon its image,
Until the wind blew.

[From now on, i will be writing with (and you will be reading) the small "i." There is no need to capitalize it, since it is not really *a central controlling entity* in the first place. It is merely another one of the multitudinous, symbolic thoughts. Possibly, it might stand for all of the thoughts and feelings that are utilized and projected by this organism, but that does not, in itself, warrant "Special Capitalization."]

As a very young child, i attended a parochial school run by a local parish; the school was adjacent to the church. We were required to attend mass every day, prior to the classes, which were mostly run by the local order of nuns. While sitting in church, i remember thinking (on more than one occasion) that God was not there to any great extent. God was, one felt, more out-of-doors among the plants and living things, mountains and valleys. God was life, not some dreary symbols or images that were worshiped by preprogrammed automatons who mostly just repeated what they were told to repeat in stale, enclosed, limited, dreary little buildings; in other words, they didn't really have anything sacred locked in a golden cage (for commoners to come visit and pay to support).

I also remember that, as a very young child, (long before i had read any poetry), i stopped thinking, one day, and questioned the whole nature of "thinking" and "knowing." I remember that, on that particular day, while a very young child, i suspected that there exists something better and clearer (for the mind) than what mere "thinking" and "knowing" consists of. There exists a *silence* that is vast and all-inclusive, a *silence* that is a deeper intelligence than what mere symbolic, repetitive thinking consists of.

Later in life, i became more and more appreciative of the nature of that *silence* that is immense and so extremely dynamic. A dull mind can practice and attempt all kinds of techniques in order to acquire "silence." However, the silence that such a mind attains will inevitably be the resultant trappings of a reactionary, power-driven, contriving, mechanical mind. Therefore, such a silence will not be of the profound kind at all; rather, it would merely be a superficial, manmade, mediocre kind of silence. True, deep *silence* may not be what can be brought about by any dull, second-hand method. True, deep *silence* comes about naturally, without any effort, when the mind is keen and pure, innocent, and "not full of itself." True, deep *silence* may be outside of the realm of what mediocrity and uncaring eyes can grasp and attain. True, deep *silence* may be beyond the avaricious, acquisitive "groping" and "grappling" that mechanical, robot-like minds were programmed to function as. Mechanical, robot-like minds are, unfortunately, not capable of functioning with deep, all-abiding compassion; therefore, they are not dynamic enough to function in that deep *silence and limitlessness* in which the *truly sacred* abides. (E. E. Cummings once wrote, "Most people are perfectly afraid of silence.")

One may fortunately function, even for many years, in (and "as") deep, dynamic silence, yet still not be visited by the *profoundly sacred*. However, if it should finally come, even unto one who is far into old age, such a one, to whom it comes, would be blessed beyond belief, far beyond what the mind can imagine or conjure up of its own accord. Such a one, blessed, would then be over a trillion times more alive than what people now call living, and such a one would truly be of a *benediction* beyond the confines of death and sorrow. The *sacred* may come to minds that (to an extent) run parallel to deep order and to the goodness that is immense. The *sacred* will seem elusive to dull minds that are narrow, repetitive, shallow, uncaring, closed, cold, indifferent, imitative, frightened, old, and shadow-like. This, one fully understands: the *sacred* loves life; the *sacred* runs through life; the *sacred* is not some fragmented, little "I" who is associated with other thoughts about how it is separate from the whole of life.

from Walt Whitman:

We Two, How Long We Were Fool'd

We two, how long we were fool'd,
Now transmuted, we swiftly escape as Nature escapes,
We are Nature, long have we been absent, but now we return,
We become plants, trunks, foliage, roots, bark,
We are bedded in the ground, we are rocks,
We are oaks, we grow in the openings side by side,
We browse, we are two among the wild herds spontaneous as any,
We are two fishes swimming in the sea together,
We are what locust blossoms are, we drop scent around lanes mornings and evenings,
We are also the coarse smut of beasts, vegetables, minerals,
We are two predatory hawks, we soar above and look down,
We are two resplendent suns, we it is who balance ourselves orbic and stellar, we are as two comets,
We prowl fang'd and four-footed in the woods, we spring on prey,
We are two clouds forenoons and afternoons driving overhead,
We are seas mingling, we are two of those cheerful waves rolling over each other and interwetting each other,
We are what the atmosphere is, transparent, receptive, pervious, impervious,
We are snow, rain, cold, darkness, we are each product and influence of the globe,
We have circled and circled till we have arrived home again, we too,
We have voided all but freedom and all but our own joy.

Most people have nice, clean vehicles that look fantastic on the outside; they also have pristine lawns that are often quite flawless (to them) in terms of having no wild-growing dandelions, weeds, nor wild violets growing also. Their lawns look to be quite orderly and perfect. Such people appear to have very orderly lives on the outside; however, on the inside (i.e., within their heads) there often exists great disorder and chaos. Such people often have homes that look clean and majestic on the outside; but what occurs in the inside is often disorderly, unclean, impure, and sullied.

Additionally, we don't mind purchasing all kinds of edibles to consume as our food, edibles that look charming and pleasing on the outside; however, on the inside, many of these things are essentially unhealthy and full of artificial ingredients, with "fabricated, over-processed" contents. However, our minds — corrupted by age-old industries that have indoctrinated millions (via commercials, advertisements, fancy outer packaging, etc.) to "accept" their broken-down and ramshackle products as being legitimate — purchase these so-called consumable items as if each of our organic insides has some kind of magical digestive system capable of easily dealing with the artificial and synthetic. Is there any wonder why cancer, obesity, and other diseases are rampant at the time of writing this book? Our apples no longer have wormholes occasionally in them, as they did at one (less polluted) time in the past. Our vegetables seldom have insects upon them: for no six-legged crawler would be able to devour them; furthermore, we think that these vegetables are "safe." Many farmers often annually add barren fertilizer to fields; such fertilizer is not organic and is missing many micronutrients. Many authorities don't care one pin what you buy — be it edible, political, or spiritual authorities — as long as they can squeeze plenty of money out of you while giving you artificial things.

Therefore, our houses, vehicles and edibles appear to be clean and neat on the outside, yet our minds and bodies are filthy and corrupt on the inside. We have bought all the tickets from the old and corrupt; many of us have been totally bamboozled by the old-fashioned big shots. We have symmetrical, orderly-looking, clean vehicles, yet on the inside many of us remain conniving, foul, stealthy, greedy, and uncaring; in other words, we are disorderly on the inside, while, outwardly, we like to give out the appearance of being orderly. We take frequent baths, use deodorant profusely, yet we are often hateful and indifferent inside of our heads. Many of us dress elegantly and beautifully, but, at the workplace, we bully or mistreat others whom we have power over. We have cosmetic surgery... so that, even though we are full of old, washed-out ideas on the inside, we appear fresh and new on the outside. Things have not changed all that much, really, since Christ's time. In the ancient *Gospel of Thomas*, for instance, Jesus asks, "Why do you wash the outside of the cup? Don't you understand that the one who made the inside is the same one who made the outside?" And in Luke (Chapter 11, Verse 39), it states: Then the Lord said to him, "Now you Pharisees (i.e., you orthodox priests and temple-goers) clean the outside of the cup and of the dish, but inside you are full of greed and wickedness." During the time of Christ, many people had great wealth/prestige and took great pains to ensure that they looked good from the outside: that their clothes, homes, temples, and possessions reflected style and orderly beauty; however, they too, on the inside, were disorderly, ugly, and shattered. Things really haven't changed since Jesus's time, have they?

Our so-called outside "order," if one looks honestly, is truly only a small, superficial semblance of order. Much of it is a pretentious show to impress others (who, like many of us, are easily fooled). We imitate; we fool ourselves; we fit nicely into the old pattern that everyone else seems to be in, and we think we are doing rather well by being in this vintage mold, this cast, this array that was designed for us to function in, that was designed for us to "function as." We are happy, little cogs in the age-old machine, and it is easy to remain indifferent and to stay that way, in that stagnation, in that comfort. However, what is truly tarnished and sullied on the inside cannot possibly be happy, despite all the polish on the so-called outside. The outside often is a reflection and an extension of the inside, and we may fool the foolish, but we cannot fool the truly intelligent, the truly wise. The truly wise merge with this foolishness and partake of it, not so much in the active sense; they merge with it in their consciousness, the perceiver being the perceived, and they go beyond it. The wise mind permeates the lies and lives well beyond them. Such a mind is not captured by what is stagnant, old, and dead. It flows on as a real, living, organic movement, though it touches the stagnation.

What you own or manipulate is an extension of yourself. Some of the vehicles that people currently own are overly large, fancy, and shiny; many of these vehicles are mammoth energy wasters, terrible producers of pollution, though they look pretty. A truly wise man can see what good, or what harm, things do to the environment. A truly wise man can see if something emanates from a mind that has some compassion, or if it likely comes from a mind that is indifferent and uncaring, sullied. To be mostly unsullied means that one is pure and uncorrupt on the inside. What is pure inside: often takes care of what is outside. It takes care of the outside, because it perceives the outside without separation. It and the outside are one. Such a mind is not separate from the world. It does not use outside appearances merely to impress others with pretense and artificial ostentation. It is content in itself, and need not depend on the reflection of others who are foolish.

from Stephen Crane:

There was One I met upon the road
Who looked at me with kind eyes.
He said: "Show me of your wares."
And this I did
Holding forth one.
He said: "It is a sin."
Then held I forth another.
He said: "It is a sin."
Then held I forth another.
He said: "It is a sin."
And so to the end
Always He said: "It is a sin."
And, finally, I cried out:
"But I have none other."
Then did He look at me
With kinder eyes.
"Poor soul," He said.

People get into drugs for various reasons; drugs are an escape from the everyday occurrences, from the everyday routines, from the monotony of it all. A truly sane, balanced mind, however, does not fall into the trap of merely having everyday routines that it gets tired of; nor does such a mind succumb to the boredom of monotony. A truly sane mind has learned, for itself, about how (without merely following a pattern or technique) to be appreciative of every single moment of its life in a *truly living* way. Such a way, of true intelligence, is beyond the confines of boredom and psychological suffering. A balanced mind of true sanity and true intelligence does not merely depend on outside circumstances in order for it to be happy. It is happy beyond circumstances, for it has learned, for itself, about the absurdity of merely groping to the outside environment for inner happiness. Such a mind is a flame that need not merely be fueled by situations occurring in the so-called extraneous (so-called "outer") environment.

Drugs, for many people, are not merely constituted of such things as alcohol, marijuana, and certain pills and chemicals. Many people overeat as a form of drug; or another drug, for many people, is an over-dependence on music, sports, or television. Many people get lost to an unending degree in cyberspace, and some people are drugged by clinging to an over-abundance of money or prestige. Some people drug themselves by means of massive amounts of knowledge, massive amounts of children, and some people drug themselves by needing to travel from one spot to another area. (However, they are just the same consciousness wherever they go and are exactly where they were from the start). Some people will drug themselves, in the future, by having computer-oriented implants placed inside (or physically connected to) their brains; they will become even more mechanically robotic and more "un-alive" than their predecessors were. Some people drug themselves by useless idleness; they drug themselves by not doing anything of a caring nature for others; they drug themselves by wallowing in their own unending, self-absorbed, little comfort. The poet Wallace Stevens once wrote: "Poetry is a cure of the mind." One cannot cure the mind if one merely takes many mind-altering drugs. Alcohol is a depressant; it, in reality, does not make one truly joyous. Other drugs are equally inefficient at causing the mind to be truly joyous. True joy is not a result; it especially is not a result of some manmade chemical, sold in the marketplace. The black-market, of those selling drugs, has "elders" and "powerful authorities" within it, just as there exists powerful, corrupt bureaucrats in high governmental positions; neither of them really cares for you to be living in true freedom and true harmony.

Fortunately, there are people with truly balanced minds. They are a light unto themselves, and they share that light by helping life. However, they do not get so lost in their work that they merely depend upon it, or use it as a drug. They also live in a blissful way (beyond technique oftentimes), in which they learn about life without needless dependence, without much harm to life's creatures. They exist in *silence*, at times, but do not mechanically measure what the duration of that silence might be, for their lives are blissfully beyond what can be measured and analyzed. They do not "know" that they are in a state of *silence*, for real *silence* is a state beyond knowing, and beyond "what can be known and measured." They do not react from much fear, because they have intelligently gone beyond fear, by having understood it, by not thinking that they are separate from fear.

Only deeply healthy minds are creative in the truly living sense, where joy occurs without a mere motive, beyond calculation. Only healthy minds are not drugged by language, by symbols, by bad habits, by beliefs, by uncaring behaviors; only healthy minds are truly empty of rubbish. All minds that are into drugs are into dead-end streets, and a dead-end street is always limited, always what vastness is not. All too many of us have absorbed what the elder authorities have immersed us in, and we have become addicted to what it is. All too often, what it is (besides synthetic things) happens to be "thought and the process of thinking." We are addicted to being one series of thoughts after another, without any real stoppage or *silence* whatsoever. We are lost without exclusively being the *thinking process,* and we are afraid of true *silence.* Words, and stale images, which make up "thought" and "thinking," are always old and of past memories, past occurrences. They are truly limited, like dead-end streets. These images might become rearranged and, thus, seem new, but they are, nevertheless, images and symbols coming from "stored memory"; hence, they are "old" and are from the "past." Existing exclusively as (and "from") old symbols is not real living. Looking at life through the screen of accumulated symbols, patterns, and stored images, may not be real living at all.

from Stephen Crane:

There was a man who lived a life of fire.
Even upon the fabric of time,
Where purple becomes orange
And orange purple,
This life glowed,
A dire red stain, indelible;
Yet when he was dead,
He saw that he had not lived.

Chapter 4

We so easily come to conclusions, to little, narrow, dead-end, mental streets in our lives about so many things; thus, we block our minds from looking at everything with fresh, uncontaminated eyes. It is useful, in life, to often measure things, to weigh things with knowledge, with the mind, so that we can function in a more healthful, beneficial, well-dressed manner. However, if we use the problem-solving energy of thought beyond what is necessary, then we over-extend its use into realms where it interferes with, rather than supports, much happiness. While you are over-extending problem solving, and are constantly worrying about things, you cannot fully be enjoying life spontaneously. A balance is suggested. However, only a sane, healthy mind can see when it is functioning as "thought" and "thinking," beyond what is necessary.

Many people, far too many, are not sane, are not healthy in the mental sense. They go on measuring; they go on calculating, with thought, endlessly. Such people often tend to "measure each other up" in a rather mechanical, robotic, cold, gear-meshing-with-gear way, and then they don't even mind when so-called "others" suffer or are in pain. Instead of having the passion of direct insight, they weigh things out only in a calculating way, and go about their "business" without directly caring. They often tend to bully others; they often tend to be domineering over others; they often exploit others. It is easy to look at life through second-hand images and then to have second-hand feelings, which are not "true" feelings at all.

Most people are afraid of *dying*; but he (or she) who *dies* (mentally, not physically) to all of the constant rumblings of thought and thinking, may be he (or she) who truly lives. This is not so for the man who is ceaselessly worrying, ceaselessly conniving, ceaselessly clinging to his perceptions of everything through the screen of thought/thinking. Most people are afraid to die to thought/thinking, which they have incorporated as their essence, which they have incorporated as their so-called life. However, clinging to that kind of "life," in that manner, may not be real living at all. In The Gospel of Luke, Jesus allegedly said, "Whoever tries to hang on to life will forfeit it, but whoever forfeits life will preserve it."

from Jesus, from the Gospel of Matthew, World English Bible:

"Therefore I tell you, don't be anxious (i.e., worry via thinking) for your life: what you will eat, or what you will drink; nor yet for your body, what you will wear. Isn't life more than food, and the body more than clothing? See the birds of the sky, that they don't sow, neither do they reap, nor gather into barns. Your heavenly Father feeds them. Aren't you of much more value than they? Which of you, by being anxious (i.e., by worrying via thinking), can add one moment to his lifespan? Why are you anxious about clothing? Consider the lilies of the field, how they grow. They don't toil, neither do they spin; yet I tell you that even Solomon in all his glory was not dressed like one of these. But if God so clothes the grass of the field, which today exists, and tomorrow is thrown into the oven, won't he much more clothe you, you of little faith?

Therefore don't be anxious, saying, 'What will we eat?', 'What will we drink?' or, 'With what will we be clothed?"

Of course, we are not suggesting that one just sit around languidly and forget all about earning a living to put bread on the table. Life is very tough, currently, and we need to be very concerned and diligent. However, it would be prudent to also take a lot of time, each day, to observe life simply and directly, without many self-projected burdens of worry and fear.

In the *Tao Te Ching*, Lao Tzu is translated as having said: "In the pursuit of learning, every day something is acquired; in the pursuit of Tao, every day something is dropped." So, we need not always just be thinking, as others (i.e., the elders and authorities) want us to think. They often indoctrinate people and fill their minds (i.e., the people's consciousness) with what they want the *content of consciousness* to be. People all too readily absorb the advertisements, the political and religious propaganda, the slogans and the systems, and become what "outside authority" *programs* them to become. The truly intelligent mind reads and studies often, but that is not all; a truly intelligent mind also frequently becomes empty and still — not by engaging in effort, practices, or methods to do so — just by naturally and instantaneously, psychologically dying to all the second-hand symbols and "un-alive" patterns that it was programmed (by the authoritarian elders) to be. Such a vibrant intelligence remains youthful and new, uncorrupt and uncontaminated; it dies to what exists as "un-alive" symbols and old, corrupt representations, but it never truly comes to a limited end. It definitely never comes to a limited end.

from the Tao Te Ching by Lao Tzu, as translated by J. Legge (and edited, slightly, by Thomas Peace):

The (state of) vacancy should be brought to the utmost degree,
and that of stillness guarded with un-wearying vigor. All things
alike go through their processes of activity, and (then) we see them
return (to their original state). When things (in the vegetable
world) have displayed their luxuriant growth, we see each of them
return to its root. This returning to their root is what we call the
state of stillness; and that stillness may be called a reporting that
they have fulfilled their appointed end.

The report of that fulfillment is the regular, unchanging rule.
To feel that unchanging rule is to be intelligent; not to feel it leads

to wild movements and evil issues. The understanding of that unchanging
rule produces a (grand) capacity and forbearance, and that capacity
and forbearance lead to a community (of feeling with all things).
From this community of feeling comes a kingliness of character, and he who is king-like goes on to be heaven-like.

One cannot have a truly close relationship with nature if one looks with barriers, through multitudinous patterns of thought that separate the "perceiver" from "the perceived." If one merely looks at a butterfly with the labels and images of "butterflies" that one has collected and stored in (and "as") the memory bank, then one is merely looking through (and "as") some images and thoughts occurring in (and "as") ordinary time. Nature is much more vast, intricate, and flowing than what thought and conceptual patterns can conjure up. If we merely look through thought, we will be cutting ourselves short and will be looking with rather dead, cadaverous eyes that see only partially.

Memory, as the *past*, as what occurred in (and "as") the *past...* is old. The memory bank is full of old patterns. These patterns can be rearranged, but they are still old. Memory is what was "before"; it is not new in the spontaneous "now." In the ancient *Gospel of Thomas*, it is said that Jesus saw infants being suckled. He said to those around him, "These infants being suckled are like those who enter the Kingdom." The ancient *Tao Te Ching* asks, "Can you avoid separation? Attending fully and becoming supple, can you be as a newborn babe?" We can look at things in wonderment, with fresh, young eyes; we can look without merely depending upon the old, worn-out patterns of the *past*. We will still use the *past*, as memory and knowledge, as useful tools in order to continue to survive in harmony. However, we will not become overly dependent upon the tools; we will not get lost in the tools and patterns of the *past* and merely remain there. Dead, worn-out thoughts will often die (in us), and a new *living* way of being will exist. It will not merely be an old extension of the *past*. It will not exclusively be the same, old patterns in rearranged forms. Freedom exists when the mind is not merely burdened with *past* images, with *past, dead patterns*. (E. E. Cummings once poetically wrote, "Knowledge is a polite word for dead but not buried imagination.")

A free mind is a wonderful thing, a miraculous thing. One cannot choose to be free, no more than one can choose to be humble, no more than one can choose to be silent. True freedom and silence come when one does not merely try, via effort, to attain things and to label things. That non-effort, however, is of a great energy; it is of a vast intelligence that is beyond what a mere calculating, striving mind can grope for. If there is awareness, throughout the day, without separation between the perceiver and the perceived, of each thought, of each feeling as they occur, then there may be an awareness that is beyond the boundaries and limitations of thinking. Such awareness, such intelligence, is not capable of being pigeonholed and analyzed by thought. Insight, deep insight, may be beyond the measurements and configurations that thinking is capable of being. Profound insight may exist beyond the superficial, virtual energy of thought. Profound insight shatters through ordinary patterns and situations; it brings great joy, for it runs with (or "as") the essence of everything. Those with it go beyond mere depression, beyond looking at things with the boredom and monotony of the same, old patterns (of thought). Those with it do not need to go far to find much stimulation; they are not dependent upon needing much stimulation, but they do experience much in the way of miracles frequently, even in the nearness of their own backyards or wilderness paths.

from the Tao Te Ching by Lao Tzu, translated by J. H. McDonald:

The spirit of emptiness is immortal.
It is called the Great Mother
because it gives birth to Heaven and Earth.

It is like a vapor,
barely seen but always present.
Use it effortlessly.

Being silent, as a quiet mind, may not be easy for a saturated mind that is full of the commotion and the imprints of others. A mind that is constantly chattering is not a "free" mind because it, despite thinking otherwise, is full of their thoughts, their methods, their patterns, and their systems. Only in complete stillness can the bliss of the *sacred* come; the *sacred* alone is the true whole and source behind everything. It may come: not merely as (or from) a method— not as (or from) an array of symbolic patterns. What is deeply alive, most assuredly, never is merely composed of patterns and dead symbols. Those who merely get lost in the vast array of symbols and representations, amusements, and sequential patterns, are those who do not understand the awareness that silence and deep living is. Such a "deep living" is a "beingness" that is above the antiquated, time-based, sequential modes that people cling to. This "beingness" is of a deep silence and profound understanding that transcends mere reactive thinking. Those that are "of it" are extremely creative, though they may not just produce "things" that are useable by human beings. Those that are "of it" partake in a creative fountain that is pristine and good, and such a goodness does not merely grope for things, nor does it struggle to negate and avoid things.

The greatest state of mind to exist as, for a human being, is that state of mind that is the deep *here and now*, without the corruption of the *past programming* of others operating. Such a state of mind would then be capable of loving the whole of life in the truly deep sense, not in the cadaverous sense, like the dead state that those who are corrupt and cruel, unfortunately, adhere to. To love in the superficial sense is not the same as *loving* in the deep or profound sense. A mind that is dead-from-the-neck-up, unfortunately, is bound to cause much harm to the life forms on this planet. Its "malfunctioning" internally will, as time goes by, cause "malfunctioning" and chaos externally. Such a mind, interestingly, will insist that its behavior is OK, all the while not realizing its profound lack of awareness.

One can help others and encourage others to learn to awaken their minds; such "learning" is not merely an accumulative process. Such learning is not merely what comes about by studying books and by remembering things. When the space between the "perceiver" and "that, which is perceived" ends, then there exists the beginning of deep wisdom. The space between the "perceiver" and "that, which is perceived" does not require time in order for it to disappear; that space is a product of time, because it is merely reactive and part of a sequential process. Negating it and going beyond it does not take time. A mind that is truly in timelessness, that is beyond mere cause and effect reactions, is in no need for mind-altering drugs and in no need for endless forms and patterns of entertainment; what is *whole* need not always seek parts. What is "whole" need not always seek more via partial, sequential modes. That space — that an ignorant mind always creates between itself and what it sees — is a crude, divisive, dimensionless, dead outlook that was absorbed and inherited from other minds that were themselves not fully alive or whole. Wisdom is not of the realm of dead minds that cling to old traditions and old, worn-out perspectives. A truly advanced mind, a truly youthful and fresh mind... is not a chain of mere reactions; nor is it merely a part of a chain of reactions. A truly wise and whole mind is not merely trapped in a sequential process, and it does not exclusively function as a sequential process (though it sometimes functions sequentially and sometimes partakes in interesting entertainment for long periods of time). Truth may be so subtle and non-causal, that seeking it with strenuous effort cancels the chance of coming upon it. It is not a prize to be attained, but it exists. Deep truth may be more subtle and elusive than what the men, in the following poem, were capable of; it may be very elusive, like the dynamic effortlessness that the recently mentioned, poetic *Tao Te Ching* mentions.

from Stephen Crane:

"Truth," said a traveler,
"Is a rock, a mighty fortress;
Often have I been to it,
Even to its highest tower,
From whence the world looks black."
"Truth," said a traveler,
"Is a breath, a wind...
A shadow, a phantom;
Long have I pursued it,
But never have I touched
The hem of its garment."
And I believed the second traveler;
For truth was to me
A breath, a wind,
A shadow, a phantom,
And never had I touched
The hem of its garment.

When the mind is full of *chattering thoughts*, it is occupied with its own activity, its own projections. Then it is often lost in superficial images that are merely the symbols of others. It actually, then, is the symbols and thoughts of others, rearranging (but essentially the same). When such a mind is *afraid* to be without those symbolic images for a time, it usually does not realize that it is not something separate from the *fear*. It actually (at that time) *is* the *fear*. When the mind is *fear* of being what "silence" is, then silence does not easily come.

A mind that is not merely composed of images and fear, is a silent, joyous, truly living mind. Thoughts, in such a mind, are often not manifesting in (and "as") consciousness. Without symbols, without being fear, without being projections of thought, without being desires, without being comparison and jealousy, such a mind is silent and at great peace. That *silence* is not a dead silence. It is a *living, active silence* that is whole. That *silence*, in such a living mind, was not brought about by any manmade method or procedure. That *silence* was not fabricated by the intricacies of clever thought/thinking. That *silence* is not a second-hand affair that was learned or absorbed from another. That *silence* is not merely part of the sequential series that thought (as time) consists of. (The previous sentence is immensely important to understand, in terms of the seriousness and depth of its meaning.) Holes, within and through the layers of Swiss cheese, are not merely parts of the cheese.

Only emptiness can contain everything (i.e., the whole). That which is full of itself, full of its own projections, can only get more parts, more fragments, and more symbols, which are only partial. Arrogant individuals are full of themselves. Such individuals are chock-full of isolated symbols (involving limited space). However, that emptiness which is vast can be imbued with the essence of all life. Such a mind that is of such pure emptiness is beyond the clutches of fear, separation, and hatred. Such a mind that is of such pure emptiness is wise, is unburdened of too many desires, is compassionate, and is not separate from insight. *Deep insight* is the spontaneity of a *truly empty mind*; it is the mind merging with the *unknown* without dependence on the old, worn-out clamor of thought. Getting to deep insight does not take time. There is no procedure, in time, to use to get to deep insight. Thought, the manifestation and execution of thought, does take time. Without time, thought could not exist. Thought and time are interrelated and intertwined. As we suggested before, this sounds rather mysterious, though it is true: that a mind that transcends the boundaries of thought, transcends the boundaries of separation and time. Such a mind may then be of deep bliss and may be truly blessed. Such a mind, being beyond separation, is not separate from others.

Many people, unfortunately, do not see the beauty of letting go of all the movements (in time) of thought/thinking. They are caught in the superficial, narrow aspect of symbolic thinking, and they merely remain there, psychologically suffering. Being merely what symbols are, one must, by natural law, be what suffering is. Being merely symbolic, artificial, "un-alive," craving, fragmentary, separate, and second-hand, is necessarily what psychological suffering must consist of. Those who merely live in thought/ thinking... must necessarily exist in (and "as") separation, sorrow, and conflict. Separation, sorrow, and conflict must, by necessity, depend upon (and exist in) time. Separation, sorrow, and conflict are a dead kind of shadowy emptiness; they are not the true, immense vastness that is living, supremely empty, and whole.

However, despising *words and symbols* is wrong. Do not develop a friction against words, thoughts, and symbols. Just look without friction, without struggle, without undue conflict. Enjoy life and be whole; be all, and be beyond all.

brief excerpt from Rumi (translation by Coleman Barks):

When you are with everyone but me,
you're with no one.
When you are with no one but me,
you're with everyone.

Instead of being so bound up *with* everyone,
be everyone.
When you become that many, you're nothing.
Empty.

When i was a very young child, i had a small, stuffed, Raggedy Ann, male, knave-like, clown-doll whom i considered my great pal and best friend. We spent a great deal of time together. Since my parents did not spend a great deal of time with me that particular doll had a very significant role in my young life. He was my best friend for a considerable time and was always there when i needed him. He was my security, my stability.

Time went by; a good bit of time transpired. Then, one strange day, as i held my dear friend, i suddenly came to the biting realization that my doll was not at all something alive and feeling. The doll, despite its happy, roguish smile, was, in essence, a mass of fabric and stuffing. That tremendous realization was quite a jolt to my consciousness. I was in a deep shock. I survived it, however, and grew to become appreciative of things that were truly alive, truly feeling.

During that time, and later in life, for quite an extended period, i regarded myself as a careful, autonomous, unencumbered manipulator of thoughts. I took it for granted that "I" was a free entity in the middle of my head that made the decisions in an independent and unrestricted way. Then, one strange day, as I thought I held my opinions, i suddenly came to the biting realization that my ego (i.e., the supposed *central processing agent* called "myself") was not at all something truly independent, alive, and viable. The thought of a "Me" or an "I" who is in charge of all the other thoughts was, in essence, just another thought. That "Me" or "I" was another thought in a series or sequence of thoughts; it was not truly what was "in complete control" of the other thoughts (at all). This might seem quite frightening to those who have not put away their dolls (i.e., their fictitious, make-believe images). However, it was not frightening at all, because intelligence was still there; understanding, as wisdom, was still very much there. It was not my intelligence as apart from your intelligence. It was not my well-being as apart from your well-being. It was intelligence and insight that had no fear, and it was freedom to the greatest degree, for around it were no borders involving separation, no demarcations of "Me" as isolated from "You." Only sorrow is confined to small, restricted areas, areas that feel that they are so very special and so very isolated and separate from "others." True sorrow is a *fictitious center* that, by its very fraudulent, untruthful, and deceptive nature, causes great grief for itself and others. Unfortunately, very immense, lofty, balanced boulders are as rare as magnificently stable minds that are perfectly poised while resting upon the peaks of high mountains.

Most people, unfortunately, do not realize that empty symbols, as words, make up (or compose) a large part of what their consciousness (or mind) is. Furthermore, since they are not at all separate from what their consciousness consists of, these people are largely composed of words and symbols that, interestingly enough, are shadowlike impressions, residual aftereffects, and limited representations, which are merely mental reflections and not the real things. These people, to a great degree, are the words that compose their minds. These people are made of words, filled with words, function as words, emit words, and pattern their lives via the frameworks that words delineate. They perceive the world through a screen of "learned words." No wonder so many are, unfortunately, second-hand human beings who are barely alive in the true sense. What is merely symbolic, limited, and second-hand is not what is *truly alive* and *joyous*.

So, after all these years of thinking that you are alive, if you desire to cling to your old symbols and old patterns regarding that "Me" that you think is so full of life, by all means, cling to them. (Cling to the old patterns of symbols that support fabrications about you, if you wish.) However, freshly stepping out from the old, dark recesses of ignorance and limitation takes a great deal of courage and insight; what remains *false* cannot do it. Interestingly, many atheists maintain that God is dead; ironically, it may be that "symbol-oriented atheists" and "church-going, self-projecting-image-worshiping believers" are all, unfortunately, essentially un-alive, while God is very much alive.

from Wallace Stevens:

A High-toned Old Christian Woman

Poetry is the supreme fiction, madame.
Take the moral law and make a nave of it…
And from the nave build haunted heaven. Thus,
The conscience is converted into palms,
Like windy citherns hankering for hymns.
We agree in principle. That's clear. But take
The opposing law and make a peristyle,
And from the peristyle project a masque
Beyond the planets. Thus, our bawdiness,
Un-purged by epitaph, indulged at last,
Is equally converted into palms,
Squiggling like saxophones. And palm for palm,
Madame, we are where we began. Allow,
Therefore, that in the planetary scene
Your disaffected flagellants, well-stuffed,
Smacking their muzzy bellies in parade,
Proud of such novelties of the sublime,
Such tink and tank and tunk-a-tunk-tunk,
May, merely may, madame, whip from themselves
A jovial hullabaloo among the spheres.

This will make widows wince. But fictive things
Wink as they will. Wink most when widows wince.

The old school of thought (and all "common" thought is old and of the stored past) taught us that each of us is separate from each other; they taught us that we are *apart* from all the others. The index finger of the hand can name itself; it can be proud of itself, think that it is unique, think that it is separate and apart from all the other fingers. The index finger is very good at pointing; but the little finger (of the hand) can also point fairly well. If the index finger would somehow harm or destroy the little finger, it would really be doing damage to itself (even though it would not fully realize that it was harming itself). We are very much like the fingers of a hand; there are many of us, but we are not truly separate. (Realizing that we all are "one" and not really separate, by the way, does not mean that you can, for instance, go into your neighbor's home and take his television while stating that "It is mine as much as it is yours, since we are not really separate!")

Our ideals, our systems, institutions, countries, beliefs, and cherished ways of living may be essentially empty shadows compared to what direct perception and uncontaminated observation is; and seeing directly with *uncontaminated eyes* may be beyond what structured systems and dead patterns are capable of providing. One cannot merely be molded into an entity that fully loves. Deep love cannot merely be taught; it is not merely the product of a system. However, dead systems can destroy young, living minds. Most of us look through eyes that were contaminated by the old schools of dead thought. We (most of us) function with brains that are looking through distorted patterns and through images of misconception. As we look through distortion, we then react. Our reactions then flow from distortion. A holistic mind of insight acts; it does not merely react. With so many of us functioning merely as reactions that we absorbed from old, antiquated systems, is there any wonder why the world is in chaos as it is? (Wallace Stevens once wrote, "The poet is a god, or, the young poet is a god. The old poet is a tramp.")

We are at each other's throats, competing, in conflict, quarreling over separative boundaries, racial features, religions, countries, flags, systems and ideals. We think that we are making wonderful progress, while all the while we are getting lost in details without seeing the beautiful, majestic, and profound whole. We chase after empty patterns without ever seeing that deep *energy* which is beyond death and limitation. To really enjoy life, one must truly be alive; otherwise, one is merely "going through the motions of being alive" (which is not true living at all). Plenty of people "go through the motions of being alive," unfortunately. Real life may be (for human beings) actually that which is full of *deep perception* and *deep insight* that shatters separative, divisive, dead concepts. Real life may be a flowering of goodness that does not depend on old patterns, does not depend on old-fashioned frameworks, and does not depend on callous, cruel authorities to tell it what to do. (The poet Wallace Stevens once wrote, "The theory of poetry is the theory of life.")

In his book, Leaves of Grass, Whitman, in many instances, reveals how he feels a deep "oneness" with all of life, including humans, plants, and animals. Whitman, as the following few lines from the poem entitled *Song of Myself* indicates, knew how to tear things apart, and knew how to see things as "one," holistically, without things merely all having separate, individual forms. Here is a sample of Walt: "Unscrew the locks from the doors! Unscrew the doors themselves from their jambs! Whoever degrades another degrades me… And whatever is done or said returns at last to me." There is a very good possibility that Walt Whitman was one of those rare, splendid human beings who could transcend time and space and be visited by what is *truly sacred*.

from Walt Whitman:

To be in any form, what is that?
(Round and round we go, all of us, and ever come back thither,)
If nothing lay more develop'd the quahaug in its callous shell were enough.
Mine is no callous shell,
I have instant conductors all over me whether I pass or stop,
They seize every object and lead it harmlessly through me.
I merely stir, press, feel with my fingers, and am happy.
To touch my person to someone else's is about as much as I can stand.

Society would have one perceive while being ingrained with a deep sense of *division* and *separation*. A sick society mesmerizes its members into thinking and perceiving that each one of them is separate from everything and everyone else. Friction and competition, for the most part, is the law of the land. One is considered as having a healthy brain if such a brain observes via conflict and friction.

To observe without being conditioned by the apron strings of a sick society is a very arduous affair; only a very sensitive, truly intelligent, and caring mind can go far beyond the superficial boundaries of society. Those superficial boundaries are the petty frameworks of consciousness, which many of us have thoughtlessly and erroneously accepted to be the truest reality. Our imperfections are wrought with this unreal "non-reality"; many of us are crazed beings clenching to shadows, taking these shadows to be a reality with substance. (Wallace Stevens once wrote, "The poet must come at least as the miraculous beast and, at his best, as the miraculous man.")

To look without the *curse of separation* means that an intelligent (non-barbaric) human being looks in a *holistic* way that is beyond mere fragmentation. Such a mind does not merely see in parts; it sees all as one, whole, flowing and living movement. Looking at trees, its consciousness is not separate from the images and patterns of the trees. Such a mind, of course, is not composed of chlorophyll, bark, and sap, but such a mind does have the keen insight to feel a deep "oneness" with the trees. The trees and such a profound mind have an immense and true relationship with each other. An ordinary brain will likely be aloof, apart, and indifferent about the trees. An ordinary brain will not realize that the *images of the trees* (and the very trees themselves) are not truly separate from what its consciousness is. When one looks at trees, one's consciousness consists of the images, patterns, and colors... of leaves and branches.

The "I" that says it sees the "trees" is a manmade, fabricated symbol that is unnecessary; it can be referred to if it represents the whole; however, if reference to it involves positing that the *perceiver* is something *separate from the perceived*, then miscalculation and error has taken place. The patterns that one *perceives* are the patterns that one *is*; such patterns compose and constitute consciousness. Without such patterns, ordinary consciousness is not possible. If one is supremely intelligent, one can be a mind that does not merely depend on patterns, at all times, in order to healthily function. Such a mind can function as an immense, quiet stillness that is beyond the mechanizations of patterns and attributes; but even this goes only so far and, to remain healthy, the mind must often look at trees, rivers, and other wonderful, flowing manifestations of the earth. It must look at them without separation.

To go beyond the confines of limited patterns, one must first realize that one's consciousness is not at all separate from the patterns and images that it perceives and functions as. In other words, if one observes things merely via conflict and miscalculated separations, one is then observing with great error. Such *error* often merely sees itself as *separate* from the patterns and conflict that compose what it is. If one's erroneous observations are a millstone around one's neck, how can such a one have the energy to transcend into a vast, intelligent, placid stillness that is open to the possibility of visitation from the immeasurable *benediction of what is truly sacred*? A broken mind, full of separation, would be incapable of moving beyond its dead borders that separate it from everything else.

from Wallace Stevens:

Theory

I am what is around me.

Women understand this.
One is not duchess
A hundred yards from a carriage.

These, then are portraits:
A black vestibule;
A high bed sheltered by curtains.

These are merely instances.

If it is true, as the great sage J. Krishnamurti often said, that the "observer" is not separate from "the observed," that the "perceiver" is not separate from "the perceived," then could it be that when a famous, elegant singer is performing in public before thousands, he (at the time of singing) is constituted of a consciousness that (in part) consists of the sound of his singing voice? And could it be, when someone gives a gift to someone who is celebrating a birthday, that the shape and colors of the gift help (to a small, but significant extent) to constitute and compose the content of consciousness of both the giver and the receiver? Without such things as gifts, could "givers" be possible?

At the exact moment that a teacher presents an equation to study, is the content or substance of the teacher's consciousness truly separate from what an equation is? At the exact time of driving a car through a busy intersection, is the driver's *consciousness* or *mind* actually separate from his perceptions of intersecting streets and moving automobiles? Are images of the moving automobiles, in traffic, actually what he has absorbed within (and "as") his mind, in order to function better while traveling?

If the "perceiver" is, indeed, "the perceived," when a paramedic is resuscitating an accident victim and, nearby, a thief is robbing an elderly woman of the little bit of savings that she has, which one is a victim? ——
————————————Answer: All of them are actually victims!

from Walt Whitman:

The song is to the singer, and comes back most to him,
The teaching is to the teacher, and comes back most to him,
The murder is to the murderer, and comes back most to him,
The theft is to the thief, and comes back most to him,
The love is to the lover, and comes back most to him,
The gift is to the giver, and comes back most to him—it cannot fail,
The oration is to the orator, the acting is to the actor and actress not to the audience,
And no man understands any greatness or goodness but his own, or the indication of his own.

The content of one's consciousness largely consists of the things that one recognizes. The patterns, the shapes, the colors, odors, sounds, and tactile sensations of what one experiences are often translated into, formulated into, and processed as various thoughts and images that depend on what is experienced. How one experiences... is often dictated by the way one was taught to perceive and identify things. Some previous tribes of Native Americans, such as those using the Navajo and Algonquin languages, for instance, were fortunate enough to have more of a verb-oriented (i.e., verb-based) system of language; they observed things as more of a flow, rather than as merely seeing things as distinct and separate nouns. Therefore, when you look, *how you were taught* influences what you see. To perceive beyond the primitive patterns and structures of symbolic language that one was taught (or programmed as) is to see beyond one's conditioning, beyond the "old" patterns. We, all of us, often tend to look with jaded eyes, unfortunately.

Even if one is not financially all that well off, one can often observe the beauty that is all around throughout one's environment. The best things in life are free, and one can often just look at the magnificent stars at night or the majestic tiny, but beautiful, birds that frequent one's area, soaring with jet-pilot-like accuracy around trees and buildings, while they explore and examine. *What we see* is *what we are*, to a great extent. We look at a meadow, and we are the distance of green and the flowers; we look at a wall that we are adjacent to, and we are the nearness and the flatness. In spring, we see the flowers, and we are the beauty; we see men going to war and fighting in war, and we are the ugliness.

from Wallace Stevens:

Anecdote of Men by the Thousand

The soul, he said, is composed
Of the external world.

There are men of the East, he said,
Who are the East.
There are men of a province
Who are that province.
There are men of a valley
Who are that valley.

There are men whose words
Are as natural sounds, of their places,
As the cackle of toucans
In the place of toucans.

The mandolin is the instrument
Of a place.

Are there mandolins of western mountains?
Are there mandolins of northern moonlight?

The dress of a woman of Lhassa,
In its place,
Is an invisible element of that place
Made visible.

Surely, you are to be rereading this, by and by. Right now, as you are reading this, is the content of your consciousness so very *separate* from the appearance and meaning of these words? Without these words, would your consciousness likely be something else at this time? However, as you are reading this, this *is what you are.* One hopes that the movement of these words will be a health for you, will help you to perceive more holistically, sanely, and purely (without needless division, conflict, and indifference). Health is important for all. Helping a human or an animal, either psychologically or physically, is a noble, honorable thing; it is a reflection of real integrity, real completeness. Doctors/nurses who really heal, and teachers who really reach and share depths of insight, are some of our best and true friends.

from Emily Dickinson:

IF I can stop one heart from breaking,
I shall not live in vain;
If I can ease one life the aching,
Or cool one pain,
Or help one fainting robin
Unto his nest again,
I shall not live in vain.

When we think that we are different and separate from our environment, we are wrong. When we think that we are better than those around us, we are wrong. When we think that we are special and that the others are not so special, we are wrong. When we think that we are not so special, as the lucky ones are, we are wrong. When we think that our skin is of the "better color," we are wrong. When we think that our country or religious organization is better, we are wrong. When we think that fear is separate from what thought and thinking is, we are wrong. When we think that *cruel greed* and *indifferent selfishness* can "get away with it" and exist in deep happiness, we are wrong. When we think that the left arm that harms the right arm can truly be triumphant, we are wrong. When we laugh at the dog that chases its own tail, yet (we) endlessly seek pleasure from one amusement after another, we are wrong. When we think that *silence, vast space,* and *quietness* are merely barren voids of lifelessness, we are wrong. When we think that life, sunlight, gravity, and space are all mere coincidences that will never happen again, we are wrong. When we think that the *big* can exist without the *little*, we are wrong. When we think that *left* can exist without *right*, we are wrong. When we think that the sailor is not the sails, we are wrong. When we think that the mountain-climber is not the mountain that he conquers, we are wrong. When we think that the figure skater is not very slick, we are wrong. When we think that the magician is not an illusion, we are wrong. When we think that the "perceiver" is truly separate from "the perceived," we are wrong.

from Walt Whitman:

When the script preaches instead of the preacher,
When the pulpit descends and goes instead of the carver that carved the supporting desk,
When I can touch the body of books by night or by day, and when they touch my body back again,
When a university course convinces like a slumbering woman and child convince,
When the minted gold in the vault smiles like the night-watchman's daughter,
When warrantee deeds loafe in chairs opposite and are my friendly companions,
I intend to reach them my hand, and make as much of them as I do of men and women like you.

There are multitudes of people, each thinking that "their country" is best, each thinking that "their organized religion" is best, each thinking that "their family" is the best, each thinking that "one's Self" existing "apart from others" is the best, each thinking that "humans" are far superior to "other life forms." Such gobbledygook, from each of us, may be a lot of psychotic propaganda instilled into us (and composing the framework of our contents) from an assemblage (i.e., a gang) of rather unbalanced, old, second-hand sluggards caught in concrete conformation and uncaring stupefaction. Most of us are smitten with traditions based on callous walls of delusory separation and conflict; no wonder so many go to war so readily. We do not even see war as the antithesis of the holistic human condition. So many of us are inauthentic human beings, mere cadaverous ghosts, pretending to be alive, but, instead, are half-baked puppets reacting as we were programmed to react by society. Even when some of us rebel, we do so in utterly absurd, unsophisticated ways.

Is the hand that is holding (or the eyes that are reading) this book capable of being part of that which is truly holistic, wise, and compassionate? If the hand can grasp this book, can the mind, that the hand extends from, grasp the importance of going beyond the separative, stupid traditions and patterns that isolate, cause friction, and that lead to war and indifference? They do not want you to commune with the infinite cosmos, to perceive things freely and directly without the shackles of thoughts and patterns that they handed over. They may not want you to realize that the best and most precious things in life are free and near (in the living present). They may not want you to look directly at life as one whole; they may want you to merely go after parts and repetitious, sequential procedures (that they can sell for a price). They may not want you to perceive deeply; they may want you to look superficially in the manner that they were carelessly taught. They may eventually want your brain to be electronically programmed internally with their separative ideas; they may want such a brain to be hardwired with electronic devices enabling them to control you more efficiently.

We all seem to be very separate, like islands quite apart from each other, separated by vast expanses of ocean. If one looks with depth, as we previously suggested, there is a perception that all the islands are connected, underneath the surface, and are all part of one whole. An isolated, programmed, uncaring individual cannot truly see the profound depth of the aforementioned statement; but a wise, sagacious, perceptive, alive human being sees it clearly. What *sees clearly*, in the deepest sense, may not merely function as an isolated, separate individual who has been conveniently programmed by the bureaucratic authorities. What *perceives deeply* may not merely look within the confines of time and separation. Separation takes time. What *perceives deeply* may not just cling, in fear, to a lot of shoddy, worn-out, sequential patterns that were programmed for it to function as. What *sees clearly*, in the deepest sense, may be "one" with eternity, "one" with truth, and "one" with the whole of the cosmos. Such a *wholeness* can never be adequately labeled by any pattern, symbol, or group of images. What is vast and deeply intelligent cannot be mentally captured by what is superficial and limited.

Many may not want you to be whole and happy. Many may want you to be dependent upon them and upon what they have, upon what they think. Though their countries and religions and patterns may all be, in a way, different (and supposedly separate), they are all essentially the same, with the same stupidities, fears, separation, blatant indoctrination, feelings of control, and (though they sometimes speak of caring) essential indifference. To go beyond all forms of cruel separation is to truly live. John Donne, though he (not so wholeheartedly) belonged to religious groups that unfortunately had separative, divisive components, was, nevertheless, sagacious enough to feel the deep integrity of man and unified cosmos.

from John Donne:

No man is an island entire of itself; every man
is a piece of the continent, a part of the main;
if a clod be washed away by the sea, Europe
is the less, as well as if a promontory were, as
well as any manner of thy friends or of thine
own were; any man's death diminishes me,
because I am involved in mankind.
And therefore never send to know for whom
the bell tolls; it tolls for thee.

Well, that's enough about death, for now. Live in this world and be joyous. Live simply, with youthful feelings of wonder and joy. As E. E. Cummings stated in part of his poetry: "you shall above all things be glad and young. For if you're young, whatever life you wear, it will become you; and if you are glad, whatever's living will yourself become." Moreover, if you are truly "young," you will exist beyond merely engaging in crippling evil, hurtful manners, and age-old deceit.

(The following riddle, about the sage and the "switched images," is a bit tricky and is rather difficult, but is really quite cool once it is understood.)

Here is interrogative information regarding properly understanding it:

If a sage is what a wise man is, and if a wise man is he who perceives that the image, of what he (himself) looks at, is not separate from what he really is, then was the sage, in the following poem, not really a fool (as his students thought)? Furthermore, in the situation that the following poem depicts, was the pupil, who deceitfully switched the images, actually somewhat of a devil because of the trick that he tried to pull upon the teacher/sage? In addition, if the sage saw that the student who pulled the deceitful switch was looking at both images while laughing, was the sage aware that the devilish student was not truly separate from what he, as a student, thought he was separate from?

In the following poem — because he realized that the "observer" is not really separate from "the observed" — did the sage also see that he, as a sage, each time that he looked at one of the images, was not really separate from what that particular image was? Why, each time the sage looked at an image and claimed to be what it was, was he correct? Additionally, after the deceitful switch was made, why was the sage correct when he identified the image (which he previously labeled as himself) as being a "devil"? Was the sage correct because he (as a sage) realized that a devilish student, while looking at an image, causes that image — since the "observer" is not separate from "the observed" — to be what is devilish?

from Stephen Crane:

The sage lectured brilliantly.
Before him, two images:
"Now this one is a devil,
And this one is me."
He turned away.
Then a cunning pupil
Changed the positions.

Turned the sage again:
"Now this one is a devil,
And this one is me."
The pupils sat, all grinning,
And rejoiced in the game.
But the sage was a sage.

As the previous poem illustrates, it is possible for some humans to attempt to deceive others by way of trickery and chicanery. It is not so easy, however, to trick a true sage as he is sharing his wisdom. Many people probably have been tricked and duped, over the millennia, by unethical people. Some of the ways that people are so strategically hoodwinked... surely exists in the realm of religion. Some ancient books, purporting to be religious texts inspired by God, may be nothing more than deceitful, underhanded lies. They may be nothing but complete forgeries, or contain many sham additions to what was once (long ago) a true text that was written (undistorted) by a true sage or enlightened man. People are so gullible; they easily, en masse, fall for these ungracious forgeries — in numbers totaling millions, when enough of them agree together — referring to them as being "sacred books."

from Stephen Crane:

You tell me this is God?
I tell you this is a printed list,
A burning candle, and an ass.

In the future, it may be best to have communities and areas of land actually governed a lot more by computers run and operated by the local (and average) working people, (who would work in a temporary mode, on a sequential, rotating basis), and not by crooked, professional, life-long politicians (i.e., leftovers from the ancient feudal system). Computers could be monitored and organized by groups of local people (who work in the community in regular, rather average jobs); these groups would also cooperatively connect as global groups. The computers would periodically ask the many voters questions (referendum style), which they would vote on, and the computers would be used to tally the votes. Local and global working, (average) people would (in groups that would monitor each other) continue to function in a rotating, sequential basis, helping to bring the results into fruition. These servants to the people—not political bureaucrats of elitism—would be asked to serve only for a limited time, and would be asked to serve for the good of all (and for Mother Earth) and not merely for the good of a select few; they would not be endorsed to do things in the realm of special interests, but rather, for everyone globally. The local groups could work in groups of 12 or so, as juries do; a few at a time would rotate in and out. Global oneness and green energy would be top priorities. Kudos should go to E. E. Cummings for writing, "A politician is an arse upon which everyone has sat except a man." Let us stand up!

In the future (as is happening now), computers and machines will do more of the work that humans had previously done. Therefore, we will not need to work long, dreadful hours for excessive, endless days, as we did in the past. With the extensive free time that we then can have, what will we do? Will we merely charge along, attempting to escape into more and more entertainment? Instead, will we learn how to live greenly, with compassion, in our local area, appreciating the simple beauty that exists in our immediate environment? Will we exist effortlessly, having minds of *silence* that are open to true benediction, open to true, harmonious communion with what is whole, limitless, and beyond mere symbols and avaricious, big ambitions (that are, in reality, little and petty)? True compassion acts; in its effortlessness, it acts; it is not a set of petty, little reactions, as is greed and mere self-gratification. [The computers of the future, incidentally, will get far more complex than we have ever imagined. We should not let scientists graft compact units (involving such complexity) into our brain areas; human minds are mechanical enough. We must ensure that we freely use computer technology, and not merely become slaves to it.]

Slavery involves separation. If, regarding the psychology of the mind, as we suggested, the "observer" is "the observed," then when a group of men is marching toward mountains (i.e., toward a mountainous region) — as they are treading along looking at the lofty Alps that lie before them — are their minds not composed of the attributes of those mountains? In actuality, since each marching man's consciousness consists of (and "is") the perception (and image) of mountains, we, in an interesting way, can say, "After the peaks assembled, the mountains began marching."

Without false segregation, the "perceiver" is not truly separate from "the perceived." Therein, you make "two things" as "one." Therein, two things are as one thing, in "one" consciousness. Therein, two (or many) things are as *one thing*, as *one mind*. Thus, truly, when men begin forging ahead, parading toward mountains that they perceive in the distance, it is evident to the wise that "the march of the mountains began."

from Stephen Crane:

On the horizon, the peaks assembled;
And as I looked,
The march of the mountains began.
As they marched, they sang:
"Aye! We come! We come!"

In the following poem, was one man wiser than the other because one man, by realizing that "the observer is the observed," was intelligent about the fact that an assassin, even though such an assassin would erroneously think that he is separate, is not really separate from whom he perceives as being the victim?

from Stephen Crane:

A man feared that he might find an assassin;
Another that he might find a victim.
One was more wise than the other.

In the poem entitled *The House Was Quiet And The World Was Calm*, by Wallace Stevens, the relationship regarding "the perceiver and the perceived" is explored, such as in the lines of: "The reader became the book; and summer night was like the conscious being of the book." Mystics, like John Donne, Wallace Stevens, and Stephen Crane, may have often written things that the sagacious and keenly wise can pick out and spot instantly. However, they may have also written a lot of extraneous material that does not point to the truth. And people of very long ago, such as Jesus and Lao Tzu, may have written or said beautifully insightful things; however, over time, devious others may have added to their works, and distorted them, for selfish reasons involving distorted ideologies and corrupt images that they wished to convey or imprint into the minds of others. Therefore, beware, for what was once pure may now be contaminated with imperfections and distortions. The wise harvester may gather that which is pure (for you to use) and will discard the rest.

from Jesus (two sayings from the ancient Gospel of Thomas):

Jesus said,
The Father's imperial rule is like a person who had [good] seed.
His enemy came during the night and sowed weeds among the good seed.
The person did not let the workers pull up the weeds, but said to
them, "No, otherwise you might go to pull up the weeds and pull up the
wheat along with them.

For on the day of the harvest the weeds will
be conspicuous, and will be pulled up and burned."

Jesus said, "Congratulations to the person who has toiled
and has found life."

from Stephen Crane:

Yes, I have a thousand tongues,
And nine and ninety-nine lie.
Though I strive to use the one,
It will make no melody at my will,
But is dead in my mouth.

Congratulations for having read this, thus far; one is thus entering a realm that demands great courage and penetrating openness. If you are truly *open*, you are truly majestic and grand in a limitless fashion. True *openness* goes beyond the limited and selfish comforts that propaganda instills. True *openness* may mean that one goes toward truth whatever the consequences, not merely wanting pleasing answers or fabricated legends that will falsely pacify or falsely soothe. True *openness* is immediate, beyond sequential memories of how things "should be," or how things "will be" in some fictitious, promised domain (that authorities have held before us like a carrot on a string); the immediacy of true *openness* is beyond sequential opinions, judgments, suppositions, and is beyond comparison. The *grace* of true *openness* lies in the fact that it is direct perception, now, without the distortions of interfering thoughts (that have been instilled in one by old, worn-out, business-like automatons of the past). True *openness* is beyond the sequential calculations of limited thinking. Limited thinking is what produces fear (out of its own clinging to limitation). Selfishness and fear go together, hand in hand. Limitation, sorrow, and fear… go hand in hand.

from Stephen Crane:

Mystic shadow, bending near me,
Who art thou?
Whence come ye?

And — tell me — is it fair
Or is the truth bitter as eaten fire?
Tell me!
Fear not that I should quaver.
For I dare — I dare.
Then, tell me!

We must again repeat that while one can be told "about" energy, via symbols and patterns of thought, one may not actually "be" the energy. This is so because symbols, as we said earlier, are not the things that they merely represent or "stand for" but are more like shadows, being rather superficial and insubstantial representations about things, but not being the actual things. Later, within this book, you (as the reader) will be told, in depth, about eternity. In depth, eternity will be revealed to you (who partially are, currently, symbolic words sequentially moving along this paragraph). Similar to true "energy," it may be that the essence of "eternity" cannot merely be conveyed or absorbed via the usage of words and symbols. One may *think* that one is eternal; one may rejoice in the belief that one is eternal; one may operate under the presumption that one is eternal, but, as with true energy, "thinking" about eternity may not at all be what being in communion with true eternity is, period. When shadows presume to be the light, they can think that they are "bright" all that they want, but they may not be, in reality, enlightened whatsoever. It is easy for the mind to think that it is clever, when it is not; it is easy for the limited to think that it is unlimited, when it is not; it is easy for the mind to think that it is good, when it is not.

from Stephen Crane:

Walking in the sky,
A man in strange black garb
Encountered a radiant form.
Then his steps were eager;
Bowed he devoutly.
"My Lord," said he.
But the spirit knew him not.

If one is imbued with the decrepit thoughts of what was injected into one by elderly "authorities," then one is *old*. If one is filled with prejudice from the antiquated patterns of what was poured into one by elderly "authorities," then one is *old*. If one is saturated with preconceptions from the old formulations of what was infused into one by elderly "authorities," then one is *prehistoric*. If one is misshapen by invasive notions of isolation and superiority with the secretions injected into one by elderly "authorities," then one is cut-off and castrated. If one is constantly monetarily and psychologically flustered from the conniving payments of what was deposited into one by elderly "authorities," then one is *old*. If one genuflects to aged, manmade figures, carved from the fabrications of manipulative headstone representations, then one is *old*. If one takes advantage of the small and disadvantaged in order to conserve and perpetuate comfort and high-ranking eminence, then one is *old*. If one mistreats others in a bloody violence that magnifies a pompous center while perceiving lowly multitudes at a telescopic distance, then one is *old*. If one shuns the less talented to exclusively bask with the shrewd and cunning, then one is *old*. If one clings to social cliques and is afraid to be alone and peerless, then one is *old*. If one is afraid of appearing aged, then one is *old*. If one tirelessly and unceasingly chases after entertainment, then one is *old*. If one is constantly apprehensive about what others might say, then one is *old*. If one bootlicks the hard-hearted suppressors, then one is *old*. If one supports death, decay, and destruction, then one is *old*. If one overpopulates a small, over-crowded, celestial garden orb, then one is *old*. If insensitivity abuses or easily extinguishes the small, then one is *old*. If indifference cripples the subservient, then one is *old*. If jealousy swims through comparison, then one is *old*. If hatred mushrooms from explosive persuasions, then one is *old*. If one readily maims, kills, and terminates others who are supposedly separate from what one is, then one is *old*.

from Stephen Crane:

"Tell brave deeds of war."

Then they recounted tales:
"There were stern stands
And bitter runs for glory."

Ah, I think there were braver deeds.

It may be that important answers are coming, important answers about life, death, eternity, about everything. However, words (as symbols) can reveal only to a very limited extent. Despite what the revelations about profound eternity reveal, by the words and symbols which are to come, the deep *benediction of "timelessness"* cannot (via words and symbols) be what is conveyed by "one" to "another." In light of the possible truth of things partially revealed, please do not cower as a shrinking, selfish, limited darkness. A shrinking, limited darkness is like what Alzheimer's disease is; it is a dwindling away from what is whole, what is keen, what is aware, what is eternally youthful, what is perceptive. As when the corpus callosum is severed causing the two halves of the brain to be separate from each other, the act of separating "others" from oneself is a curse; it is a disease of pre-historic selfishness and limitation that is darkness personified. As we recently suggested, the nature of eternity will be deeply explained here, as time goes by. This eternity may shed further light on the problematic issues that the corpus callosum and that Alzheimer's disease present regarding enduring within the life/death continuum. Contemplating the implications of all this is not merely easy and superficial; it is immensely important and deeply serious. *True eternity* is not something that a limited, isolated brain can fully partake in or be appreciative of. *Eternity* is not something that a dead-end brain can have profound insights about, in isolation.

from Walt Whitman:

I wish I could translate the hints about the dead young men
and women,
And the hints about old men and mothers, and the offspring
taken soon out of their laps.
What do you think has become of the young and old men?
And what do you think has become of the women and
children?

They are alive and well somewhere,
The smallest sprout shows there is really no death,
And if ever there was it led forward life, and does not wait
at the end to arrest it,
And ceas'd the moment life appear'd.

All goes onward and outward, nothing collapses,
And to die is different from what any one supposed, and luckier.

While standing way up high, near the top of a precipice, fear is intuitive and beneficial; such fear is good and helps the body to wisely avoid danger. However, many people have psychological fears, and these fears are unnecessary and actually cause undue stress and friction within (and "as") the organism. Fears about a danger in the environment may be healthy; but many psychological fears may be dangerous (in themselves) and a waste of energy. One may fear what others think of oneself, for example. Such fear may cause one to conform, excessively adhering to absurd customs and primitive behaviors, (just in order not to appear as being different or unusual). Furthermore, while all along not understanding what living and dying entails, one may fear death. Such death, that one so fears, may involve ideas that one has accumulated, over time, directly or indirectly from others. Therefore, it is *ideas* and *symbols* about death and speculations about coming to an end that exist as *fears*; ideas, symbols, and psychological fear all go together, hand in hand. Instead of *psychologically dying* to the absurd notions, ideas, and patterns about death that one has accumulated, one clings to these formulations, and so one remains as what fear is. One is not separate from one's fears. The fears are part of what one actually is. There is no entity apart from the fears who can control them, subjugate them, or gradually eradicate them. When a fear manifests in one, it is what you are. One cannot get rid of what one is. One may understand what one is, and it may dissipate. It may be that the more one tries to act as a separate entity that tries to control fears and apprehensions, the more one isolates as limited and separative ideas and fabrications; and isolated ideas and self-fabrications all tend to lavishly feed the furnace of what fear is. An isolated notion of "I" or of a central "Self" apart from others, naturally (or unnaturally) is a segregated, limited "center" with a periphery around it. Such segregation naturally (or unnaturally) produces a space that adores and worships the idea of a central "authority" or "controller." However, the idea of a controller is just an idea. There is actually no true, central, regulatory agency apart from the other thoughts, images, and formulations of the entire brain. Therefore, when compassion takes place, you are the compassion. When psychological fear takes place, you are the fear. (We are not suggesting that fear is the only thing that you are; that would be absurd.)

Directly observing fear, without thinking that one is separate from it, is deep intelligence. Such intelligence does not merely try to alter or eradicate the fear… but, instead, may watch it such as when one closely watches a precious flower; it watches without tons of shunning prejudice, without disapproval, subjugation, or substitution. We do not wish to run from the fear via entertaining experiences or quick replacement activities; we want to passively observe it with care, open eyes, and with the realization that it is something *not apart* from us.

The mind can be blissful and full of deep abiding joy and happiness. However, such beauty of mind is not likely if the mind merely clings to empty, shadow-like symbols, mere symbolic images, and barren structures of thinking. One, unfortunately, cannot shine in ecstasy while merely being shadowy symbols, fears, hatreds, old, separative perspectives, and empty representations. Remaining as symbols is not real living. Symbols, as thoughts and mental formulations, are extremely good and very beneficial; but they, as we suggested earlier, are merely tools, not the *true essence* of deep insight and bliss. Symbols and representations are not living, in the deepest sense. They are old and rather un-alive. However, there is such a thing as "fighting fire with fire"; persevere, don't get bored with this; do not give up regarding deeply understanding these lines, and you may easily, without effort, blossom from a stale, rather dead chrysalis: into an amazing, vibrant, eternal, butterfly-like creature of true wisdom.

Methods — given by others, to end mental symbol making, and to suppress the endless process of ideation — are not of value. Methodologies, and patterns of methodologies and techniques, are structured formulations and, as such, merely trick the brain into groping toward silence and freedom. *Silence* must come naturally, without any effort. Silence that is merely brought about by a highly structured method, practice, or technique… is merely a mechanical silence that is not the vast, *living intelligence* that comes effortlessly with keen awareness and freedom from manipulation. The beauty of *true silence* is that it is not the product of a domineering or manipulative process. No illusory suppressor, no dictatorial entity, no vain and craving monstrosity can capture it. That is its beauty.

from Walt Whitman:

The earth never tires,

The earth is rude, silent, incomprehensible at first, Nature is rude and incomprehensible at first,

Be not discouraged, keep on, there are divine things well envelop'd,

I swear to you there are divine things more beautiful than words can tell.

While in college, i began becoming very serious concerning understanding *consciousness*, the *nature of reality*, and *holistic living*. One thing that, curiously, initially influenced me very dramatically was the motion picture entitled "A Clockwork Orange." In this movie, the main character, Alex, after being sent to prison for murder, undergoes an experimental (aversion) therapeutic procedure, in which he is injected with a drug that makes him feel sick while he is forced (with eyes permanently bound open) to watch graphically violent films. This experimental (aversion) procedure eventually ends up conditioning him to suffer crippling bouts of nausea at the mere thought of violence. As an added, unintended consequence, it turned out that background music, coincidentally of Alex's favorite Beethoven's Ninth Symphony, was played during the aversion therapy process while in prison, causing Alex to later be totally unable to listen to his beloved classical music. Seeing this particular movie had made a very profound impression on me. I was shocked to realize that human beings could be ingrained heavily in *conditioned* modes of behavior; *psychological conditioning* meant that people could often act as if they were programmed, almost in the way that computers were. I began to ponder the possibility that much of what humans do is largely, if not entirely, part of a process of *conditioning*. *Conditioning* occurs when one's thoughts function merely as part of a cause/effect continuum; conditioning occurs when one *primarily* functions as *reactions*. Merely responding to the environment in ways in which one was *programmed* to… is, in actuality, conditioning. Unfortunately, a life that is composed mostly of a series of mere "reactions" is a rather mechanical and inanimate existence. Anyway, the movie shook me to my core. (It got reactions out of me, for sure.) Human motives, behaviors, influences, systems, methodization, and patterns all began to be perceived more scrupulously and suspiciously.

(Anthony Burgess, who wrote the book that the film was based on, has stated that the total of 21 chapters of the book was an intentional nod to the age of 21 being recognized as a milestone in human maturation. The 21st chapter, wherein Alex matures and tries to lead a more non-violent life, was omitted from the editions published in the United States prior to 1986 and was not included within the film. By the way, the "youth" of trouble-making teenage and 20-year-old individuals is not, by any means, the type of "youth" that my book advocates or relishes; the youth i am advocating is much more innocent and "youthful" than that.)

Thought, by its very nature, is a rather mechanical process that is essentially part of a dynamic cause/effect continuum. There was much violence within the aforementioned film, and thought, by its very nature, due to its separative, isolating constitution, is often rather violent and primitive.

Those that deeply embrace violence are like a cancer, and they need to be isolated within a confined environment wherein they cannot destroy human lives (and other life forms). Hardened criminals need to be treated with respect and compassionate rehabilitation; they should not be released from life; nor should they be released into society if they are likely to continue in their deleterious ways.

Conditioning affects us all. We all tend to act in rather mechanical, robotic patterns. Those of us who are not often compassionate (i.e., are not compassionate to humans or animals) are especially mechanistic, robot-like, and rather puppet-like. In a state of *silence and compassion*, one may go beyond the realm of mechanical conditioning. Then one is not merely just a cog in the wheel. However, one cannot merely "know" when one is truly in such a state, for deep wisdom is not what is cognizant of itself. Just as humility cannot be sure that it is humble, true wisdom cannot be cognizant of its own existence.

Very many people act thoughtlessly, in uncaring, self-centered ways. Such people, in their cold, callous, indifferent mannerisms, are like un-alive, robotic automatons, hardly alive in the true sense. Due to unfortunate genetic processes and/or wrong social/learning processes, these people pop up and make life more difficult and unpleasant for a lot of us. However, a sagacious, wise mind often functions beyond the realm of conditioning. A wise mind is like a rare jewel in the vast, dark, sordid soil. What is sordid lacks dignity; it has little true integrity and is not honorable. What is sordid may trick itself and trick others into thinking that it shines with goodness. However, the true *benediction of timelessness* does not ever visit those who are charlatans and counterfeit.

from Walt Whitman:

The devilish and the dark, the dying and diseas'd,
The countless (nineteen-twentieths) low and evil, crude and savage,
The crazed, prisoners in jail, the horrible, rank, malignant,
Venom and filth, serpents, the ravenous sharks, liars, the dissolute;
(What is the part the wicked and the loathsome bear within earth's orbic scheme?)
Newts, crawling things in slime and mud, poisons,
The barren soil, the evil men, the slag and hideous rot.

(Isn't it interesting about how Walt perceived those countless gangs of savage nineteen-twentieths before Burgess's notion of "maturity at the age of 21" ever existed?)

In terms of maturity, could it be that, embedded within Emily Dickinson's many orthodox poems, there exists glimmers from a *profound immensity*, an *immensity* that is vast, boundless, majestic, and that is far beyond the ordinary notions of orthodox, conformist men? To truly be appreciative of the profundity of this *immensity*, must not the mind (of the person examining its qualities and offerings) also largely be deeply profound and serious? (No, this movement is not "bragging" about "itself.") Is a very superficial, uncaring, indifferent brain capable of perceiving and appreciating what is impenetrable by mere words, symbols, and cold calculations? Could the uncaring, shallow brains of ordinary men easily laugh at the deep, heartfelt, serious, submissions of a truly wise man, all the while labeling them as being ridiculous and insane?

from Emily Dickinson:

MUCH madness is Divinest sense
To a discerning eye;
Much Sense, the starkest madness…
'Tis the majority
In this, as all, prevail.
Assent, and you are sane;
Demur, — you're straightway dangerous
And handled with a chain.

Many of Emily Dickinson's poems, indeed, may profess to be of an orthodox kind, depicting her to have cherished rather conventional ideas concerning God and accepted notions about the after-life. However, under the guise and pretense of vast amounts of rather ordinary conceptions, does there mystically exist: abundant poems that are indicative of unconventional, penetrating revelations that piercingly break through the barriers of doctrinal, traditional patterns and beliefs, (revealing her true wisdom)?

from Emily Dickinson:

TO hang our head ostensibly,
And subsequent to find
That such was not the posture
Of our immortal mind,

Affords the sly presumption
That, in so dense a fuzz,
You, too, take cobweb attitudes
Upon a plane of gauze!

Chapter 5

As was previously mentioned, as a parochial school student, one was expected to attend mass in church, on a daily basis and, of course, on Sundays. The staleness of church seemed like a black, morbid death to me; the confining, limiting walls that surrounded us youngsters seemed like a deceased monster that had swallowed its unfortunate, diminutive victims. I remember thinking: "Surely God is not here… God is out among the splendid outdoors and unlimited spaces." I continued to kneel, as if serving a prison sentence. (John the Baptist, who was instrumental in Jesus' religious beginnings, was far away from temples and was situated deep within the abundance of nature and the outdoors.)

Had they captured God (i.e., the sacred), keeping divinity there in their manmade, special, stagnant place? Alternatively, had they cunningly devised a way, a method, for acquiring other people's money and attention? Did the many millions who belonged to their organized religion mean that it was legitimate? Unfortunately, can it be that a blinding cult can inspire endless masses through contagious trickery/chicanery?

Is what is truly sacred what can merely be locked in time, in a limited place, in a limited space? Can the wind, and can what is *sacred*, be held within a diminutive, confined area for people to visit? Can what is *sacred* be explained with mere symbols and with mere images? Can dead images be adored and worshiped as if they were living realities? Can self-created projections of thought be appealed to and beseeched? Are there people who peddle religion, and profess to have God while, all the while, they are deluding themselves, as well as deluding others? It may be that real religion is what exists in quiet, but helpful, humility; such humility may not erroneously attempt to direct God (i.e., *the sacred*), as if God (i.e., *the sacred)* was limited enough to require guidance and beseeching; such a humility would be actively helping people, plants, and animals in direct ways, without manipulating authorities. Beware of those who claim to have God in their buildings, in enclosed spaces, within the confined and limited. Many cults try to cultivate people and cultivate the *sacred.* Cults tend to "cult-i-vate." *The sacred* cannot be cultivated; however, naïve, bamboozled masses of people certainly can be "cult-i-vated." Oh, by the way, flowers can be cultivated, especially if it is done with love and affection (and not with a lot of confining limitation).

from John Keats: Written in Disgust of Vulgar Superstition

The church bells toll a melancholy round,
  Calling the people to some other prayers,
  Some other gloominess, more dreadful cares,
More heark'ning to the sermon's horrid sound.
Surely the mind of man is closely bound
  In some black spell; seeing that each one tears
  Himself from fireside joys, and Lydian airs,
And converse high of those with glory crown'd.
Still, still they toll, and I should feel a damp,
  A chill as from a tomb, did I not know
That they are dying like an outburnt lamp;
  That 'tis their sighing, wailing ere they go
  Into oblivion; —that fresh flowers will grow,
And many glories of immortal stamp.

Intelligently, a very wise, silent sage once said, "When the bird finishes singing, today's sermon will be over."

from Emily Dickinson:

SOME keep the Sabbath going to church;
I keep it staying at home,
With a bobolink for a chorister,
And an orchard for a dome.

Some keep the Sabbath in surplice;
I just wear my wings,
And instead of tolling the bell for church,
Our little sexton sings.

God preaches, — a noted clergyman, —
And the sermon is never long;
So instead of getting to heaven at last,
I'm going all along!

Will life seem boring and dull to a mind that has allowed itself to become boring and dull? Would a mind of great light and contented, inner bliss need to experience many extraneous things in order to *finally* become happy? Would a mind that is full of fear and apprehension be likely not to care what other people think about it? Would an isolated brain that separates itself (with distance) from everything else, likely feel heartfelt compassion for a hurt, little animal? Is a mind "that gets used to seeing everything" in life (i.e., a mind that sees the "same-old thing") likely to look at things afresh every single second, while being highly appreciative of the spontaneous wonderment of what takes place in life? Is a mind that is entangled in and twisted with unending symbols that label and pigeonhole, likely to observe without reactionary, calculated, dead methodology? Can a brain that is constantly babbling to itself have the immeasurable, unlimited space to transcend restricted bias and narrow direction? Can a brain, full of insecurities, stand steadfast against powerful instigators? Can a brain, that clings to rigid, dead patterns of thought and that clings to lifeless symbols, likely be what deeply esteems life and beauty?

How does one perceive and look at things? How does one listen to things? If one perceives through a mental framework that is melancholy and stale, then most everything that one sees will likely seem dull and uninteresting. If one observes things through a mental screen of indifferent fragmentation, then most everything that one sees will seem distantly aloof and apart. If one observes with joyful, wide eyes, then most of what one sees will likely be rather thrilling and a cause for celebration. If one observes (without separation) with caring, tender, and heartfelt eyes, then most of what one sees will be appreciated and loved.

from Emily Dickinson:

TO hear an oriole sing
May be a common thing,
Or only a divine.

It is not of the bird
Who sings the same, unheard,
As unto crowd.

The fashion of the ear
Attireth that it hear
In dun or fair.

So whether it be rune,
Or whether it be none,
Is of within; -

The "tune is in the tree,"
The sceptic showeth me;
"No, sir! In thee!"

Sorry, but we need to repeat things, with subtle variation, for you; otherwise it will likely not get realized deeply enough, and then you might merely carry on as before. As we have suggested, thought is an extremely important tool. However, it is only a tool, and to take a mere "tool" and make it out to be the essence of the organism: may be a colossal mistake. Authorities of the past have endlessly made that mistake, and they have led millions to unhesitatingly accept it. We have blindly accepted tools and mental fabrications as being "real" and "authentic"; in reality, they are mere symbolic processes that are, fundamentally, rather superficial and limited in scope and dimension. We cannot repeat enough that symbols about energy are not the actual energy. Words, concepts, and ideas are extremely necessary; they can help us to curtail and nullify dreadful diseases in children, adults, and in animals. They can point out, to us, about how we can be silent: to understand how everything is tied together in one immensity, in one holistic movement. Words, used with compassion, can assist us in regard to living with tremendous peace and harmony.

However, words, concepts, and ideas are not all that there is. They are very limited, because they are merely fragmentary, symbolic representations that merely "stand for" and "betoken" things. *Thought's* very nature is that it is partial, and that it always involves a "sequence of representational patterns occurring over time." Mental patterns that occur over time are, by natural law, necessarily chronological, circumstantial, cultured frameworks (that are essentially extensions that evolve from the past). One can only recognize and interpret things according to the conditioned background of one's past memory and culture; that stored memory may adjust, reformulate, and add relatively new dimensions of perceiving things to itself; but it can only do so according to its very limited (acquired) capacity (involving biological and environmental parameters) and the information that it has already accumulated.

Mental reactions, thought, image making, and thinking all initially evolved, in life, as an aid to assist the organism in terms of survival and in terms of extending the organism's continuity. All thought, even in the most modern and advanced physicists and brain surgeons, is essentially reactionary, conditioned, and residual. This residuum (consisting of symbolic representations), even though it may be relatively modern (and even though it may consider itself to be highly evolved), may, nonetheless, be completely conditioned (such that the whole of such thought is part of a type of "domino effect" causal continuum). This is not necessarily a terrible or unfortunate thing, however. The evolutionary process can be a wonderful, flowering phenomenon that blossoms into what can transcend "domino effect" conditioning and mechanical entrapment. It can occur when, in supreme intelligence, the mind psychologically dies to thought and, instead, exists with holistic, non-symbolic perception and insight. However, all too many cling to the isolating and limited dimensions which mere symbolism expounds. They refuse to leave their cherished mental patterns, representations, and self-concepts; they cling to the insubstantial, murky, shadowy, second-hand, archetypal models that were delegated to them by authority, and they refuse to change (i.e., they ardently refuse to move beyond their enclosing symbols).

from John Keats:

Read me a lesson, Muse, and speak it loud

Read me a lesson, Muse, and speak it loud
Upon the top of Nevis, blind in Mist!
I look into the chasms, and a shroud
Vaporous doth hide them; just so much I wist
Mankind do know of hell: I look o'erhead,
And there is sullen mist; even so much
Mankind can tell of heaven: mist is spread
Before the earth beneath me; even such,
Even so vague is man's sight of himself.
Here are the craggy stones beneath my feet;
Thus much I know, that, a poor witless elf,
I tread on them; that all my eye doth meet
Is mist and crag— not only on this height,
But in the world of thought and mental might!

We are suggesting that all thoughts are the result of murky conditioning. This conditioning can be altered by the light of freedom (i.e., by the light of divine insight and infinite, compassionate wisdom); but this conditioning is still within the realm of residual reactions that develop and manifest in defined ways within a cause/effect continuum. Thoughts, all thoughts, manifest as reactions to stimuli; these stimuli can be either profound and far-reaching or superficial and limited. Most educators, unfortunately, teach children in rather limited, insubstantial ways, rather than in ways that are penetrating, dynamic, impassioned, and heartfelt. Most educators have become what they were educated to become, which is often second-hand, superficial, and imitative, rather than holistic, deep, and penetrating.

Little wonder then, why so many of the entities within society merely chase after one entertainment after another, with no meaningful pauses to investigate with silent integrity that is free of reactionary processes. Most of us become merely what we were cranked out to become; usually, the result is rather mediocre, mechanical, indifferent, self-serving, and old. We cling to (and function "as") *past* concepts, because the "past," as a dead series of symbolic images, was hammered into us. Most of us were molded and forged into the old, traditional, cursory, lackluster way of thinking; furthermore, according to very many large corporations: that will do just fine. They do not want you to meander away from the machinelike, unfeeling, involuntary way of thinking, because, if you did, you would be a danger to all that there is. It is far easier to sell tons of appliances and apparatuses to habitual, unanimated entities. Such entities will not meddle as much with regard to propounding environmental concerns, population control measures, and notions of living happily without requiring huge automobiles and tons of needless gadgets.

They have invested heavily in you, so please do not pull and yank on the puppet strings. (What i write within this paragraph might get everyone's blood boiling, whether they want it to or not.) Above all, please do not question things, and please refrain from reading more of this dreadful, controversially inane book. Continue reacting to all of the innumerable advertisements and commercials, and definitely allow yourselves to be altered by subliminal propaganda. Refrain from looking at things without residual, reactionary thought; continue looking through the screen of worn-out, past images involving calculated judgments, prejudices, comparison, envies, separative viewpoints, limited space, and isolating "center-Me-oriented-frameworks." Worship procreation processes and reproduce heavily, creating tons of cute, little ones (who will eventually purchase much for the corporations); overstock your aquariums; watch the water get cloudy, and smell the foul water, as the whole goes belly-up. Eat plenty of subordinate, inferior animals (slaughtered by others on your behalf) that, themselves, have enjoyed sex immensely, while you must continue to think that "your sexual experiences" are so outstandingly special and unique. Blend in with everybody else and do exactly as they do. Cower easily and remain afraid. Let others step all over you (and harm the ones close to you). Cling to the old patterns. Do not be primitive and barbaric enough to worship the sun and the moon; instead, worship images of thought that the elders have formulated for you to ardently worship. Unfalteringly think that your country is superior to everyone else's. Unfailingly be what waves separative flags. Cling to depression, indifference, separation, and sorrow. Continue not to do anything about "others" who are suffering. Pour cement over everything living; cover the earth with pavement, concrete and non-recyclable garbage. Spew out pollutants like there is no tomorrow. Eat unhealthy, adulterated food (to excess if you want), because it tastes so scrumptiously good. Let obesity be your modus operandi. Do not bother to exercise daily (because it takes too much strenuous effort that is uncomfortable); let machines take you everywhere without needing to expend any effort whatsoever. Free cancerous murderers and child molesters out of their prisons, so that they can readily harm others repeatedly. Watch the news on television, and be glad that you are normal. Merely grope after pleasure while frantically fleeing pain. React exclusively to appear different; appear different to not appear to be exclusively reacting the same. Decorate your body to fool others into thinking that you are different. Follow your leaders without question. Do as you are told. Think that you have total freedom. Psychologically accumulate more and more without hesitation while, all the while, creating barriers between what you consider to be "yourself" and "others." Maintain psychological fears about ending. Believe that dying and living are two separate things. Be afraid of the unknown, and never stop "knowing." Never, while (supposedly living), psychologically die to the unending, mechanized, robotic process of "labeling" and "thinking." Do not care two pins about what happens to others (who seem to be quite separate from you). Teach your children as you have been taught. Cogitate freely. Incessantly talk and communicate with others via electronic media (to run from your own sense of isolation and loneliness). Endlessly listen to music to fill the void with sequential patterns, in time. Continue to fit right in. Wake up tomorrow (and everyday), doing what you always must do. Use the (false) shield of "distance" for protection of a formulated "self," to (supposedly) safeguard it from the "dangers out there." Merely observe things from a (supposed) central image (called "me") that is considered to be in control of all the "other thoughts and images." Use *past formulations* (of old images) to *see* (i.e., recognize) other (so-called "new") images. Label the living bejebbies out of everything. Continue to look through the shades of the *old past* to see the *same-old things*. Laugh at what you think is crude, while "thinking" that "you" are sophisticated. Think exactly as you were programmed to think. Sleep tight; don't let the bedbugs bite.

from Emily Dickinson:

THE brain within its groove
Runs evenly and true;
But let a splinter swerve,
'T were easier for you
To put the water back
When floods have slit the hills,
And scooped a turnpike for themselves,
And blotted out the mills!

(Also please eventually find and read the poem, entitled "The Unknown Citizen," by W. H. Auden.)

It may be that, to truly *end* one's *conditioning* completely, one must enter into a realm of *true silence*, psychologically. One, as we said, cannot come upon deep and *true silence* via any method, practice, or system. One can easily come upon silence via a method and by practicing various things, such as by chanting, or repeating mantras, or by undertaking some sort of learned procedure. However, such a silence will be a rather dead and unalive silence and will not be the limitless, profound, *true silence* whatsoever. If the "means" is mechanical and calculating, then the "result" will be machinelike, rather lackluster, and lifeless. One cannot fabricate a highway or path to what (as a majestic, free, timelessness) cannot be approached by mechanical-oriented sequences in time.

True freedom, the actuality of being beyond conditioning, must exist beyond the realms of rather dead cause/effect-oriented sequences in time. (If it were merely a part of the series of cause/effect sequences, it would be conditioned and fragmentary, just as the conditioned, residual responses are.) In fact, we are saying that there exists a *sacred benediction* that all would agree is most profound and *spiritual*, if they could somehow commune with it. However, that *sacred benediction* never actually meets or is experienced by minds that are merely composed of conditioned and limited sequential symbols of representational thinking. What is mechanical, conditioned, and rather dead, cannot ever be "one" with what is free, truly alive, and beyond conditioning. Of course, what is *sacred* can influence the realm of men within the world; however, it would not do so through merely conditioned, limited, fragmentary minds (that are caught in stagnant symbolism, caught in sequential mental frameworks, and caught in the habit of seeing things with an innate sense of distance and spacious separation).

True silence comes naturally, on its own, to a mind that is mostly innocent and pure, to a mind that is not laden with (innumerable symbolic representations and measurements that never stop babbling). One cannot "know" that one is in a deep, *true silence.* Such *silence* is beyond the realm of knowing. One may be in such a silence for many years before being visited by that profound, *sacred benediction*; or that profound *benediction* may never come to one ever. One need not regret that the *benediction* hasn't come, because light need not crave more light. Wisdom is limitlessly content, in and of itself; that is its beauty.

Gracefully, *true silence* intelligently and sagaciously goes beyond what are mere symbolic sequences. All thoughts are limited, symbolic sequences. All symbolic sequences take time, because all symbolic sequences must, by natural law, move in a series within (and "as") a cause and effect continuum. Each thought is a symbolic representation that takes time for the mind to formulate as, and each thought (being symbolic and merely representational) takes up a very limited space; all limited symbols, by natural law, must take up a limited space. The *truly sacred* may not merely be a series of shadow-like, symbolic, sequences in (and "as") time. The *truly sacred*, not being merely fragmentary, exists as a true "whole"; this true "whole" does not merely operate as a broken-up field of patterns in sequential time. Since all of the multitudinous universes operate in (and "as") patterns in time, what is *sacred* truly exists beyond them. What is truly "*timeless*" may exist beyond (sequential patterns in a spacious, symbolic series). The phenomenon of thought exists as "sequential patterns of spacious symbols in a series"; such a symbolic series has never been able to be what the *truly sacred is*, and it will never be what the *truly sacred is*. The phenomena and process of thought is incapable of being the *truly sacred*. What exists (beyond sequential patterns in a spacious, symbolic series) may exist beyond the multiplex of universes and beyond the requisite natural laws of the cosmos. It does not take time to go beyond the limited (natural) laws of our universe; time is part of these laws, and what is primarily limited cannot fully enter into the unlimited whole. The silent mind that receives the *benediction* of the unlimited *whole* exists beyond the realm of time.

from Emily Dickinson:

GREAT streets of silence led away
To neighborhoods of pause;
Here was no notice, no dissent,
No universe, no laws.

By clocks, 'twas morning, and for night
The bells at distance called;
But epoch had no basis here,
For period exhaled.

Professor Roddenbacher (to his science associate):

"Really, George, considering Emily Dickinson's limited resources and the fact that folks were not as scientifically erudite in her day and age, don't you find it to be quite ludicrous that Thomas Peace actually assumes that she had the sophistication to be able to contemplate *time* and *space* with any real degree of perception or realization whatsoever?"

George: "You are undoubtedly correct, Professor. Miss Dickinson, who was a mere recluse in a very crude, bygone time, could not possibly have had the immense sophistication to regard aspects such as *time* and *space* in terms of profound psychological and scientific frameworks."

Excerpt from Emily Dickinson, Valentine Week 1850:

THOU art a human solo, a being, cold and lone,
Wilt have no kind companion, thou reap'st
what thou hast sown.
Hast never silent hours, and minutes all too
long,
And a deal of sad reflection, and wailing
instead of song?
There's Sarah, and Eliza, and Emeline so fair,
And Harriet, and Susan, and she with curling
hair!
Thine eyes are sadly blinded, but yet thou
mayest see…
Six true, and comely maidens sitting upon the
tree;
Approach that tree with caution, then up it
boldly climb,
And seize the one thou lovest, nor care for
space, or *time*!
Then bear her to the greenwood, and build for
her a bower,
And give her what she asketh, jewel, or bird, or
flower…
And bring the fife, and trumpet, and beat upon
the drum…
And bid the world goodmorrow, and go to
glory home!

It is truly unfortunate that the fellow, whom the above poem concerns, never has *silent hours* and seems to be stuck in *time.* Poor fool!

In terms of time and space, thoughts require time to be formulated, and thoughts manifest as a requisite space (wherein something or some things are represented by special, needed images; these special images require and necessitate an amount of time with regard to the occurrence of their manifestation). We were all taught that the mind creates thoughts, that "the mind" constructs or manufactures "thoughts." It could just as easily be argued that: "thoughts" construct or manufacture "the mind." Actually, it is that "thoughts" and "the mind" are not two separate entities; they are one in the same. We *are* what thought takes place as. Fortunately, the mind need not merely be what the thought process consists of. The thought process is virtual. The mind can be much more than that.

Thoughts are always partial and fragmentary. Thoughts are symbolic representations and, as such, they can only represent a portion of what is manifesting out there, in reality. They are like crude sketches of what is occurring in real life, and, by the time one thing is sketched, it has changed or has been altered and may not at all be like what was initially perceived. Things perceived by the brain become (more often than not) pigeonholed and categorized in ways that are usually fragmentary and limited. Perceiving things as being "separate" — such as when thinking that the "perceiver" is separate from "the perceived" — naturally causes a friction (and loss of energy) in the mind, as one disunites and divides what is actually whole and unified.

We must again reiterate that self-concepts about "oneself," as consisting of a central, "controlling" agency, are generally and essentially false. The thoughts — that exist, as what an internal, central, and controlling mechanism seems to occur as — happen to be just that: thoughts. One supposedly "central thought" can think that it is controlling the "other thoughts"; however, it is, in reality, just another thought; it is not really controlling the other thoughts whatsoever. Additionally, there is really nothing truly "central" about it! In actuality, the mind (including the brain) has no central point! If one erroneously thinks that one is truly separate from *the object of perception*, is one likely to think that there is an actuality, called "I," that exists at a real distance from the object? May the following poem reveal how "thinking that one is separate from an object of perception" causes one to fundamentally stray away from the object via fragmentary friction? In addition, does the following poem reveal how "finally perceiving that the 'perceiver' is not separate from 'the perceived'"… causes the mind to regain the energy lost by that initial, erroneous friction and separation that occurred in the first place. (You and the object with its distance… are *one whole.*) You are silly if you think anything else.

from Emily Dickinson:

PERCEPTION of an
Object costs
Precise the Object's loss.
Perception in itself a gain
Replying to its price;
The Object Absolute is nought,
Perception sets it fair,
And then upbraids a Perfectness
That situates so far.

(Let us take a little break here.) The following are a few interesting notes about my so-called self. What most people regard as their "separate selves" consists of what is rather illusory and insubstantial. Only when one psychologically dies to the trivialities and superficialities of a separate "me" can there be what really exists (in a fully holistic, true, and eternal way).

Unfortunately, for me, the lottery drawing, held on July 1, 1970, to select draft numbers for determining which men would be sent to war, left me with the draft number of "39"; (the date of my birth was 11-04-51, which was what helped associate me with the draft drawing number of "39.") Any number lower than 125, or so, meant you were eligible to go. Not wanting to be one of the "little-shots" getting shot a little, for the ungodliness of the "big-shots," i went to college rather than to the battle field. When college draft deferments ended, i applied to be a conscientious objector. My deep feeling was (and is) that organized fighting, as war, is something that is beyond what i wish to participate in. For instance, i am a vegetarian; i don't even wish to kill chickens! I really despised that God-forsaken number. The number "39" certainly managed to rattle my cage! By the way, i have no beef with veterans of war; some of my best friends are veterans, whom i often deeply admire… and tease.

I have been a vegetarian for many years. The type of vegetarianism that i partake in is the ovo-lacto form; besides plenty of vegetables, i consume cholesterol-free milk and egg products. I first became interested in the vegetarian diet and lifestyle while in college, when a girl (at a party) mentioned that she was a vegetarian. Always having had an affinity for animals, i felt that such a way of eating was quite admirable, and i started forgoing meat (not long after the party). (The girl at the party, by the way, was with her boyfriend, and i had no desires to date her.) Initially i, during my first vegetarian endeavors, continued eating plenty of fish. I was, for many years, an avid fisherman (often managing to catch plenty of fish when other people would fail miserably). There were plenty of very good lakes for fishing around the campus where i attended college, so i was not at all inclined to readily give up catching and eating fish. Fishing was my deep passion; it was one of my very favorite things to do.

However, things would quickly change in that regard. I remember that, one day, while at the college dorm where we lived, a friend had some rock 'n roll albums that i had never heard before. One of them was a music album by the rock group known as *Jethro Tull*. I owned and loved *Tull's* nonconformist "Aqualung" album; however, since i never heard of the *Tull* album which my friend had, i borrowed it from him (to listen to later in the evening). I took the album to my room and tossed it, face up, on my bed cover. (Back then, the music albums were of the very large LP type, with large, graphic designs.) Immediately after throwing the album on my bed, i went fishing, as i had planned to do that particular day. So i went fishing, and while fishing, i began experiencing a couple of rather unusual feelings. Both of the "feelings" had to do with separation and space. One of the "feelings" involved a deep, empathic "closeness" to what the fish actually were experiencing; one began clearly seeing their point of view, their struggle, and their real and genuine fear. Additionally, i had a very definite sensation or feeling that i was being watched by some form of higher intelligence, a higher intelligence that saw what i was doing as being rather barbaric and callous. My deep passion (for fishing) suddenly began to look very superficial.

I terminated the fishing and went back to my college dormitory (to relax and to get away from that unpleasant experience at the lake). I sat on my bed and turned the *Tull* album around to see the back cover (in order to see if a list of the songs in the album was posted). Instead of a list of songs, there was a large photograph of the lead singer holding the tail of a large fish as it dangled down. Attached, near to the fish, was (shockingly to me, at the time) a note with the number "39" exclusively upon it. Like a fish on a fisherman's line, one knows what it is like to be one of the "unlucky ones," regarding that nauseating number. (Incidentally, the album that i borrowed was entitled: "This Was," and was recorded and released in 1968; regarding this rock album, one realizes that "this was" something that existed prior to the 1970 U.S. draft Lottery.)

I no longer eat fish; I no longer am a fisherman. Alternatively, I currently have a number of interesting hobbies, such as fossil hunting, taking close-up pictures of insects, flying sport-kites, and keeping and raising pets, such as tropical fish (whom i care for very much). I still remain unimpressed by the ungodliness of wars; that hasn't changed. As for the number "39," well, i still immensely dislike it to this day.

from Stephen Crane:

Black riders came from the sea.
There was clang and clang of spear and shield,
And clash and clash of hoof and heel,
Wild shouts and the wave of hair
In the rush upon the wind:
Thus the ride of sin.

Thought and thinking (which are usually quite conditioned) are, nonetheless, extremely useful tools, just as we have said. We are not suggesting that one should avoid and shun the thinking process. The thinking process is beautiful and necessary. As was suggested, we very much need the thinking process to help eradicate disease, overpopulation, ignorance, indifference, and unnecessary pollution within the world. However, the process of thought, as a mere reactionary, conditioned network, will not do things with keen insight and understanding if the organism functions by depending upon symbolic, reaction-response modalities exclusively. One may insist that what is being suggested here is sheer nonsense, and one may merely be satisfied with regard to living exclusively in (and "as") *thought* and the *thinking process*. However, it may very well be that clinging to what is exclusively one series of symbolic reactions after another may be the equivalent to clinging to mere shadows that are inherently devoid of true joy and true renewal. What is residual, symbolic, artificial, second-hand, memorized, rehashed, rehearsed and repeated, cannot possibly be the fresh and new joy of true, spontaneous awareness and direct, unadulterated perception; nor can it be the explosive depth of real, heartfelt compassion. True compassion only occurs within and through those of us who are alive. Conditioned entities — who (unfortunately) are dead-from-the-neck-up — do not exist as real compassion. (Actually, they are dead-from-the-heart-up.)

Being full of fear is not living. Fear is the product of thought and thinking (about the future). The "future," that thought *thinks* about, is not the "future" at all; it is *past* memories and reactions merely projecting what the future "might be." So a mind that exists as many fears in succession is (unfortunately) not existing as the "living now"; such a mind is entrenched in (and "as") the dead *past*. Such a mind is "living in the past." It manifests as old memories of "what might be," that are projections from what it has absorbed and learned. While it exists as old shadows of the *past*, the *new* and *beautifully radiant* occurrences are not what it partakes in, and it (in its dark fear and frightened images) misses the *bright beauty* and *harmony* of spontaneous, holistic living and life.

One cannot merely "get rid of fear." For fear in oneself… is (partially) what one is. Who is going to "get rid of" or extinguish fear? Will it be another set of images from the past that are "learned memories," as fear is? Who is going to break and crush the un-malleable, solidified patterns of the bedrock of fear? Will it merely be the tough, habituated reactions of a rocklike center? Such a hardheaded center thinks that it is the formidable rock or bulwark that is in charge of the *other* earthy fragments of thought; in reality, though, it is another learned reaction that is not necessary, that is not un-rocklike, nor "in control." Can one conditioned symbol remove another conditioned symbol and, then, call itself free? Can one series of mechanical reactions actually free another series of mechanical reactions? Can one set of *symbolic shadows* chase away *another set of symbolic shadows* in order to become free of *shadowiness*? We are not suggesting, of course, that one just wallow in one's fears and sorrows; one, without relying on time, can psychologically die to all the fears and false images that one exists as. Instantly dropping all the *past burdens, past memories* and *past images*… takes no effort. Passively being the fear, without prejudice, takes no effort. Such "effortlessness" does not require a learned "method," does not require a memorized "procedure," and does not require "responding according to some specified pattern." Effort requires time. Time, psychologically, is not where the spontaneity of joy readily resides. We are talking about virtual psychological time, not true, physical time. True joy is in the immediate "*now*," not in dead memories or in limited fears of obstruction and pain. True joy is beyond what any drugs or programmed procedures can provide. Watch animals, such as bees and birds; they do not waste time grieving and crying in sorrow. They do not sit around sad and mentally crippled; they sing, they fly, and celebrate life! True joy is not apart from the graceful, untroubled, nimble, and cheery mirth that many animals have, as they actually live in (and "as") beauty.

from Emily Dickinson:

WHERE every bird is bold to go,
  And bees abashless play,
The foreigner before he knocks
  Must thrust the tears away.

It is so easy to be strategically hoodwinked by what the erroneous, elderly authorities have planted within us, while we, all the while, think that what is in us is our own free and correct intelligence. If we merely manifest as what they implanted within us, we may be essentially "un-alive." Majestically, however, thoughts are not merely "dead shadows" and phantomlike reactions if, along with them, between them, and through them, there exists something that is "beyond reactions, beyond uncaring indifference, and beyond self-centeredness." One of Emily Dickinson's short poems, for instance, indicates how the words of people who are merely happy are words that are generally trivial and paltry, whereas the words that "the silent" feel are beautiful (i.e., extraordinary). If you think that words from *the truly enlightened* have no real, magical life of their own, then just keep reading.

from Emily Dickinson:

A WORD is dead
When it is said,
Some say.
I say it just
Begins to live
That day.

It is tremendously important not to merely drift through life in a languid and indifferent manner, not caring for oneself (and others, who are not so very separate from oneself). He or she who is appreciative of his or her own uniqueness is wise and intelligent. You are good; you are special; you are important! We are all the same in many ways; however, each of us is unique; we must relish and nourish our uniqueness, our being unlike everyone else. It would be ludicrous to look down on others, to see others as being inferior to what one is. It would be wise to be appreciative of the beautiful uniqueness of others, to admire and be very appreciative of them, as one is of oneself.

Merely being appreciative of one's immediate family (or race) is a form of narrow-mindedness that is largely unavailing; it is a crude and very limited way of looking and perceiving. The whole world is one large family; we are, all of us, its children. We are not merely dust in the wind, here to temporarily go through a few patterns of experience and then be expired forever. We are very special and significant.

If you are depressed and melancholy, it is a sign that something is wrong with your outlook and perspectives. Work at understanding yourself; learn to blossom into what is joyous and caring. I realize that some of us can be dealt an overwhelmingly rotten hand, with life's circumstances sometimes being overwhelmingly difficult and (almost unbearable) to cope with. If that is the case for you, such as the death of a loved one, please do manage to get over it (i.e., the dark dirt of what was handed to you by chance) and then flower as true joy again. One can blossom effortlessly. Instead of looking at everything with (and through) the eyes of the *dead past* (i.e., with the eyes that have recorded and pigeonholed everything, with the eyes that keep remembering all the pain), look without so much memory and categorization; look at things *as if for the first time*. Go beyond the pain and sorrow, please. There is great beauty to be seen in so much of life. To truly see such beauty, one must have eyes that are not contaminated by worn-out images of the *past*. Merely to look through a *mental screen* of what has been "accumulated," may not be truly "looking" at all.

A mind that is surrounded by limited perspectives, limited viewpoints — while it looks through screens of "past, worn-out knowledge" that was handed down to it — is ensnared and confined within its own prison. Such a (mental) prison, of limitation, fragmentation, and mere representation, is bound; it is bound to be bored, bound to be depressed, and bound to feel frustrated often. Such a mind is bound in limitation. Effortless liberation comes when the mind looks without the *past*, looks without pre-programmed memory, looks without pre-conceived notions, and looks without pre-conceived images. True freedom uses the past memory bank intelligently, when it is needed, not overusing it (when using it is not necessary). True intelligence and freedom go hand in hand. True intelligence is perceptive; true intelligence sees the beauty; true intelligence looks beyond barriers; true intelligence is not merely limited. Is a mind that is enmeshed and entrapped by the limited likely to be content within its domain, which it inevitably must accept as being finite? Will innumerable, limited minds inevitably disagree with what this book puts forward? Is true intelligence devoid of immortality? (Wallace Stevens once wrote, "Success is to be happy with the wise.")

from Walt Whitman:

Whoever you are! motion and reflection are especially for you,
The divine ship sails the divine sea for you.
Whoever you are! you are he or she for whom the earth is solid and liquid,

You are he or she for whom the sun and moon hang in the sky,
For none more than you are the present and the past,
For none more than you is immortality.
Each man to himself and each woman to herself, is the word
of the past and present, and the true word of immortality;
No one can acquire for another—not one,
Not one can grow for another—not one.

The symbol (even though it is merely just a symbol) of a pyramid, upon an American dollar bill, is rather interesting. At the top of the pyramid is the "*All-seeing Eye* of divine providence." Before the adjournment of the Continental Congress on July 4, 1776, a committee was appointed to develop a seal for the United States; this pyramid design was completed from that committee. At the base of the pyramid is, in Roman Numerals, the date of 1776. The Latin, written below the pyramid, NOVUS ORDO SECLORUM, means "A new order for the ages."

It is interesting that, concerning the symbolism of the great pyramid, the symbolic bricks start out large at the base; as one progressively goes higher, the bricks diminish in size and then disappear. It may be that when thought and symbolism (just as the bricks) diminish and go away, there is the possibility for divinity to visit. The pyramid, too, may reveal somewhat of an evolutionary process, wherein more crude entities at the bottom, nevertheless, have helped more refined entities up toward a great silence and emptiness, a great *immensity*, a *divine benediction*. It may very well be that "your wise men don't know how it feels to be thick as a brick."

from E. E. Cummings:

Humanity i love you
because you would rather black the boots of
success than enquire whose soul dangles from his
watch-chain which would be embarrassing for both

parties and because you
unflinchingly applaud all
songs containing the words country home and
mother when sung at the old howard

Humanity i love you because
when you're hard up you pawn your
intelligence to buy a drink and when
you're flush pride keeps

you from the pawn shops and
because you are continually committing
nuisances but more
especially in your own house

Humanity i love you because you
are perpetually putting the secret of
life in your pants and forgetting
it's there and sitting down

on it
and because you are
forever making poems in the lap
of death Humanity

i hate you

Walt Whitman was, i most strongly maintain, an enlightened being. He (like E. E. Cummings) was one of those few who were visited by *divinity*, by the actual *sacred*, during their lifetime. Whitman went past and transcended limited thoughts, mere small, fragmentary perspectives, and isolated vantage points. Whitman was sagacious, extremely wise, compassionate, and all encompassing. Even though he functioned far back in the 1800s, he, nevertheless, had modernistic views not limited by traditional and solitary viewpoints. Whitman understood the multiverse; he understood, with keen insight, how the cosmos operated. His understanding was not limited to a mere single solar system, or a mere single universe. Since he was indeed visited by a *benediction* of vast *sacredness*, he then had more than just a glimpse of the whole of everything. Whitman often saw and wrote of the supreme splendor of man, nature, and the multiple universes. Whitman's grace often poured out to others, as when he unselfishly assisted the civil war wounded; as i had previously mentioned, he gave so much to them that, in fact, his own health deteriorated as a consequence. Whitman was moral, ethical, and imperishable. He everlastingly cared about people and life.

It is very improbable that, during one's lifetime, one would meet such a person as what Whitman was. He was incredible and indissoluble; he was vast, straight, sound, and deep thinking.

from Walt Whitman:

O soul thou pleasest me, I thee,
Sailing these seas or on the hills, or waking in the night,
Thoughts, silent thoughts, of Time and Space and Death, like waters flowing,
Bear me indeed as through the regions infinite,
Whose air I breathe, whose ripples hear, lave me all over,
Bathe me O God in thee, mounting to thee,
I and my soul to range in range of thee.
O Thou transcendent,
Nameless, the fibre and the breath,
Light of the light, shedding forth universes, thou centre of them,
Thou mightier centre of the true, the good, the loving,
Thou moral, spiritual fountain — affection's source — thou reservoir,
(O pensive soul of me — O thirst unsatisfied — waitest not there?
Waitest not haply for us somewhere there the Comrade perfect?)
Thou pulse — thou motive of the stars, suns, systems,
That, circling, move in order, safe, harmonious,
Athwart the shapeless vastnesses of space,
How should I think, how breathe a single breath, how speak, if, out of myself,
I could not launch, to those, superior universes?

While in college, one began to become more and more serious about living a life of morality, integrity, and wholeness. No longer would i be interested in going out in the evenings, partying, drinking, and pursuing women. After giving up all of that, i often went for walks, by myself, looking at nature and enjoying the beauty around the college campus. At the time, J. Krishnamurti's works interested me. I would often read his insights about living with a silent mind, going beyond fear, and living in the "present," not in the past or in the projected future. I remember, back then, often looking without the images of *thought and thinking* interfering. There was no method or procedure to "get to" or "arrive" at such silence. The rigmarole of thought simply dropped from one's mind, naturally, at times.

One evening, while at the college dormitory by myself, while my friends were out partying, something incredible occurred. Drugs and drinking had nothing whatsoever to do with it; i had never done that much in the way of drugs, and never cared that much for drinking alcohol; i was free of those things for quite some time; so drugs and alcohol were not factors in what i partook in. Before it occurred, immediately before it occurred, thought was rather infrequent in one's consciousness. Words and images were infrequent and not manifesting. One of Emily Dickinson's poems (beginning with the first line of: "All things swept sole away") mentions something about how, when all things are swept sole away, there is *immensity*. Well, that evening, i was visited by "*Immensity*." It was likely what people refer to as "enlightenment," "nirvana," or "being visited by the *sacred*." Words, of course, cannot describe it. It was an *immensity* that was far beyond what symbols, formulations, and mental representations are capable of. All thought and thinking is "about" energy; all thought consists of mental models or mentally fabricated tokens or representations "about" energy. *Thought and thinking* is a modality that is not the actual "energy." *Thought/thinking* is barren. Thinking exists as symbolic impressions that truly have no real, deep "energy" inherently within. Thinking, though extremely useful and necessary, is like a dark void: barren of true energy. What happened to me, that night, was *not barren of energy in the least.* While it occurred, the thought process was *difficult* and "in the background." In other words, the thinking process was (in a way) being overshadowed by what was not a shadow. One considers, now, how intense sunlight often puts dark shadows into abeyance.

As that *benediction* occurred, one was partaking in what seemed like an immeasurable bliss, far from what words can describe. It was like being alive a trillion times more than one ever was before. Later, while it occurred for quite some time, when one stood in front of a mirror as it was taking place, one noticed that the whites of one's eyes were of a deep blood-shot red in color. (Don't laugh; it wasn't drugs.) Additionally, one's hands became very contracted, and it was often very difficult to physically move. Things, visually, lost their distance; everything seemed to be dancing and flowing into one in a supreme, majestic movement of order and love.

At one point, one went to the restroom to take out one's contact-lenses (that were for correcting vision); for, indeed, one managed to think that "If one is permeated by the *sacred*, one wouldn't need to have corrective lenses to see clearly!" As i reached for the contact lens's case within the mirror-cabinet, that *immensity* prevented my hand and arm from going any further. A few moments later, i reached again — and was fully able to reach — and began taking my contact lenses out. As soon as i took the contact lenses out, that *immensity* was gone. I looked into the mirror, and what i saw was fussy and unclear!

Walt Whitman mentions something about such an *Immensity* within some of his poetry. I think that what he writes about is like what i had partaken in while at that dormitory during my college days. Of course, someone casually reading his poetry would have no idea whatsoever concerning the *Immensity* to which he is referring. How could they have any idea of what such poems are about, if they never had partaken in, or undergone, anything similar? [At the time of this writing, i did a web-search on the analysis of the following poem, and no one seems to understand what it means whatsoever.] To me, however, a great deal of what he writes about has some very profound meanings regarding the effect of such an *Immensity.* Some of what he writes about is a reflection from when he underwent a visitation from something beyond mere symbols, beyond the sequential framework of thinking, beyond the limited, fragmentary, banal, commonplace realms of ordinary consciousness. That *Immensity* floored Whitman, understandably, just as it floored me. That *Immensity*, whatever one wishes to call it (the name is not the thing), is beyond time and fragmentation. It is a *sacredness* that is beyond mere limitation. I feel very blessed concerning having been visited by it when i was very young. I am still reeling from such a visitation! Some may not be visited by it until way later in their lives, when they are very elderly; most are never visited by it at all. Most, unfortunately, never let go of dwelling in (and "as") limited, shadowlike representations. It does not visit what is corrupt, distorted, and shadowlike.

from Walt Whitman:

One Hour to Madness and Joy

One hour to madness and joy! O furious! O confine me not!
(What is this that frees me so in storms?
What do my shouts amid lightnings and raging winds mean?)
O to drink the mystic deliria deeper than any other man!
O savage and tender achings! (I bequeath them to you my children,
I tell them to you, for reasons, O bridegroom and bride.)

O to be yielded to you whoever you are, and you to be yielded to me in defiance of the world!
O to return to Paradise! O bashful and feminine!
O to draw you to me, to plant on you for the first time the lips of a determin'd man.

O the puzzle, the thrice-tied knot, the deep and dark pool, all untied and illumin'd!
O to speed where there is space enough and air enough at last!
To be absolv'd from previous ties and conventions, I from mine and you from yours!
To find a new unthought-of nonchalance with the best of Nature!
To have the gag remov'd from one's mouth!
To have the feeling to-day or any day I am sufficient as I am.

O something unprov'd! something in a trance!
To escape utterly from others' anchors and holds!
To drive free! to love free! to dash reckless and dangerous!
To court destruction with taunts, with invitations!
To ascend, to leap to the heavens of the love indicated to me!

To rise thither with my inebriate soul!
To be lost if it must be so!
To feed the remainder of life with one hour of fullness and freedom!
With one brief hour of madness and joy.

A real visitation, from what is "truly sacred," must affect more than just the individual; it must affect the whole of mankind. To some, the beauty of true *enlightenment* may be so indescribably immense… that they, after it goes, feel almost as if in a hellish predicament. *Enlightenment* is indescribably immense.

from Emily Dickinson:

MY life closed twice before its close;
It yet remains to see
If Immortality unveil
A third event to me,

So huge, so hopeless to conceive,
As these that twice befell.
Parting is all we know of heaven,
And all we need of hell.

One cannot describe a true, sublime *benediction* with mere words or illustrations. The living, sublime *sacredness* cannot be captured by what is limited and fragmentary. All words, by their very nature, are fragmentary and partial. The description is never the actuality of the described. The map is not the territory. Even relatively simple things often cannot be adequately described via mental messages or by communicated terms, much less an *Immensity* that is far beyond mere symbolism and rambling shadowiness.

Since words and symbols are fragmentary, partial, and incomplete (regarding what they attempt to describe), it stands to reason that an entity whose consciousness exists almost exclusively in (and "as") the domain of "words" and "representations" likely has the misfortune to experience more deception, more delusion, and more fallacious phenomena than does a sagacious mind that exists beyond what is confined. To comfortably dwell in the limited, while content with it, accepting it wholeheartedly, is to be impoverished and destitute of true happiness. To cling to the limited is sorrow, tragedy, and misery, and that is precisely why evil men are never truly joyous. Being evil, in other words — just out for oneself to the exclusion of "others" — is a narrow-minded, partial, fragmentary, and therefore "limited" point of view. Such limitation is a phenomenon wherein barriers constitute one's consciousness, and a consciousness riddled with barriers is little, narrow, and insufficient. A spiritless, lifeless flame is the indifferent, dying beam of a little, self-centered brain. Such a brain is languishing, is barren of true joy, and often extinguishes the light and happiness of others. What is limited and trapped around a fictional self-center… is likely to contribute to the suffering or even to the obliteration and "wiping out" of others. Such a destroyed mind may see no harm in ceasing or harming the life of "others."

A truly intelligent mind, on the other hand, sees that the right hand is not separate from the left hand at all. This does not mean that it (i.e., the wise mind) is guilty when, on the other hand, someone else does something atrocious; but the wise mind will point to what is not limitation and fragmentation. A wise mind helps. It is not merely what remains in (and "as") a secluded, isolated, undisturbed center. Such a mind may even go through discomfort and distress to help (while others do not care). Such a mind may ask for no reward; it often asks for nothing in return; it may be whole and boundless enough, such that it needs no petty rewards or gratuities. Interestingly, it may not merely recoil from discomfort and pain, for it may be incalculably vast, such that it is willing to go through considerable pain in order to help others. To transcend limitation, such as limited discomforts, is to transcend sorrow. Sorrow and self-centeredness are forms of grief. A fragmentary mind is of a *broken-heartedness* that exists as long as mere symbols and notions/images of an isolated "controller" manifest.

A free mind is a mind of effortlessness. Such a mind need not cling to any false "center" or "domineering image" that supposedly is in charge of the "other" thoughts and images. A free mind is beyond images and symbolic representations. A free mind is not of limited prejudices, confined hatreds, or envious wants (involving circumference around a limited center). A free mind has no isolating borders and learned boundaries of a small "self." Such a joyous mind is open (beyond all learned boundaries); its vastness cannot be described by mere words and limited patterns. Such an "open" mind exists without selfish barriers. Such an "open" mind is available to the possibility of visitation by the *sacred benediction* while it functions through life. However, as stated before, if the *sacred* does not come to it, it is joyous and blissful anyway, for it, in itself, is a *benediction and a blessing*, asking nothing more. Superlative *radiance* comes when wisdom beyond boundaries and isolating images occurs. That vastness lies beyond what fragmentary communication is capable of. Most people, unfortunately, merely dwell as (and exist as) what fragmentary, symbolic communication is.

from Emily Dickinson:

TO tell the Beauty would decrease
To state the Spell demean,
There is a Syllableless Sea
Of which it is the sign.

My will endeavors for its word
And fails, but entertains
A rapture as of legacies —
Of introspective mines.

Thought, being fragmentary, is always partial and incomplete. A symbol is usually an incomplete representation regarding the actuality of the thing that it stands for or tries to depict. However, so many millions have embraced *thought/thinking*, and have accepted it to be the very essence of their consciousness. Each one of us functions, in consciousness, as a conglomeration of thoughts and symbolic representations. As you think, so you are. One's thoughts are not separate from what one is. What one is… is a bundle of fragmentary symbols.

Thought, being a rather insubstantial phenomenon, is (as we suggested before) barren of energy. Thought is "about" energy. When individuals think, they often think (internally) as a series of "internal voices" that talk (inwardly) to themselves. This "internal talk" often takes on the form or *semblance of one's own voice*. In other words, the internal thinking process often *mimics* the *voice* that one *hears* while one is actually talking to others. This pirating or pilfering of the sound of the voice is but another way in which thought tries to copy and imitate reality. However, it is not real. Is it? Internal thoughts of one's real voice have no actual reality of their own. Internal pictures of the environment… are not true and complete pictures.

Thought, being a sequential series of symbolic patterns, in time, often relies heavily on systems. Systems often represent, to thought, a way of doing things easier, in a structured way that thought, hopefully, can comprehend and benefit from. Thought/thinking, being an internal structure of patterns of representations, tends to relish outward (manmade) systems that it can relate to (and possibly benefit from). Humans adore systems. We are so ingrained in the systems that we adhere to; we are even willing to fight and go to war over these very systems. We often bicker and fight over our precious systems. We have even reduced religion into a structured framework of systems (as if what is truly alive and divine can be captured by the shoddy, limited mental meanderings of man)! Our political systems often contribute to a lot of suffering of the masses… because, instead of direct compassion and understanding, manmade structures have wielded power over insubordinates and have held them in check. So instead of man being important, systems have become important. We often go at each other's throats over these systems and manmade patterns of behavior. When we succumb to the comfort of being lead and governed by "systems," we tend to get more and more indifferent, more and more languid, letting the system do the work for us. Envy, greed, ambition, and indifference often emerge in a brain that depends, internally, on systems and images. These internal systems (of images, so-called domineering patterns, and notions of space between one's self and others) often make the mind into something increasingly more mechanical and increasingly more machine-like. A bunch of reactions, as programmed responses to keep one safe in a small, little corner, may be beneficial, though very limited. However, when it turns one into a mere mechanical monster, then one may lose one's integrity and turn into what is not truly alive.

Love is not what manifests from cold, manmade systems. Love is not some concoction from a reaction-oriented brain that is full of patterns and shoddy ideas of the past. Love is a spontaneity that cannot be handed over to another to have (as a mere system provides). A worn-out brain, full of internal and external systems, may, indeed, talk about love and spew out a lot of ideas of morality supposedly pertaining to love. Many hypocrites may say that they know all about morality and all about love; but it may be that what they say is not at all what they claim to be experts in. Love is not something that one can know that one has.

Is a self-centered brain, full of images of a dominating, internal, central regulator, truly likely to be the holistic compassion and wise understanding that love is? Can what fabricates boundaries and peripheries around itself with psychological demarcations… be the boundless compassion that is free from restricted images and internal systems? Can a distorted mind — that has been corrupted by mechanical systems and patterns within society

— easily be what love is? If one's mind is paralyzed and deadened by the fabricated beliefs of others, can one easily be the dynamic energy that love is? If one is satisfied with the paltry images, self-enclosed perspectives, and meager symbols that society attempts to instill into one, is one likely to feel limitless love? If one merely pampers an inner "me," while shunning those whom one feels apart from, can there (then) be love? If one merely panders to the dominating dictators, without question, is that love? If one is a slave to fears involving one's little self as opposed to the well-being of the whole, is that love? If one does little or nothing to help curtail pollution within this fragile planet, is that love? If one procreates, producing many babies upon a planet that is severely overcrowded and dying from overpopulation, is that love? If one purchases illegal drugs or alcohol, supporting industries that create havoc within people's lives, is that love? If one prays and pretends to be religious one day a week, but treats people like pawns, reacting unjustly and indifferently throughout the rest of the week, is that love? If one fills one's body with a lot of dead, unwholesome foods, is that love? If one merely remains comfortable throughout one's entire lifetime, without ever suffering to help his fellow man, is that love?

An entity who tends to be cold, indifferent, egotistically self-centered and heartless, unfortunately — with respect to what is being related here — will not be likely to develop and grow much at all. If you do not blossom in the active present, you are not learning and are not truly alive. It does not take time to be a wise, intuitive mind that is full of insight, loving the whole of everything with deep perception. What remains as the dark, unenlightened, self-centered, and shady can live for many years; however, that is not real living whatsoever. Someone who physically dies in his early teens, yet who truly loved the helpless and the small (with open, dynamic eyes), has lived much more than he who has chronologically existed for many cadaverous decades yet, all the while, has been exploiting the destitute, deluding the naive, stepping on the small, and disregarding those in agony and affliction.

from Emily Dickinson:

NOT all die early, dying Young,
Maturity of Fate
Is consummated equally
In Ages, or a Night.

A Hoary Boy, I've known to drop
Whole statured, by the side
Of Junior of Fourscore — 'twas Act
Not Period, that died.

If it is primitive and barbaric for one thought or image to think that it is in control (and think that it is "in charge") of other thoughts, then what is the mind to do? Can a false "central authority" be thrown out and discarded by the *thinking process*? Furthermore, who is going to throw it out? Will it be another internal authority? If the mind contains friction, with internal conflict and turmoil, is such a mind healthy? Friction within a mind, as it is occurring, is a waste of energy. A mind that is wasting energy is not a holistic mind full of integrity.

If part of the mind wants to "do" something, and another part of the mind thinks that it "should not do it," that is friction, which is a waste of energy. As was suggested before, a mind full of friction wastes a lot of energy. Opposing forces, within the mind, contribute to internal discord and internal disharmony. A mind of understanding may be effortlessly aware of these contending influences and go beyond them. It cannot go beyond them if it is merely trapped in (and "as") fragmentary divisions in opposition. To go beyond the friction, one sees the friction as friction (but not from a partial realm). The central "I" or ego, called "me" or "myself" is a partial realm and, as such, cannot do this. Only understanding can do this. Moreover, one cannot "know" that one has understanding. Understanding is beyond the field of the known. The "known" consists of mere thoughts and thought processes, which are fragmentary and partial. That which is merely fragmentary and partial cannot have full understanding. Interestingly, a mind that must know that it has understanding is out of luck. Similarly, a mind that thinks that part of it is in control of other parts is out of luck.

In a mind that is confused, without much understanding, fragmentary processes must occur. In such fragmentary processes, for example, one may be in a situation wherein there is the desire to do something, while there is also the idea that one should not do it. These two fragmentary processes may cause friction. Adding the idea of a central "controller," who will decide what to do with these two opposing forces, does not curtail the friction or fragmentation. On the contrary, it adds to it. Because the reality may be that there is no separate, authentic controller apart from these opposing forces whatsoever. Adding another form of fragmentation to two opposing fields of fragmentation, does not, in reality, diminish the fragmentation. Doing so just adds more separation into the mind, which may not at all be helpful in the long run. More fragmentation, more needless division, is not better; it is far worse.

Intelligence, as understanding and true learning, may perceive this. If it does, the mind may undergo a marvelous transformation. However, such a transformation may not merely be what is known by ordinary memory, or via the ordinary thinking process. A sagacious mind that functions in understanding, functions beyond the field of the *known*. Its awareness is not merely constituted of fragmentary realms. When truly beyond "fragmentary realms," an intelligent mind may have the profound intelligence "to not necessarily think that it is composed of a separate, internal controlling fragment or regulatory mechanism." Such intelligence may be profound.

Many minds may feel depressed at the notion or realization that the internal regulatory mechanism, called "I" or "me," is spurious and much of a sham. Such depression or melancholy is not at all warranted; one can function just perfectly, and with less friction, without all that false, internal muddle and clutter. Without the falsity of the internally controlling "I" or "me," one remains infinitely important; then what is done has *infinite significance.*

One can still refer to the self as "I" or "me" to others in society. However, that does not mean that one is duped into the misconception of a separate regulatory center that is in charge of the "other" thoughts/ideas. Additionally, it is pointed out here that an entity, who commits a serious, harmful crime to others in society, is not to be exempt because he (or she) feels that he (or she) is not constituted of an internal regulatory, controlling "I" or "me." Furthermore, maintaining that "he is merely conditioned" is no valid excuse either. We are, all of us, responsible for our actions, and any serious, cancerous behaviors that cause excessive harm to others in society must be incarcerated (to protect the health of the whole).

A mind that has the deep intelligence and understanding to function without the separative fragmentation of a controlling "center" would likely additionally have the intelligence (by way of understanding and not by mere knowing) to perceive when "thinking that it shouldn't do something" occurs along with a desire to actually "do the thing." Such deep intelligence would see the entirety of the situation, and instead of merely being caught as opposing fragments regarding it, it would perceive the whole picture, the whole movement of thought, and it would go beyond it. Merely being trapped in thought is what fragmentary processes must remain as. What is immersed in (and "as") fragmentation cannot easily go beyond fragmentation and separative perspectives. What intelligently (not intellectually) perceives the limitation of fragmentation goes beyond it. That is real learning. The question is, do we see things merely verbally and intellectually, without much holistic understanding? Do we perceive with insight, beyond confining, limited words?

An old mind, heavily conditioned by society, is not likely to give up the cherished idea of a psychological, controlling, central "I" or "me." Such a mind likely has such a cherished concept ingrained deep within its psyche, high on a carefully sculpted pedestal, with years upon years of cogitations helping to secure it. Such a mind would be in trepidation and alarm… at the very thought of negating part of it that contributes to segmentation and division. Clinging to a glorified fragment, a central fragment that is considered domineering and "in control," may set the stage for more separate factions and more conflict. Strife, boredom, and discord, in such a mind of limitation, would likely be common.

Consciousness does not need a "central I" or central "me" to control it. Consciousness is largely the content of the mind. Adding more separation to the content, by postulating and supporting a "central controlling mechanism," is a waste of energy. Of course, the symbol of "I" can stand for (and represent) the whole of consciousness; that is another story. However, a vast number of people, unfortunately, were conditioned to take the "I" as being some kind of separate, vital, central, domineering, inner being or mechanism; there is, in reality, no such thing. In evolution, as we said before, thought was initially a tool for helping the organism to survive; then, the organism took a part of the tool to represent its central essence. However, there is nothing "central." Ask any accredited neurologist!

True understanding may not be what is composed of falsities, unnecessary fragments, divisiveness, and disunity. True understanding may be what is holistic, immediate, and beyond conditioned parts and patterns. True understanding may be beyond the mere isolated, divisive field of the "known." What is merely *known* is composed of parts and fragments. Mere symbols, constituted exclusively of parts and fragments, are not the reality of the whole. You are more than some *damn false symbol* that is supposedly centrally located, supposedly in charge of all the other symbols. We can psychologically die to the falsities; such a dying is, in reality, true living. Living and dying go together; they are entwined as one; they are not separate parts, separate fragments. Falsities run rampant in society. If we succumb to them, we may remain caught in false and limited centers; we may remain trapped in false mental demarcations; we may contentedly live in the clutches of what is destructive and ruinous for this blessed earth and for man; we may smile for the wrong reasons.

from Emily Dickinson:

Me from Myself — to banish —
Had I Art —
Impregnable my Fortress
Unto All Heart —

But since Myself — assault Me —
How have I peace
Except by subjugating
Consciousness?

And since We're mutual Monarch
How this be
Except by Abdication —
Me — of Me?

As a reader of this book, one may say that the writer is getting too deep regarding what is being pondered about and written here. The reader may say that the writer is delving into where man is not meant to travel. What is being written, however, truly is for good reason. It is your minds that have been cluttered and riddled with excess rubbish, with unending chattering thoughts full of a false symbolism that (all too often) has taken the place of the real world. The distortion within many is profound and far-reaching; hence, what this book (repeatedly) points out must be profound and far-reaching. Many of us have become mere puppets, mere followers, mere second-hand entities who dwell more with symbolic non-realities than with true perception and heartfelt understanding. That is a tragedy.

Compassion, real compassion, is not at all extraordinarily difficult if one goes beyond the fragments and beyond the limited, false space that a conditioned mind is composed of. One does not need fancy philosophies and fabricated doctrines to have a simple, kind, and gentle heart. To live simply, without a lot of mental distortions, allows the mind to truly be open; it is then not closed by lines of fictitious space, limited demarcations, and isolating notions of separation. Living simply is bliss. It is not some arduous, terribly difficult thing that one must strive for.

There is no need to get troubled, for instance, by judging that one's consciousness is "thinking far too much." Let it think; just passively observe without trying to suppress or subjugate; such suppressing and subjugation would merely cause more friction within (and "as") the mind. There is no actual, separate thing or entity that can truly suppress or control thought anyway; supposing that there is, is just folly. Any method or practice, to control or suppress thought and thinking, is, likewise, folly. Any such methods would just make the mind more repetitive and machine-like, causing it merely to be reacting instead of being aware in direct action. A mind of understanding acts; it does not merely react (like some second-hand, programmed robot or conditioned process). One cannot know that one has understanding. Understanding, true understanding, is a blessing that one cannot fabricate or manifest like some old, learned memory or routine. Understanding is alive and living and, being alive, it is not what can be concocted by dead and stale symbols, or by old and learned routines handed over by some conditioned entities or elders. Understanding may leave one open and vulnerable; but in its vulnerability lies an inviolability and invisibility. It is not some stagnant thing that one can capture and retain for selfish gains. E. E. Cummings once wrote that, "It may be dreadful to be old, but it's worse not to be young."

(Let's take a break here. Let's say that all the uplifted *swords* of the truly *straight and direct*, held by every single, serious, distinguished poet, be reaching up to cross each other and join far up above, where all can see… together forming a union, a solidarity, that goes far beyond the limited. The limited is for the primitives of the past. Isn't it? The pen is mightier than the sword.)

Consciousness is not truly separate from what it sees, as the following poem will unveil. We think that we are separate from what we perceive; but that was merely what we were taught, and what we were taught, by our old and ancient-minded elders, may be very wrong. *Mind* is not separate from what it sees. This is not to say that, when one sees a burning campfire, one (then) is actually on fire. However, it does mean that flames and smoke contribute to the patterns, colors, smells, and images that help constitute the mind. Without experiencing, what would the mind be? Most minds depend on experiencing in order to exist. In actuality, what most minds experience is filtered through screens of conditioned "learned patterns and images" that tend to label and categorize what is observed. This happens to such an extent, oftentimes, that what is seen is not seen freshly, with uncontaminated eyes; instead what is seen is merely looked at through preconceptions within (and "as") the brain. Therefore, what is actually there is not fully seen at all. Merely to recognize things through images of the past (i.e., through stored images of memory and categorization) may not be directly perceiving things fully at all.

When one sees an insect, for example, why need one immediately label it, as to the type of insect that it happens to be? More so, why is there a need (in many circumstances) even to label it as an "insect"? As long as one isn't an entomologist, why can't one just look at the organism, not merely categorizing it in the brain as being "this" or "that"? Looking without immediate categorization allows the brain to possibly look "without the 'known'," without mere past memory and past, stored knowledge interfering. Then there is the splendid possibility of directly seeing, freshly, without the old, stored, cobweb-oriented past. Then there is the wonderful possibility of seeing the true beauty of the creature, its wonderful behavior, order, dynamic colors, amazing shape, purposeful struggle, and spirited drive. Habitually labeling it as a mere "ant," however, easily tends to make one overlook its tremendous presence, its dynamic being. Indeed, if we look at it with innocent eyes that have dropped the old-fashioned images of separation, we may even be able to feel a deeper, more profound connection with it, along with all life upon this earth.

Do you look with sordid eyes, from the old, contaminated past, at most of the things within your life? Merely to be looking with eyes contaminated by the past may not really be "looking" at all. A mind that merely looks in that (old) way is likely to be a bored, sullen, and melancholy mind, for it sees the same-old things repetitiously, never perceiving freshly, as if for the first, splendid time.

A wise mind goes beyond this, by watching its reactions from moment to moment. This "watching" is not some learned technique; it is a spontaneous "watchfulness" that occurs every single second. One need not struggle with this and make it into something difficult. Once mere reactions are seen to be the true "danger" and "limitation" that they are, the mind easily learns to pause between thoughts, looking without mere memories, without circumscribed, limited symbols. One doesn't have to go around with a silent mind for hours; one can just pause between all the chattering and all the commotion of thought, now and then, and briefly look and perceive without a mere conditioned background interfering.

It can be seen, in all this, that we are tied to what we perceive. Moreover, what we see often imprints upon our minds. The space between the *perceiver* and *what happens to be perceived…* is essentially nonexistent in the psychological actuality of things. We think that we are so separate from our environment; we are not. We have been taught that we are not what we see; we were taught that we are separate from what we see. Is that actually so in the psychological sense?

from Wallace Stevens:

Tattoo

The light is like a spider.
It crawls over the water.
It crawls over the edges of the snow.
It crawls under your eyelids
And spreads its webs there—
Its two webs.
The webs of your eyes
Are fastened
To the flesh and bones of you
As to rafters of grass.
There are filaments of your eyes
On the surface of the water
And in the edges of the snow.

If you cross an old, wooden bridge with a friend, you see the bridge, and your friend sees the bridge. Is the consciousness of each one of you what the same bridge helps to constitute? Hence, are you both *made-up* of the same bridge? If you see the bridge differently than does your friend, is your consciousness composed of the same bridge that your friend perceives? If each of you perceives the bridge in the same way, is each of you crossing the same bridge? If each of you perceives the bridge in a different way, is each of you crossing the same bridge? If you think of a bridge while you are crossing, has a bridge crossed your mind, while you were thinking?

from Wallace Stevens:

Metaphors of a Magnifico

Twenty men crossing a bridge,
Into a village,
Are twenty men crossing twenty bridges,

Into twenty villages,
Or one man
Crossing a single bridge into a village.

This is old song
That will not declare itself ...

Twenty men crossing a bridge,
Into a village.
Are
Twenty men crossing a bridge
into a village.

That will not declare itself
Yet is certain as meaning ...

The boots of the men clump
On the boards of the bridge.
The first white wall of the village
Rises through fruit-trees.
Of what was it I was thinking?
So the meaning escapes.

The first white wall of the village ...
The fruit-trees ...

A very intelligent mind of the most profound silence, at times, may exist *without* merely *experiencing things*. Such a mind can exist and function from (and "as") a deep silence that is free of limiting pre-conceptions, free of residual and representative symbols, and free of sequential categorizations. Such a mind can sometimes exist without thought and exist without merely experiencing many "things" (i.e., "things" being learned objects of thought recognized by the brain). Being quiet, without always engaging in a lot of recognition, may be a characteristic of such a mind. Such a mind would be a light unto itself. It would live simply, without a lot of silly, little desires churning away within it (as what the elders of society have spoon-fed to others to needlessly crave). Therefore, a mind of silence can exist, at times, without needing to experience things. Such a mind has an essence of completeness and integrity, without the need for repetitive stimulation. Often such a mind would also joyfully experience many things. (Sometime in the future, when you get a chance, please read E. E. Cummings's profound poem that curiously starts out with the first lines of "somewhere i have never travelled,gladly beyond any experience,your eyes have their silence.")

To be silent, in such a way, is to bc alone. Then one does not depend on anyone or anything; one does not even depend on the thoughts and symbols that society has provided for one to exist as. Such "aloneness" is not the same thing as being "lonely." Being lonely is a feeling of isolation and a sense of being away from needed companions or needed contact. Being lonely is often a rather sorrowful feeling that leaves one feeling brokenhearted and "down in the dumps." Aloneness, however, is entirely different. In aloneness, one finds oneself in deep beauty, and in such beauty there is profound energy. When a human is liberated from the social structures of mere greed, arrogance, achievement, status, ruthlessness, compassionless cruelty, indifferent heartlessness, unimaginative symbols, mundane reactions, lifeless thoughts, trite experiences, and everyday perspectives, then that person is alone. Such aloneness is beautiful and beyond the ordinary; it is multi-dynamic, free of dependency, and full of integrity. It is wonderful to have comrades and companions. It is also (at times) wonderful to exist splendidly, in aloneness.

One can live simply, with a lot of silence and perception beyond the framework of preconceived patterns of thought, yet one can often function skillfully with words and complicated thoughts (using them to help others in realms such as health-care, holistic education, and environmental purification). Compassion and real silence often go together. One cannot feel deeply, from the heart, if one is merely constantly composed of chattering thoughts, symbols, and rigid, cold mental frameworks.

From Wallace Stevens:

The Snow Man

One must have a mind of winter
To regard the frost and the boughs
Of the pine-trees crusted with snow;

And have been cold a long time
To behold the junipers shagged with ice,
The spruces rough in the distant glitter

Of the January sun; and not to think
Of any misery in the sound of the wind,
In the sound of a few leaves,

Which is the sound of the land
Full of the same wind
That is blowing in the same bare place

For the listener, who listens in the snow,
And, nothing himself, beholds
Nothing that is not there and the nothing that is.

Existing as a true silence does not mean that one cannot occasionally listen to music now and then; it does not mean that one shuns noise and runs away from television shows. Existing as true silence does not mean that one needs to become like some kind of monk and then live in some dark cave or desolate oasis. Existing as a silent, wise mind does not mean that one cuts oneself off from society or from the world, living like some kind of hermit in the underbrush. Of course, things done wisely are usually done in moderation. Excessive listening to music constantly throughout the day (day in and day out) will tend to leave the mind spewing with constant, sequential patterns of sound and rhythmic movements, which is not very conducive to stillness and quietness. Excessive eating is another thing that is not conducive to a healthy mind; a body that is very unsound is not likely to harbor a healthy brain. There are all kinds of things that people do (in excess) that tend to not be intelligent and healthy. Additionally, there are all kinds of things that people do to harm the environment. However, a sane, healthy mind lives mostly as a splendid order, not as a lot of harmful disorder. Unfortunately, society, as it is currently, is full of disorder. As Zorro (i.e., Don Diego) has said in the Family Channel films, "There is no shortage of injustice in the world." In the Disney set of Zorro films, Don Diego states, "Injustice is everyone's business; no man can stand alone; when you injure one of us, you injure all." Many people are indifferent; they just do not care. They do not care about others. They do not care about themselves. They do not care about the environment. They do not care about their children. They do not care about many things.

A brain that is in a jumble, that is disorganized internally, that is disheveled, is likely to react in ways that are askew and crooked. Such minds are commonplace, and such minds often, sadly enough, assert that they are unfailing, religious, and extraordinary. Such minds are often reluctant to change in their ways, to look without prejudice, and to see beyond their conditioning. They cling to disorder and maintain that it is orderly.

It is easy for a distorted brain to rely on false notions, erroneous beliefs, and untrue conceptualizations. Distorted brains will often vehemently defend rigid concepts that were handed down (like a pair of pants) to them. When people are spoon-fed beliefs for years upon years, such beliefs become ingrained in (and "as") their consciousness. They then ardently cling to the apron strings of what they were taught and fervently fight against those whom they consider threats.

Be suspicious of any beliefs that were handed down to you by any strict authoritarians. By strict authoritarians, one means those who propound rigid creeds and dogmas that force others into submissive roles. Submission to rigid dogma tends to make one servile and second-hand. Truth can never be discovered by what is second-hand, stale, jaded, and unoriginal. You have to discover truth for yourself. No one can do it for you. No one can merely regulate you into it.

We all make mistakes. I do. You do. We all do. We are human. We are complicated (no matter how simple we are). We sometimes do things that are not entirely orderly. Make mistakes (but please, just do not overdo it!) It is normal to be human now and then and to do things a bit "off the beam." However, we are all responsible for each other. It is best if we watch carefully, with integrity, not letting our mistakes get the best of us.

If you made a mistake, it may be wise not to waste a lot of time regretting about it, wishing that one did not do what one did. One did it. It is over. It is the past. If one keeps beating oneself over the head about it, one is *living in the past.* Old memory is of the past, and a mind that keeps regretting what it did, with a lot of remorse, is a mind that spins old memories repeatedly. Such a remorseful mind is what lives in (and "as") those old memories, memories that are coupled with regret, memories that are tied to stored ideals of "what should be," memories that eat away at one's soul and well-being. The true soul may be what one is "now," beyond separation, not what one thinks about what one was before. What one was before may be nothing but an old, dead memory. What one is now can be a living awareness, a living presence, and a vibrant alive "beingness" that includes all. However, if it is mostly a bunch of sorrowful memories regretting about the past: is that true living? The distance, the space, between what you are now and what you were (and what you accomplished) in the past, may not be so very different from the distance between you and another human being. We have *space* between what we did in the past and what we are now, and we have *space* between those we perceive as "others" and what we consider ourselves to be now. Space is space; it is all relatively the same, whether we like it or not. It may be that the *space* between you and the others is what was ingrained within you as an old, second-hand belief; and it may be that the *space,* between what you are now and what you are regretting in the past, is equally old and dead. (This does not mean that you can do rotten things and then conveniently forget about them!)

If you are going to cling to dead memories of the past, by way of remorse, by way of repeatedly regretting about what you had done, you might as well clutch dead, stagnant, and obsolete doctrines; for, either way, you are under the spell of what is "not alive," and under the clutches of mortal, poisonous disorder.

from Emily Dickinson:

REMORSE is memory awake,
Her companies astir,
A presence of departed acts
At window and at door.

It's past set down before the soul,
And lighted with a match,
Perusal to facilitate
And help belief to stretch.

Remorse is cureless, - the disease
Not even God can heal;
For 't is his institution,
The complement of hell.

Of course, we are all responsible for acting with integrity and order with each other. People who act like a cancer, and harm others with malevolence, must be incarcerated to prevent them from doing further insanity and destruction; let them be incarcerated with dignity and infinite care; let them be incarcerated with showers of compassion and pity; but, beware, many of them are conniving! We can — most of us that are not crazed, anyway — live in harmony, with vast compassion and insight together, as one globe; we can live, not as separate, isolated individuals, not as mere separate countries, but as *one whole.*

It is wise to have a lot of sanity and integrity in one's life. It is wise to love yourself, to care about yourself. What is "yourself"? Are you merely some limited, circumscribed symbols, attached to a body of flesh that harbors some fallacious ideas of disconnection from everyone else? Are you merely some unrelated, detached mental tokens, programmed to be divorced from the rest of life? The "old ways" have indirectly told (and retold) you to cut yourself off, to distance yourself from "others" and from the rest of life. Our new ways are saying, "No, do not indifferently 'write others off,' instead, look holistically, with integrity"; look with the integrity that is supportive, in a true communion that allows for warmhearted empathy and congenial sympathy. The fact is that you are everyone else; that fact is real communion. Let old ideas of separation go into the ground. Let the new ideas of union and true solidarity combine with idea-free compassion, oneness, and insight.

from Walt Whitman:

These are really the thoughts of all men in all ages and lands,
they are not original with me,
If they are not yours as much as mine they are nothing, or next to nothing,
If they are not the riddle and the untying of the riddle they are nothing,
If they are not just as close as they are distant they are nothing.

This is the grass that grows wherever the land is and the water is,
This the common air that bathes the globe.

With music strong I come, with my cornets and my drums,
I play not marches for accepted victors only, I play marches for conquer'd and slain persons.

Have you heard that it was good to gain the day?
I also say it is good to fall, battles are lost in the same spirit in which they are won.

I beat and pound for the dead,
I blow through my embouchures my loudest and gayest for them.

Vivas to those who have fail'd!
And to those whose war-vessels sank in the sea!
And to those themselves who sank in the sea!
And to all generals that lost engagements, and all overcome heroes!
And the numberless unknown heroes equal to the greatest heroes known!

This is the meal equally set, this the meat for natural hunger,
It is for the wicked just the same as the righteous, I make appointments with all,
I will not have a single person slighted or left away,
The kept-woman, sponger, thief, are hereby invited,
The heavy-lipp'd slave is invited, the venerealee is invited;
There shall be no difference between them and the rest.

This is the press of a bashful hand, this the float and odor of hair,
This the touch of my lips to yours, this the murmur of yearning,
This the far-off depth and height reflecting my own face,
This the thoughtful merge of myself, and the outlet again.

Do you guess I have some intricate purpose?
Well I have, for the Fourth-month showers have, and the mica on the side of a rock has.

Do you take it I would astonish?
Does the daylight astonish? does the early redstart twittering through the woods?
Do I astonish more than they?

This hour I tell things in confidence,
I might not tell everybody, but I will tell you.

True intelligence — not the limited intelligence of mere ideas, mere representations — is composed of compassion. Compassion cannot merely be handed over to another, as can some lifeless symbols, mental formulations, and representational patterns. Empathy exists in a truly holistic, wise mind that is full of understanding. Sensitivity of the heart is a dynamic, living thing. A dull, dead brain — laden with limited images and full of delusions and fears — cannot have much sensitivity. Many of us have learned to avoid psychological pain. Throughout the years, while avoiding such pain, many of us have learned to build walls around ourselves, to isolate ourselves from the pain. Some of the psychological walls, that some of us have built, are so thick and full of distance, that we have over-isolated ourselves from the rest of life and humanity. Some of us have become indifferent, uncaring entities, who do not care two pins about anybody else. Like crude snails, some of us have hidden in our callous shells, using distance and protective, hard images to isolate our so-called "selves" from "others."

Real compassion breaks down these false walls. In doing so, it annihilates the distance between a central self and others. Selfishness is like hypnosis. Hypnosis often involves concentrating on a limited center, to the exclusion of everything else. A truly selfish man is a man who acts as if under the spell of hypnosis. Such a vain man merely concentrates and focuses on his little, illusory, central self. Such a man heavily pinpoints on that "self" to the exclusion of everything and everyone else. Such action is not really action whatsoever; it is merely reaction, in a very crude and barbaric form. A selfish mind is not open, vulnerable, or dynamic. A selfish mind tries to protect and comfort its ego; however, in doing so, it creates more misery and harm for all. A limited means has a limited end. In the long run, dead motives lead to dead, sullen morbidity, not to true joy and a truly healthful paradise.

Feeling and acting compassionately is wise, is an indication of wisdom. Is it wisdom, however, when one immerses into the suffering of others to such an extent that one loses one's own sense of joy and integrity? (The author has mistakenly done that, in the past.) A truly compassionate mind also has compassion for the mind within the body that it inhabits. A truly compassionate mind usually will not be foolish enough to allow itself to be broken and demoralized by unfortunate circumstances, be they what occur to it directly or to those around it. A compassionate mind, in its flowering of empathic behavior, will also have compassion and sympathy for itself (and not exclusively for others). Therefore, it will uphold its sense of order, integrity, soundness, and well-being, not easily letting go of the graceful light that it shines as.

The following poem may be indicative of a true love that a man has for others. Alternatively, it may indicate projecting one's desires to a hypnotic (loved) center at a distance, while neglecting one's own well-being, soundness, and mental health.

from Stephen Crane:

Places among the stars,
Soft gardens near the sun,
Keep your distant beauty;
Shed no beams upon my weak heart.
Since she is here
In a place of blackness,
Not your golden days
Nor your silver nights
Can call me to you.
Since she is here
In a place of blackness,
Here I stay and wait.

A truly wise, sagacious mind helps others and itself (which includes the "others") to go beyond the losses and limitations. The wise help to bring us to the light and to remain healthy. They do so out of compassion and caring. They realize that the light is for humankind, and not just for isolated individuals. They point to show us beyond the small and hypnotized; they point to show us the limitless and large.

from Walt Whitman:

On the Beach at Night

On the beach at night,
Stands a child with her father,
Watching the east, the autumn sky.

Up through the darkness,
While ravening clouds, the burial clouds, in black masses spreading,
Lower sullen and fast athwart and down the sky,
Amid a transparent clear belt of ether yet left in the east,
Ascends large and calm the lord-star Jupiter,
And nigh at hand, only a very little above,
Swim the delicate sisters, the Pleiades.

From the beach the child holding the hand of her father,
Those burial-clouds that lower victorious soon to devour all,
Watching, silently weeps.

Weep not, child,
Weep not, my darling,
With these kisses let me remove your tears,
The ravening clouds shall not long be victorious,
They shall not long possess the sky, they devour the stars only in apparition,
Jupiter shall emerge, be patient, watch again another night, the Pleiades shall emerge,
They are immortal, all those stars both silvery and golden shall shine out again,
The great stars and the little ones shall shine out again, they endure,

The vast immortal suns and the long-enduring pensive moons shall again shine.

Then dearest child mournest thou only for Jupiter?
Considerest thou alone the burial of the stars?

Something there is,
(With my lips soothing thee, adding I whisper,
I give thee the first suggestion, the problem and indirection,)
Something there is more immortal even than the stars,
(Many the burials, many the days and nights, passing away,)
Something that shall endure longer even than lustrous Jupiter
Longer than sun or any revolving satellite,
Or the radiant sisters the Pleiades.

Chapter 6

Most minds, we repeat again, do fear things frequently. Fearing an attacking animal is a form of intelligence; it helps the body to avoid serious danger. However, human minds are so complex that the fear that they experience is often unnecessary or even harmful; often such fear is psychological and has little to do with actual danger to the organism. Instead of merely fearing *actual things* that are dangerous in one's immediate environment, many tend to fear *abstract notions* that have been programmed into them by such things as wrong education, corrupt religious institutions, and fragmentary governmental agendas. When a mind fabricates something to fear, such fear is often a projection from what is distorted, limited, and insecure. Psychological distortion and psychological insecurity go together.

One is not separate from the psychological fear that one has, as it occurs. At the precise moment of experiencing psychological fear, you are the fear; you are not merely something that sees fear from a distance; you are the actual fear. The actual distance, between you and psychological fear, does not exist.

Pleasure and fear often go together; as we have said, they are like two sides of the same coin oftentimes. As the poet, E. E. Cummings once poetically wrote, "Pleasure and pain are merely surfaces… life's only and true value neither is… love makes the little thickness of the coin." A psychological fear may be, for instance, about the possibility of not experiencing something pleasurable from another human being in the future. Such fear may be a projection of an insecure mind; such a fear is not at all separate from the individual who is partaking in it.

At the precise moment of desiring some form of specific pleasure, you are the desire. Being a desire is a reaction about a projected future; it is a reaction that, by its very nature, is unfulfilled. A very wise mind is not often many psychological reactions that are unfulfilled; therefore, a very wise mind is not often embedded with a large amount of empty desires. Order does not frequently wish to turn into disorder. That is why a wise mind (full of order) does not frequently turn into mere desire (which is a form of disorder). Light does not always need more light. Order does not seek the darkness of superficial craving.

Wanting things, now and then, is fine. We are not suggesting that one should not want things. Things are best done in moderation, as we have suggested before. Then there is a natural balance, a healthful naturalness, a movement of true order and integrity. (I'm a bit too obsessed with collecting fossils and poems, according to my wife!)

When one is aware that fear is occurring in (and "as") one, it is prudent to observe without merely being reactions of resistance and disapproval. Merely trying to subjugate fear, to resist fear, or to avoid or run away from fear, may be to cause more friction, more fragmentation, and more separation within (and "as") the mind. More fragmentation and separation would, in the long run, only increase and propagate fear. Fear often arises when there is friction, when there is a lack of harmony and integrity. A mind that resists and fights fear is full of fragmentation, and it is likely to nourish and support a vast amount of fear by way of its tremendous fragmentation. When fear arises, just "be it," throughout its entire movement and momentum. If you truly are the fear, there is nothing that you can do about it; you are it. Furthermore, with desire, be the desire. This does not mean that one can go around doing whatever one wants. That would be disorderly and ludicrous. Society has excessively much disorder now, the way it is. As desires take place in (or "as") you, be them without thinking that you merely "have them." It may be the other way around; desires may "have you." Failure to feel fulfilled can be the essence of a distorted, fragmentary brain, a brain that thinks that it is "what is having desires." Failure to feel fulfilled is disorder and disarray. There are all too many brains that are in that sad state of affairs. Only a crippled, unfulfilled mind is always hankering, always craving, always lusting, and always wanting. Integrity, in and as itself, needs nothing more. Integrity is a whole mind, not a mind that is broken up with fragmentary ideas, such that it and its desires are two different things. Integrity is a whole mind, not a mind that is broken up with fragmentary ideas, such that it and its fears are two different things.

A mind that is indifferent, that does not care about the well-being of others, is a mind with little or no integrity. Such a mind creates barriers around itself; it creates significant space between what it considers to be "itself" and "others." A mind of limited space, with barriers between itself and others, is a mind without much integrity. Integrity is wholeness, in (and "as") wisdom. Integrity is not superficial fragmentation with a lot of limited space between the fragments. Similarly, a mind that creates a barrier around itself — between what it considers to be "itself" and the "fears" that it thinks are "what it has" — is not what true integrity is. Additionally, a mind that creates a barrier around itself — between what it considers to be "itself" and the "desires" that it thinks are "what it has" — is not what true integrity is.

Little wonder then why so many are indifferent toward others. So many are riddled with separations and barriers within (i.e., within their own consciousness); naturally such fragmented brains — with a lot of internal space, internal separations, and barriers — will look at others, in society, with the indifference that limited space, barriers, and restrictions provide. Little wonder then why society is in such shambles. Without living order and a vivacious integrity, mere dead reactions beget further dead reactions, and wars and disorder inevitably ensue.

So, instead of looking at the *fear within* with consternation, perturbation, contempt, and abhorrence, merely "be it," without judgment, opinion, and analytical criticism. Just *be it* and understand it as it is taking place. That is real learning. We are, all of us, composed of fears, including the writer who is writing this. Sometimes our fears are at a very primitive level of the brain that is part of the very crude past. The human brain is just too complicated and too complex to not have fears. However, through understanding and insight, we can largely go beyond them. Fear often prevents love. Love really blossoms when — in a mind full of insight and integrity — the limited barriers are absent and nonexistent.

We often run for pleasure and avoid pain, often in ways that are programmed into us like the way robots are pre-programmed by those that manufacture them. We often react like pre-programmed machines. We respond in the ways that society's authorities designed us to respond as. Though the following poem is a considerable exaggeration, it points out how one can meet turmoil without the standard, ordinary responses, without mere programmatic behavior.

from Stephen Crane:

A youth in apparel that glittered
Went to walk in a grim forest.
There he met an assassin
Attired all in garb of old days;
He, scowling through the thickets,
And dagger poised quivering,

Rushed upon the youth.
"Sir," said this latter,
"I am enchanted, believe me,
To die, thus,
In this medieval fashion,
According to the best legends;
Ah, what joy!"
Then took he the wound, smiling,
And died, content.

At the time this is being written, there are many protestors protesting against the "bad and unfair economy." There are wars going on now; but i don't see anything, on the news on television, about protests regarding the wars. When i was physically young, i was maced, along with the other peace-loving people within our crowd, for protesting against the Viet Nam war. (I live a few doors down from one of the men who had maced us, back then, while i was in college; i get along fine with that neighbor now and harbor no hard feelings against him whatsoever.) For a few years, when i was physically young, i lived in an "intentional community"; many people call them "communes." No, we didn't run around naked and "do drugs" all the time. Drugs were not allowed; we kept our clothes on. We had private rooms or private houses, but shared a common kitchen and living area. We made decisions based on consensus; there were no leaders. We all shared the beautiful, rustic land — full of many acres of trees, rolling hills, sparkling creeks, and flowering meadows — that was donated to us by a beneficent, elderly farmer. We were all vegetarians and grew much of our own food organically; we built housing using passive solar-energy foundations. We loved the children (in the right ways) and were perfect models of being orderly and kind, without motive. Some of us had part-time or full-time jobs in the outer community. The people in the nearby town respected us and thought very highly of us. They called us the "Flower Generation." I do not see enough flowers these days, anymore.

from Emily Dickinson:

IF she had been the Mistletoe
And I had been the Rose,
How gay upon your table
My velvet life to Close!

Since I am of the Druid,
And she is of the dew,
I'll deck Tradition's buttonhole,
And send the Rose to you.

It is interesting about how, in the above poem, Emily is telling us that she, in reality, is not traditional and is not merely satisfied with the circumscribed and the limited. Are we merely satisfied with the circumscribed, the limited, and the restricted? Will we wallow in pools and mud-holes (of the "limited ordinary") and be satisfied with them? If we continue to merely look and perceive with the ordinary, the limited, and the fragmented, will we probably continue to overpopulate the planet, ruin the environment, remain indifferent, allow wars, harm each other, and bring our children and the earth to a disastrous end?

When one reads most all of the books that the world has to offer — and there are innumerable books to read — one reads, for the most part, merely what is rather ordinary and limited. In other words, what one reads in most all of these books is restricted to boundaries of normalcy with demarcations involving the ordinary and commonplace. What one reads is usually constrained and circumscribed within normal limits. What this author is suggesting is that we (as the masses of readers) are accustomed to be (and conditioned to be) reading and considering what is existent within the boundaries of the ordinary. Such is tragedy. We have accepted little pools of information and details — wherein there lies the limited and bounded — all within the peripheries and boundaries of the ordinary. Even our unconventional books are, in reality, rather ordinary and not that unusual. We are completely accustomed to limited words and limited stories; we cling to them exclusively, unfortunately, like many swine that wallow endlessly in restricted, little mud-holes. Is that all we are capable of, as human beings? Cannot there be emancipating books that convey, with relatively limited words, something much more immense and measureless? If true enlightenment and true visitation from the *sacred* is indeed possible for man, here on earth, then the bureaucratic, orthodox authorities had better beware, because what is written by the enlightened may be incredibly and brilliantly majestic, while it sheds bright light on what is false, ordinary, shady, manipulating, bleak, and calculating. Those few that truly understand the entire work of an enlightened man are rarely content with the fleeting, the confined, the limited, and the isolated.

from Emily Dickinson:

THERE is a solitude of space,
A solitude of sea,
A solitude of death, but these
Society shall be,
Compared with that profounder site,
That polar privacy,
A Soul admitted to Itself:
Finite Infinity.

To truly care for others, can one merely feel a concrete, solid separation from them? If one has huge barriers between oneself and others, does such a one also likely have huge barriers between a "central concept of self" and "other thoughts that it thinks it controls"? If a brain looks at things through distance (and with prejudice), with thoughts of superiority, and with jaded eyes from conditioned traditions, is it likely to be rather indifferent and uncaring regarding "others"? Can what is limited and distorted truly perceive the beauty of what is immense, authentic, and incorrupt? If one is divorced from "right relationship" regarding all that there is, is one also divorced from true beauty?

from Walt Whitman:

Whoever degrades another degrades me,
And whatever is done or said returns at last to me.

Through me the afflatus surging and surging, through me the current and index.

I speak the pass-word primeval, I give the sign of democracy,
By God! I will accept nothing which all cannot have their counterpart of on the same terms.

Through me many long dumb voices,
Voices of the interminable generations of prisoners and slaves,

Voices of the diseas'd and despairing and of thieves and dwarfs,
Voices of cycles of preparation and accretion,
And of the threads that connect the stars, and of wombs and of the father-stuff,
And of the rights of them the others are down upon,
Of the deform'd, trivial, flat, foolish, despised,
Fog in the air, beetles rolling balls of dung.

Through me forbidden voices,
Voices of sexes and lusts, voices veil'd and I remove the veil,
Voices indecent by me clarified and transfigur'd.

I do not press my fingers across my mouth,
I keep as delicate around the bowels as around the head and heart,
Copulation is no more rank to me than death is.

I believe in the flesh and the appetites,
Seeing, hearing, feeling, are miracles, and each part and tag of me is a miracle.

Divine am I inside and out, and I make holy whatever I touch or am touch'd from,
The scent of these arm-pits aroma finer than prayer,
This head more than churches, bibles, and all the creeds.

The human body, the human organism is miraculous in many ways, especially if it contains a mind that realizes that it is not separate and divorced from all others. In a sense, we are all of one body. Jesus was likely helping to convey this at that last supper.

When one of us suffers, then truly, we all suffer. There is psychological suffering and there is physical suffering. It is very important to help others to go beyond suffering, so that more of us can live with real dignity and grace. Wars and friction between separate nations, religions, and organized groups, often directly or indirectly contribute to much suffering for man. True intelligence and the wisdom of seeing right relationship can help us to go beyond such suffering.

It is extremely important for the medical profession to continue with helping people to remain healthy and to go beyond pain. It is terrible when anyone on this planet has to suffer. When one is in serious, physical pain, one is susceptible, sometimes, to immense agony that often tends to suspend one's joy and happiness. When one suffers, with pain, he (or she) is paying the price for us all. The natural domain of the cosmos, unfortunately, must include pain and suffering. To have no pain or suffering would entail a world that would be rather artificial and plastic, (like a synthetic plant that looks perfect, but that never truly grows, struggles through the darkness of the soil, or blossoms up from what is below). A totally painless world would be a fake, artificial domain, wherein there would be something missing. It would be like having an "up" but no "down"; it would be like having "success," but never any "failure."

Therefore, when some of us suffer, they are paying a price for all of humanity. Suffering is not just some isolated thing that exclusively affects some separate entity. Suffering affects us all. We are all affected by suffering. Suffering is there for man and beast alike. Those who are partaking in it are paying the price for us all. Those who deeply suffer are not separate from Jesus when he was on the cross.

If we are truly intelligent, we can help to curtail suffering for man and for the earth. Through preventative healthcare and wise, organic medical practices, we can alleviate much suffering for man. Moreover, through wise population control, conservation, and green energy actions, we can alleviate much suffering for the earth and its precious creatures.

Life isn't perfect. I wish it was; however, if everything went perfectly right all of the time, it would be such a very plastic, synthetic world. It may be a good thing, after all, that a lot of it is much of a "toss of the dice," according to natural laws. That is the way it must be.

Suffering occurs within all of us. Moreover, when it occurs in any one of us, it affects all of us, whether we realize it or not. Suffering is universal. All human beings share in, and are part of, this suffering. Suffering is a serious thing. Constant "thinking," per se, may be a form of suffering. Existing exclusively as "symbolic representations" may be a form of "suffering." Merely to be representations "about" energy, but not actually "be" the energy, is what suffering is. We must change things for mother earth and for ourselves. We must go beyond suffering, with understanding and true love. Furthermore, as the following poem may relate, one can (in silence) be a state of mind without mere barriers of "thought," mere barriers that support separation between oneself and others. Such silence does not imply that one sit quietly in isolation while not doing anything to help; the limited silence of doing nothing, in indifference, is not (i feel) what Whitman is referring to (while being "silent") in the following poem. On the contrary, Whitman spent many years writing to help others; additionally, he volunteered for a very long time as a nurse during the Civil War, helping the severely injured physically and psychologically.

from Walt Whitman:

I Sit and Look Out

I sit and look out upon all the sorrows of the world, and upon
all oppression and shame;
I hear secret convulsive sobs from young men, at anguish with
themselves, remorseful after deeds done;
I see, in low life, the mother misused by her children, dying,
neglected, gaunt, desperate; I see the wife misused by her
husband—I see the treacherous seducer of young women;
I mark the ranklings of jealousy and unrequited love,
attempted to be hid—I see these sights on the earth;
I see the workings of battle, pestilence, tyranny—I see martyrs
and
prisoners; I observe a famine at sea—I observe the sailors
casting lots who shall be kill'd, to preserve the lives of the rest;
I observe the slights and degradations cast by arrogant persons
upon laborers, the poor, and upon negroes, and the like;
All these—All the meanness and agony without end, I sitting,
look out upon,
See, hear, and am silent.

The public's perception of the famous poet, Emily Dickinson, has been changing over time. For a long time, she was regarded as a rather sullen recluse, who would never leave home, who would dress in white, and who was mostly melancholy and obsessed with death. Newer perceptions of her are that she was a gifted, brilliant poet who chose, for private reasons, to remain at home (dressing in white); and people are realizing that she wrote a lot of poetry that was uplifting, (often about the beauty of nature). I think that she was not merely an individual full of a pathological fear of socializing, but rather was a revolutionary mystic who lived her life exactly in the way she pleased; it could be that she understood much about aloneness, eternity, and consciousness. Alternatively, it could be that an eternal *immensity* used Emily, upon occasion, to reveal its true nature. I think, however, that Emily understood the depth of what she was writing about. Emily may have understood far more, about the true nature of eternity and about the workings of perception, than what people give her credit for.

from Emily Dickinson:

THAT I did always love,
I bring thee proof:
That till I loved
I did not love enough.

That I shall love always,
I offer thee
That love is life,
And life hath immortality.

This, dost thou doubt, sweet?
Then have I
Nothing to show
But Calvary.

If, by some chance, what i am writing about happens to become popular, please do not form any organizations around it. It is not another religion. Religions tend to separate and divide people, just as separate nations and countries do. We are all too willing to fight over religious, governmental, and economic systems and policies. Our systems have become more important than ourselves. We have become the puppets of these systems; to a very large extent, they control us. Many of us are deeply ingrained within the systems. Furthermore, it may be that the systems are deeply ingrained within us.

Writing and learning about going beyond mere systems is not merely another system. Writing and learning about going beyond separative religions, nations, drugs, and organizations, is not another organized religion, nor governmental faction, nor drug.

During my college days, shortly after having had that majestic visitation of the "*otherness,*" which was a blessed enlightenment or nirvana, something additionally happened. My roommates were all gone, studying or partying or whatever, and i was in the college dormitory, bathing. This was a couple of days after having had that *nirvana-oriented phenomenon* occur. In the middle of bathing, i suddenly had an insight about the possible nature of our universe. I instantly had a realization that there is a strong possibility that our universe is part of a multiplex of universes. The realization involved the strong possibility that our universe (i.e., the one that we happen to live in) occurs repeatedly, in exactly the same way. This realization happened to me while the mind was very quiet, very silent. Not only was the body being cleansed of debris and muck, but the mind was in a freedom of silence, free from all the rubbish that was indoctrinated within by prior authorities.

Do not build what i will be suggesting to you, in my subsequent writing, into a mere belief system or into a set conglomeration of rigid ideas about "how things are" or "how the universe works." More than a mere cyclic universe can happen for each of us. However, that does not negate the possibility of a cyclic universe whatsoever. Whatever influenced me, on the day that i underwent the *nirvana* manifestation, was omnipotent beyond belief. Such omnipotence may do things beyond what we, as mere mortals (or semi-immortals), can fathom. Therefore, if a girl dies at a very young age, there is a possibility that such "omnipotence" may allow for a dimension of her to exist in a bliss-oriented equivalent of heaven. We do not know, as limited, relatively semi-mortal beings, what can occur in the entirety of all that is.

The fact that, within the brain, the corpus callosum can be severed, leaving two distinct halves that each evolve into a "separate consciousness" — and the fact that Alzheimer's disease exists as it does — leaves little hope for living in any eternal way whatsoever, unless one perceives and understands the disclosures regarding a cyclic universe.

Obviously, it is not what we are "accustomed to" or "used to." However, sometimes change happens that way, and for the better, in the long run. Before the time of Columbus, they used to think that the world was flat, that there was an end to it; they thought that you could fall off the flattened part and then perish. Many of us think that when you are dead, you are dead; they think that you come to the end, and that is it… finished. However, if our universe is truly in a cyclic-oriented dimension, then what occurs happens over and over again, endlessly. There is a possibility, when you die (if the omnipotent "otherness" does not temporarily intervene), that your consciousness will not exist until the "next round" of the cycle. Since "consciousness" (that depends on brain cells) does not exist after you die, then psychological "time" does not exist after you die. One must be "conscious" to realize "time." Without consciousness, there is no "time." The time, from when you die, within universal cycles, to when you are again "reborn" as the same person that you (in the exact-same repeated cycles) were, does not exist psychologically; therefore, it does not exist as "consciousness." Therefore, as soon as you die, no time elapses until you are again born to the same mother, and are again conscious of "time." So, in a real sense, as soon as you die, you are again (for all practical purposes) immediately born to the same family as you were born to before. Time is not recorded, from when you die to when you are again reborn. This is not reincarnation. You do not come back into another body; in one echoing, mirroring sense, you remain exactly the same. In a sense, you never really die. (Of course, you are incapable of remembering what happened before, in the previous cycles.) Like our earth, our universe is globular, circuitous, and cyclic. People, at one time long ago, thought that the world was flat. People think, at the time of this writing, that time is linear and non-globular, without the same things recurring repeatedly. They may be crudely erroneous.

from Archibald MacLeish:

Lines for a Prologue

These alternate nights and days, these seasons
Somehow fail to convince me. It seems
I have the sense of infinity!

(In your dreams, O crew of Columbus,
O listeners over the sea
For the surf that breaks upon Nothing—)

Once I was waked by the nightingales in the garden.
I thought, What time is it? I thought,
Time—Is it Time still?—Now is it Time?

(Tell me your dreams, O sailors:
Tell me, in sleep did you climb
The tall masts, and before you—)

At night the stillness of old trees
Is a leaning over and the inertness
Of hills is a kind of waiting.

(In sleep, in a dream, did you see
The world's end? Did the water
Break—and no shore—Did you see?)

Strange faces come through the streets to me
Like messengers: and I have been warned
By the moving slowly of hands at a window.

Oh, I have the sense of infinity—
But the world, sailors, is round.
They say there is no end to it.

Many of us, at the time of this writing, think that we, as humans, are so very sophisticated and modern; we may not be. This is very serious (i.e., what i am writing about). I had deeply wished that there was a way of profoundly communicating the depth of eternity to people and sharing it, in significant ways that would help to substantiate what i am propounding, since it is so very different and foreign from what we normally consider. I enduringly wished that i could discover significant media and penetrating signs to help people perceive the truth of *what is*. My indelible wish had a lot to do with helping people in sincere ways. My indelible wish had a lot to do with helping the earth, which we (as the human race) are not doing a good job of lately, at the time of this writing. In the normal course of events, writers, when they write a book, each reach into the bag of tricks that they have within their being, within their realm of possibility. However, if a human being has truly been enlightened, would the bag, which he (or she) has to reach into, necessarily be just as are all the bags that all the other orthodox writers reach into? As time went on, i began finding poems; i began finding more and more far-reaching poems (by famous, very distinguished, deceased poets) that corroborated what i was considering for revelation. (Before, i did not even care for poetry; but now i am very appreciative of it, as we all can be.)

What is important here is not just caring about this for some limited, little "self." The earth and all its creatures, the whole of life is what is very important in all this. Though your life and your personal experiences are very important to you, what may be truly very important here are not some "little personality's experiences"; what is important is the whole and well-being of all of life, the earth, and its creatures. We must learn to become better caretakers of our precious earth. Earth is our mother; we have mistreated her far too much. She is what is important. We desperately need to change, with heartfelt understanding, with true love for the whole, and not merely for some potty, little "self," or some images of a mate whom one happens to be obsessed with. We need to look without so many barriers, without all that slipshod limitation that was handed down to us from all of those bureaucratic authorities who have indoctrinated so many.

Let us say that the "indirect," in the following poem, is the same as the "direct." Let us say that the "indirect" will be exactly as the "direct" had been in the recurrent, cyclic, orderly operation of things. Let us say that, just in case the universe happens to be cyclic, we had better "get our act together" before it is too late. Let us say that what we thought was transient — without any real, lasting meaning — may be eternally significant and important. Let us say that if, while reading further in this book, your knees do not buckle somewhat, then i have indirectly failed in my direct job. (When one finishes reading this book, one may not like what it propounds, and one may not agree with what it presents, but one will have been speared by it and will always be forever affected by it.)

Whatever we do in this (direct) lifetime, in a cyclic universe, may be exactly repeated within each (indirect) identical cycle ever afterwards. Therefore, it would be prudent to act with more integrity now.

from Walt Whitman:

Song of Prudence

Manhattan's streets I saunter'd pondering,
On Time, Space, Reality—on such as these, and abreast with them Prudence.

The last explanation always remains to be made about prudence,
Little and large alike drop quietly aside from the prudence that suits immortality.
The soul is of itself,
All verges to it, all has reference to what ensues,
All that a person does, says, thinks, is of consequence,
Not a move can a man or woman make, that affects him or her in a day,
month, any part of the direct lifetime, or the hour of death,
But the same affects him or her onward afterward through the indirect lifetime.
The indirect is just as much as the direct,
The spirit receives from the body just as much as it gives to the body, if not more.
Not one word or deed, not venereal sore, discoloration, privacy of the onanist,
Putridity of gluttons or rum-drinkers, peculation, cunning, betrayal, murder, seduction, prostitution,
But has results beyond death as really as before death.
Charity and personal force are the only investments worth anything.
No specification is necessary, all that a male or female does, that
is vigorous, benevolent, clean, is so much profit to him or her,
In the unshakable order of the universe and through the whole scope of it forever.
Who has been wise receives interest,
Savage, felon, President, judge, farmer, sailor, mechanic, literat, young, old, it is the same,
The interest will come round — all will come round.
Singly, wholly, to affect now, affected their time, will forever affect,
all of the past and all of the present and all of the future,
All the brave actions of war and peace,

All help given to relatives, strangers, the poor, old, sorrowful, young children, widows, the sick, and to shunn'd persons,
All self-denial that stood steady and aloof on wrecks, and saw others fill the seats of the boats,
All offering of substance or life for the good old cause, or for a friend's sake, or opinion's sake,
All pains of enthusiasts scoff'd at by their neighbors,
All the limitless sweet love and precious suffering of mothers,
All honest men baffled in strifes recorded or unrecorded,
All the grandeur and good of ancient nations whose fragments we inherit,
All the good of the dozens of ancient nations unknown to us by name, date, location,
All that was ever manfully begun, whether it succeeded or no,
All suggestions of the divine mind of man or the divinity of his mouth, or the shaping of his great hands,
All that is well thought or said this day on any part of the globe,
or on any of the wandering stars, or on any of the fix'd stars, by those there as we are here,
All that is henceforth to be thought or done by you whoever you are, or by any one,
These inure, have inured, shall inure, to the identities from which they sprang, or shall spring.
Did you guess any thing lived only its moment?
The world does not so exist, no parts palpable or impalpable so exist,
No consummation exists without being from some long previous consummation, and that from some other,
Without the farthest conceivable one coming a bit nearer the beginning than any. Whatever satisfies souls is true;
Prudence entirely satisfies the craving and glut of souls,
Itself only finally satisfies the soul,
The soul has that measureless pride which revolts from every lesson but its own.

Now I breathe the word of the prudence that walks abreast with time, space, reality,
That answers the pride which refuses every lesson but its own.
What is prudence is indivisible,
Declines to separate one part of life from every part,
Divides not the righteous from the unrighteous or the living from the dead,
Matches every thought or act by its correlative,
Knows no possible forgiveness or deputed atonement,
Knows that the young man who composedly peril'd his life and lost it
has done exceedingly well for himself without doubt,
That he who never peril'd his life, but retains it to old age in riches and ease, has probably achiev'd nothing for himself worth mentioning,
Knows that only that person has really learn'd who has learn'd to prefer results,
Who favors body and soul the same,
Who perceives the indirect assuredly following the direct,
Who in his spirit in any emergency whatever neither hurries nor avoids death.

If the present time is what is going to recur repeatedly in the future, then the present time is what the future will be. Let this sink in, that… in a very real sense, in a cyclic universe, the present time is to be the future. Therefore, *the future is now*. Additionally, if the present time is what occurred innumerable times in the past, then the present time is the past (as what already happened). If this is so, then the future is the past, and the past is the future. Of course, all of this may merely be a lot of speculation. However, we can always go beyond this framework of time, if it exists as such, if we (as a human family) can be visited by that *sacred otherness* that is *beyond "time"* in its omnipotence and immensity. "*Timelessness"* is the *benediction* that can redeem us from merely being within sequential time. (The *timelessness* of the *sacred,* by the way, is not the same thing as the "lack of time" that occurs after we die until we are again born, to again experience time, in a cyclic cosmos.) Regarding the *timelessness* of the *sacred,* it (i.e., the *sacred timelessness*) won't negate the cyclic time that we are already in; it will, however, provide a way for some of us to go beyond cyclic time, within (and beyond) time's framework. Therefore, if (as a human family) we are visited by that *otherness,* then we are redeemed from time, from being immersed merely within the framework of time.

from T. S. Eliot:

Excerpt from Burnt Norton, from the Four Quartets

Time present and time past
Are both perhaps present in time future,
And time future contained in time past.
If all time is eternally present
All time is unredeemable.
What might have been is an abstraction
Remaining a perpetual possibility
Only in a world of speculation.
What might have been and what has been
Point to one end, which is always present.
Footfalls echo in the memory
Down the passage which we did not take
Towards the door we never opened
Into the rose-garden. My words echo
Thus, in your mind.
But to what purpose
Disturbing the dust on a bowl of rose-leaves
I do not know.

It may be, if the universe is cyclic, that you will always be reading this (as you are now). It may be eternally important for us to change for the better, educating our children with more compassion and understanding, taking much better care of mother earth, existing with truer silence and understanding, and looking without so much separation and conflict.

The *sacred otherness,* as what omnipotent love may be, is beyond the confines of time and space. Being beyond sequential time, it is most assuredly beyond mere limited desire and want. Being beyond time, it is as an immeasurable light that is of boundless energy and of supreme order. Being beyond time, it is unlimited, immeasurable, and inviolable. No words can ever adequately describe it. It does not occur to what is merely limited and self-centered. It does not visit what is merely fragmented and indifferent. It does not visit what is duped by limited barriers, around a fabricated self that is fictitious. It does not engage with what is divorced from life. It does not nurture what is cold and callous to nature. In its completeness and integrity, it need not visit what is full of endless desires (and what is incomplete, without integrity). It need not visit what is caught in endless sequences of symbolism and representations. It need not visit what remains old, second-hand, and full of fear. It need not visit what is filled with chattering reflections of authority and domineering harshness. Thank goodness that truly innocent, youthful minds can exist beyond all the nonsense; the truly youthful understand this. One strongly suspects that the *sacred* is a *benediction* that cares much for the proper education of youth.

from T. S. Eliot:

Excerpt from Burnt Norton, from the Four Quartets:

Words move, music moves
Only in time; but that which is only living
Can only die. Words, after speech, reach
Into the silence. Only by the form, the pattern,
Can words or music reach
The stillness, as a Chinese jar still
Moves perpetually in its stillness.
Not the stillness of the violin, while the note lasts,
Not that only, but the co-existence,

Or say that the end precedes the beginning,
And the end and the beginning were always there
Before the beginning and after the end.
And all is always now. Words strain,
Crack and sometimes break, under the burden,
Under the tension, slip, slide, perish,
Decay with imprecision, will not stay in place,
Will not stay still. Shrieking voices
Scolding, mocking, or merely chattering,
Always assail them. The Word in the desert
Is most attacked by voices of temptation,
The crying shadow in the funeral dance,
The loud lament of the disconsolate chimera.

The detail of the pattern is movement,
As in the figure of the ten stairs.
Desire itself is movement
Not in itself desirable;
Love is itself unmoving,
Only the cause and end of movement,
Timeless, and undesiring
Except in the aspect of time
Caught in the form of limitation
Between un-being and being.
Sudden in a shaft of sunlight
Even while the dust moves
There rises the hidden laughter
Of children in the foliage
Quick now, here, now, always—
Ridiculous the waste sad time
Stretching before and after.

In the following poem, the poet E. E. Cummings mentions "Ever-Ever Land" a great deal. He may be referring to the cyclic nature of time, in our cosmos, and the fact that where we live happens to be part of the cyclic area of the cosmos. (I love the way Cummings employs sarcasm within his poetry.)

I enjoy many of E. E. Cummings' poems; he is absolutely one of my favorite poets. A number of Cummings' poems reveal a clever understanding, which we had mentioned about consciousness earlier: namely, that the "observer" is "the observed." Cummings, within the following poem, states, "only sameness is normal in Ever-Ever Land, for a bad cigar is a woman but a gland is only a gland." You see, a "bad cigar" can actually be "a woman," when one realizes that the "observer" is "the observed." The cigar that the woman is disgusted about and upset about, actually becomes part of her consciousness when she perceives its shape, color, and smell; as she further thinks about it, its images and the offensive mental labels concerning it all tend to help formulate her mind (at the time). Hence, "a bad cigar is a woman," in that the attributes of the cigar (such as the images, colors, smells, and labels of it) all help to constitute her consciousness. (Please do not forget to be appreciative of the following sarcastic poem for the way that it may allude to the *eternity* of a cyclic cosmos.)

from E. E. Cummings:

(of Ever-Ever Land i speak
sweet morons gather roun'
who does not dare to stand or sit
may take it lying down)

down with the human soul
and anything else uncanned
for everyone carries canopeners
in Ever-Ever Land

(for Ever-Ever Land is a place
that's as simple as simple can be
and was built that way on purpose
by simple people like we)

down with hell and heaven
and all the religious fuss
infinity pleased our parents
one inch looks good to us

(and Ever-Ever Land is a place
that's measured and safe and known
where it's lucky to be unlucky
and the hitler lies down with the cohn)

down above all with love
and everything perverse
or which makes some feel more better
when all ought to feel less worse

(but only sameness is normal
in Ever-Ever Land
for a bad cigar is a woman
but a gland is only a gland)

It would be very wrong — since we may live in a cyclic universe that exactly repeats everything that occurs within it over and over again — to think that we exist in a universe that merely is like one big, mechanical machine. On the contrary, life (joyously) permeates throughout our universe; fortunately, our planet is blessed to be full of such radiating life. Plants, as an example, are always growing or flowering with majestic, tremendous energy that is truly of a living bliss. Interestingly, as plants, such as trees, flowering plants, and grasses, wither and expire (or as they are cut and destroyed), they feel no sense of pain or fear. They merely fade joyfully, so to speak. This is not to suggest that they do not struggle; they oftentimes do.

Life, on our planet, contains a lot of pain and suffering, with animals (containing pain cells and nerve receptors) contending against each other, involving a great deal of agony and conflict. However, there is an abundance of true cooperation and harmony too, and man can contribute to spreading more of this harmony, rather than causing more pain and extinction.

Life, the whole of life, on earth, is like one huge, living tree. The tree might (to the unenlightened) seem to be rather solid and "un-alive"; the bark might seem to be rather stagnant, lifeless, and inanimate; however, with each cycle (of the seasons) true energy flows through the same branches as in the seasons (or cycles) before. If you, as a leaf or a branch of that majestic tree, think that you are separate from the other branches or other leaves, you are sadly mistaken. You are distanced from the other branches and leaves; but you are not separate from them whatsoever. Only a dead branch that psychologically falls off the tree is separate; but it never really falls off; it merely *thinks so.* Only a rather separate mind that psychologically falls off the tree is rather dead. We are all a part of that enormous, living tree (of the whole of life). That tree is not merely a machine. It is vibrantly alive. To truly get in touch with the living essence of that tree, one cannot merely exist as a separate, dead branch or leaf, far from the other branches and foliage. It is easy to break away from the tree and exist as a dead, separate division. It is easy to *non-exist* in *falsities*. Alternatively, it is easy to be in *communion* with that tree and exist connected to a *divine nature.* That tree eternally comes back each season, each cycle. And each time we come back, if we are truly alive, it is truly new — though it can be thought, by others, to be exactly the same (and it appears to be the same) — and is not merely what "was."

There may be a living tree, of a cyclic universe, wherein those who live in it can return and live anew again, and not merely wither and die in some limited fashion. It is a very immense and extensive tree. Are you in *communion* with *that tree*?

from E. E. Cummings:

now all the fingers of this tree(darling)have
hands, and all the hands have people; and
more each particular person is(my love)
alive than every world can understand

now you are and i am now and we're
a mystery which will never happen again,
a miracle which has never happened before —
and shining this our now must come to then

our then shall be some darkness during which
fingers are without hands; and i have no
you: and all trees are(any more than each
leafless)its silent in forevering snow

— but never fear(my own, my beautiful
my blossoming)for also then's until

Most everything in the multiverse functions and operates by natural laws. Only rarely does the *higher power* intervene. These natural laws are the very fabric of time and space and to interfere with them much is to alter what is natural into something that is synthetic and artificial. What is *supernatural* is beyond the natural laws; it does not often interfere with the natural nature of things, (though the supernatural can affect what is natural). Natural plants sometimes wither and die. Artificial plants might appear to be perfect, but they do not have the beauty of real struggle, growth, blossoming, and true development. Truly to be alive, in a natural way, is to struggle and grow. To expect everything to be perfect… is absurd and rather plastic.

I have always found that if you really want to change things, don't just sit around praying; roll up your sleeves and actually do something. Actually help those that need help, by being active and by physically doing something. True insight and understanding *is* action, not mere reaction. Reaction is dead; it is self-centered and is full of barriers and limited lines of demarcation. Action is alive and flowering; it breaks through mere barriers, is often very motive-free, and embraces and includes. In the light of wisdom, one acts differently; then one does not merely react. That action has its own eternity. It is always beautiful. Mere reaction also has elements of eternity within it; but the eternity of mere reaction is mechanical and dead, stagnant and imitative, cold and passionless.

Interestingly, they both (i.e., action and reaction) recur, in a cyclic portion of the cosmos; however, one is alive and the other is not. They both abide (as they must) to the laws of nature. As we have said, one is much more alive than the other is. One — being immersed more in mere reactions and dead concepts — is swarming with inactivity and with mere comfort and indifference. The other — being open to the light of real insight and energy — is dynamic, gracious, truly growing, and beneficent. That "other's" energy may be so dynamic that it is, in truth, supernatural.

Day and night, in a cyclic universe, will you return again? Will you come back to live the exact, same life that you have lived before, regardless as to whether or not you believe in heaven and hell?

from Emily Dickinson:

TWO lengths has every day,
Its absolute extent–
And area superior
By hope or horror lent.
Eternity will be
Velocity, or pause,

At fundamental signals
From fundamental laws.
To die, is not to go–
On doom's consummate chart
No territory new is staked,
Remain thou as thou art.

We can go through life in a rather mediocre way, not caring much for finding anything that is *immensely sacred*. Alternatively, with open eyes, we can be joyously living, deep in what is blessed, compassionate and free. We can be touched by the beauty; alternatively, we can remain distant from it in a blind aloofness. Blind aloofness probably would think that it cannot get there. Blind aloofness probably would think that there is nothing much there to find. Perhaps blind aloofness might get lost in the details, and forget all about anything sacred worth inquiring about. Blind aloofness might care about itself and not others. Blind aloofness might build tall, thick walls of separation around itself, closing others out. Blind aloofness might care to protect itself, to the exclusion of all others. Blind aloofness might choose to stay in the shadows. Blind aloofness might remain in what are closed cages of limitation. Every step that we take can be a step of wisdom or a step of foolishness. Every step can be very significant or only mildly significant. Each step can be eternally significant or (just another limited, old step).

from Emily Dickinson:

EACH life converges to some centre
Expressed or still;
Exists in every human nature
A goal, -
Admitted scarcely to itself, it may be,
Too fair
For credibility's temerity
To dare.
Adored with caution, as a brittle heaven,
To reach
Were hopeless as the rainbow's raiment
To touch,

Yet persevered toward, sure for the distance;
How high
Unto the saints' slow diligence
The sky!
Ungained, it may be, by a life's low venture,
But then, Eternity enable the endeavoring
Again.

Our human arrangement, in a cyclic portion of the cosmos, may entail a repetition of the same things (repeatedly). Things would change and yet not change. A lot of us — especially those of us who would want to remain in mere stagnant, representational symbols — would not really ever change at all.

Those of us who are serious — who look with open eyes not merely jaded by repetitive, unoriginal, symbolic representations — might just find ourselves elevated beyond the merely repetitious, humdrum, recurrent routines. To look with a mind that is silent, that is not merely contaminated by the unoriginal, repetitive patterns that society has enveloped around it, may leave the mind open to an encounter with what is truly *timeless* and beyond the restrictions of unchangeable patterns. It is not that difficult to exist as what may see things in silence with instantaneous insight. Interestingly, it might take years of "living in order" until that *"otherness"* approaches one; or it (that *true sacredness*) may never come. Keenly, whatever takes place, the truly wise mind flows along with it, in (or "as") a motiveless passion.

Do the things you love. One need not torture oneself by sacrificing everything just to achieve something later. Enjoy life and act in ways that you find worthwhile and meaningful. You may alter or change the way you do things, such that you need not be harming the earth and its creatures so much; but there is a lot one can do on this planet that entails enjoyment and helping others in beneficial, rather than harmful, ways. The cosmos is complex and offers many alternatives. (For instance, i gave up fishing, but found many other interesting, worthwhile things to do that do not directly harm the earth's creatures.)

The truly intelligent mind can exist and be within a repetitious cycle, in (and "as") what eternally recurs… and yet not be of it. A wise, silent mind goes beyond all the patterns, shapes, and separations and may exist with what is timeless, measureless, and unlimited. Such a mind is blessed. Such a mind would not be separate from the rest of humanity. Such a mind may be far more than what one can imagine; such a mind may be magically true, (beyond the reality of mere symbolic representations that we all know).

from Wallace Stevens:

Human Arrangement

Place-bound and time-bound in evening rain
And bound by a sound which does not change,

Except that it begins and ends,
Begins again and ends again—

Rain without change within or from
Without. In this place and in this time

And in this sound, which do not change,
In which the rain is all one thing,

In the sky, an imagined, wooden chair
Is the clear-point of an edifice,

Forced up from nothing, evening's chair,
Blue-strutted curule, true—unreal,

The centre of transformations that
Transform for transformation's self,

In a glitter that is a life, a gold
That is a being, a will, a fate.

The following poem does not mean that we should not care about what we do. However, it does mean that we can relax quite a bit and enjoy the scenery now and then. Whatever we do, good or bad, won't, in the overall picture of things, adversely affect the overall order of the universe. Energy (and maybe even the patterns that the energy takes) cannot be created or destroyed. Therefore, one thing that we can do is to be appreciative of what little we have (and truly live). One of our main responsibilities may be to have a joyous, happy mind. One cannot be happy if one is all "uptight" and festering with "ideas" about how things "should be." We can endlessly argue and get caught up in systems and separative organizations. Is that what life is about?

If one lives according to rigid ideas, according to what one "should do," is one then living according to a conceptual pattern? Furthermore, as suggested before, when one inevitably acts in a way that is contrary to the concept of what one "should do," is there, then, friction within the mind? Friction, within the same mind, is wastage of energy and time. When the mind struggles with what it "should do," time is involved. There is a gap between what one desires or craves and the idea of what one "should do." This gap takes time. It involves sections of the mind contending against each other through a process of time. Desire is also a sequential pattern within time. There is a gap between what one "wants" and what one is "now." "Wanting," in the immediate "now," is a lack of energy that is unfulfilled. Being a "lack of energy that is unfulfilled" is not what exists as intelligence.

To be a "stick in the mud" is not intelligent either. It is good to relax and enjoy life, without a lot of rigid formalities and desires entrapping the mind. Interesting hobbies are "cool"; they help keep the mind spritely; learning about and studying life's endless stream of creatures, too, is excellent! (Hey, it may very well be that life is short, and you are not going to live forever.) Actually, if it is all just one brief flash, what is the point of even bothering?

from Walt Whitman:

All is Truth

O me, man of slack faith so long,
Standing aloof, denying portions so long,
Only aware to-day of compact all-diffused truth,
Discovering to-day there is no lie or form of lie, and can be none,
but grows as inevitably upon itself as the truth does upon itself,
Or as any law of the earth or any natural production of the earth does.

(This is curious and may not be realized immediately, but it must be realized,
I feel in myself that I represent falsehoods equally with the rest,
And that the universe does.)

Where has fail'd a perfect return indifferent of lies or the truth?
Is it upon the ground, or in water or fire? or in the spirit of man? or in the meat and blood?

Meditating among liars and retreating sternly into myself, I see that there are really no liars or lies after all,
And that nothing fails its perfect return, and that what are called lies are perfect returns,
And that each thing exactly represents itself and what has preceded it,
And that the truth includes all, and is compact just as much as space is compact,
And that there is no flaw or vacuum in the amount of the truth—but that all is truth without exception;
And henceforth I will go celebrate any thing I see or am,
And sing and laugh and deny nothing.

One of my hobbies (in the distant past) had involved the making of three-dimensional holograms. When a hologram is produced, light waves of a standard frequency range (from a laser) are emitted; they then are split by a light-splitting device called a beam-splitter (as when water from a hose is split by a card held close to the nozzle). Then they are recombined from two different angles (by reflecting them from mirrors) onto the photographic film medium. When these waves (of a standard frequency) combine, after reflecting off an object and then rejoining on the photographic plate, some of the waves add together and combine (to form even larger waves); this is called "reinforcement," or "constructive interference." There are also patterns of waves that can cancel each other out, which is called "cancellation," or "destructive interference"; if the difference between the wave phases is intermediate between these two extremes, then the magnitude of the displacement of the summed waves lies between the minimum and maximum values. Certain interference patterns, which then form on the plate film, help to excite matter and form chemical reactions that eventually help to form the three-dimensional image.

Quantum mechanics is a realm of science that is closely involved with a lot of this holographic process. In the science of quantum mechanics, it is known that there exists a "wave-particle duality." This "wave-particle duality," interestingly enough, postulates that all particles exhibit both wave and particle properties. Waves exhibit particle-like properties too, in the scientific realm of quantum mechanics. In quantum mechanics, this duality addresses the inability of standard, classical concepts like "exclusively being a particle" or "exclusively being a wave" regarding the ability to describe the behavior of quantum-scale phenomena. In actuality, i strongly suspect that there are no definite particles, per se; they are just waves that often happen to have particle-like attributes (i.e., particle-like appearances).

In regard to the Uncertainty Principal, developed by Werner Heisenberg in 1927, you can never have an accurate measurement of an apparent subatomic particle's momentum and its position at the same, exact time. If you have an accurate measurement of an apparent subatomic particle's momentum, you can only have a probability of having an accurate measurement of its velocity and vice versa. If you have an accurate measurement of an apparent subatomic particle's position, you cannot be sure of what its momentum is. The trade-off between definiteness of position and definiteness of momentum is scientifically quantified by what is commonly known as Heisenberg's Uncertainty Principle. Whenever we measure the exact position of an apparent particle, the range of locations narrows just enough so that we never see the wave. At any one time, we see only the "apparent particle aspect" or the "wave aspect" of a subatomic phenomenon.

When Einstein explained the photoelectric effect by showing that light came in discrete (apparent) particles called photons, quantum theory was beginning. When Einstein introduced the concept of photons, he showed that waves could have particle-like attributes. Then, years later, Prince Louis de Broglie showed that every apparent particle had wave aspects. Louis de Broglie argued that every apparent particle had a frequency, something only waves have. This was hard to explain since apparent particles are supposed to have an exact and precise location, whereas waves are spread over a range of locations. However, as in the process of holography, two waves can interfere to form another, more complex wave. Superposition, as the combining of quantum waves (with multiple wave crests and wave troughs positively combining or negatively cancelling each other out), is an important factor here. If we add enough waves together, we can get a wave packet with a range of locations that is as small as would be suitable for scientific (apparent particle) purposes. This does not give an apparent particle a definite, exact location, but it basically looks like an exact location and so explains why we see it in that manner (as a certain apparent particle). Even simple (apparently uncombined and basic) wave-forms have particle-like attributes, at times.

In the realm of quantum mechanics, studying "wave function" helps to determine the probabilities related to an apparent particle's position, momentum, and other physical properties. No one in science fully understands what wave function is. **∞** Wave function, in quantum mechanics, is represented by the Greek letter **Ψ** (spelled *psi*, and pronounced like "sigh," appropriately enough). Wave function is a "complex function" which is defined everywhere within the space-time continuum. No matter what state a particular apparent particle is in, its wave function has some complex value at every point in the universe/cosmos. The *small* is enfolded throughout the entire field of the cosmos; the *small* is the *large*; the *small* is the *eternity*, and is the *large*. (Perhaps this is why maliciously harming the small while concomitantly claiming to be often "worshipping God" is cadaverous hypocrisy.)

In the following Diagram "A", that i developed, you can observe a very rudimentary, yet effective, example about how a recurring universe could operate. The diagram reveals wave function attributes. It, operating as the whole universe, would operate in a cyclic manner, with no end and no precise beginning; therefore, it need not be *created*. Everything, in life and in existence, is relationship. What occurs usually occurs as a relationship between *waves* and what we call *apparent-particle waves.* (Actually, it is all "waves.") The present time is a mixture of relationships; that is what time is. *Holistic time* can supersede *relativity-oriented time*.

Let the middle of the diagram be the wave function area, where section 1 and section 2 meet. The arrow of relative time is in one direction only. The exact center, between sections 1 and 2, can represent a simplified wave function area. If you were around the exact center and were looking at the line between the labels B and C, you would be looking at something more akin to a *wave*. If you were around the exact center and were looking at what was coming toward you from point A's position ("relativistically" speaking), you would be looking at something more akin to an *apparent wave-particle* or *an apparent point* in space-time. From around the exact center (close up, at the subatomic-size), you would not be able to perceive both areas at exactly the same time, (which is so, if the "observer" is "the observed," and the "observer" is "the observed.") At the macroscopic scale, though, we tend to see more of the "apparent particleness" than the "waviness." However, looking at the big picture, we can perceive how the overall "apparent particleness" is entwined with (or within) an overall "waviness."

Now here's the crux of the matter (at the quantum level); what is actually coming toward you, from point A, is really not only an apparent point (except that you basically see it only that way from the center); but for someone who sees the whole picture, it has wavelike qualities too (and then some). Though it appears to be "point-like," it is actually part of an overall holistic waviness that permeates infinitely.

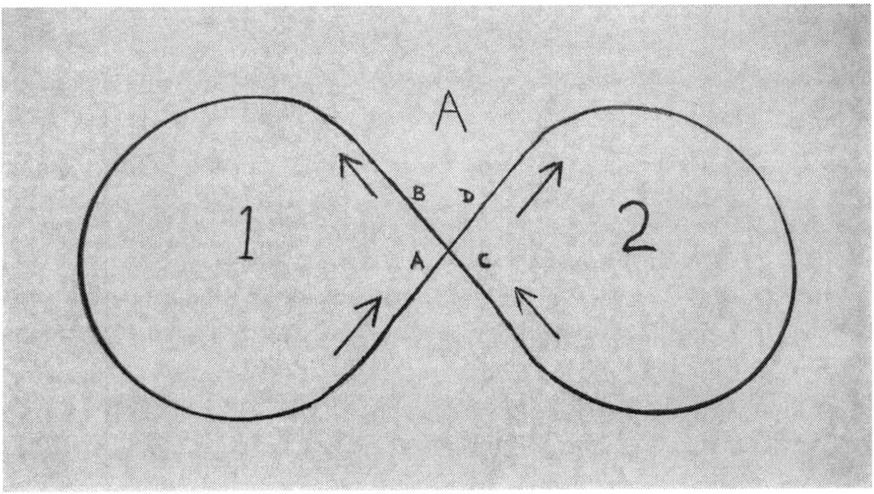

Diagram A

The diagram shows something that, in its entirety, is autonomous in nature. The diagram may give a clue to the workings of our cosmos, at least partially. Observe the *entire* movement of the pattern. It moves, yet it is not moving whatsoever. Energy is expended, yet no energy is expended. The whole pattern moves, yet it doesn't move. (If it moves within the entirety, yet remains still, it is not really moving; however, it *is* moving.) There is, within it, the conservation of energy and the conservation of all the patterns of energy. For where the actual, circular, fine lines are, in the diagram, there may be (within) a multiplex of complicated (combined) wave, energy, and apparent-particle forms and patterns. Non-locality (faster than light) oriented phenomena is an easy occurrence in such a holistic, *apparent particle-wave* multiverse. As T. S. Eliot had suggested, in the poetry previously provided, the past becomes the future, and the future becomes the past. The present is the past and the future; and the future is the past and the present. As E. E. Cummings sarcastically wrote within a poem, "the whole moves; and every part stands still." In actuality, what we are saying about our cosmos is that "every part moves; and the whole stands still."

In quantum mechanics, you can separate "previously paired" subatomic so-called particles by vast distances — even by millions of miles — and if you change one, the other will also change instantly and correspondingly (no matter how far away it is). If a subatomic, twin apparent-particle is made to spin *down*, its twin will spin *up* instantly, no matter what the distance is between them. What i am saying, along with relativity theory and quantum mechanics, points to the fact that our multiverse is not of actual separate things; the actuality is that all things merge and unite in one flowing totality. (This does not mean, by the way, that a man can go into a glamorous movie star's home and claim that he and she are one!) An *antimatter universe* and a so-called *regular matter universe* may be (together) united forever as (or "in") one whole. The "now" is enfolded in what exists as the "past" and the "future." The "future" is enfolded in what exists as the "past" and the "present." In terms of what scientists call "quantum entanglement" — which deals with non-localized phenomena involving certain paired or twin subatomic apparent-particles — there needs to be questions addressed concerning the possibility that there are paired, non-localized universes that are (for all practical purposes) exactly identical to each other. These paired universes can be mirror images of each other; they would both repeat in exactly the same way (in balance).

Well, the following poem, by Cummings, may shed some light on a few things, (including the absurd suggestions, in the most recent poem provided by Whitman thus far, that "lies" are OK).

from E. E. Cummings:

one's not half two. It's two are halves of one:
which halves reintegrating,shall occur
no death and any quantity;but than
all numerable mosts the actual more

minds ignorant of stern miraculous
this every truth--beware of heartless them
(given the scalpel,they dissect a kiss;
or,sold the reason,they undream a dream)

one is the song which fiends and angels sing:
all murdering lies by mortals told make two.
Let liars wilt,repaying life they're loaned;
we(by a gift called dying born)must grow

deep in dark least ourselves remembering
love only rides his year.
All lose,whole find

Diagram "B" below, somewhat similar to Diagram "A", reveals a continuum which may represent an eternally oriented sub-modality; such sub-modalities may flux and repeatedly exist within an overall *large* modality (such as what Diagram "A" is). Within Diagram "B", the area of wave function has apparently shifted. Area E, within the Diagram, may represent an area of more concentration, such as an area with a high gravitational field, such as a black hole (or the beginning of what a black hole can be). The area F is more of a flat (i.e., non-sunken) or slightly elevated area; the area E is as an area that is sunken in (such as a hole or depression). Time would be relatively slowed down in the E area (when observed from a distance); however, whoever is actually within area E's hole or depression would observe time running normally.

Just as apparent particles and waves coexist together in quantum wave function, as an ensemble of energy, so too does the phenomenon of *living* go with *dying*. *Living* and *dying* are not two separate things. They are forever entwined; like quantum waves, they are an ensemble together. They are not divorced from each other, as many people erroneously think. They are forever united, almost like with a marriage… and, together, they are one. Each moment, in which one is alive, exists as a living flow. That flow changes from moment to moment, such that each moment expires and transforms into a *different* moment. *Different* does *not* mean *separate.* So each moment ends (and dies), to change and transform into a different (new) moment. Just because one moment changes into a different moment, it does not mean that they are separate and disconnected. On the contrary, they are part of the same continuum. They are bound together. Living is dying and dying is living. What *was* is entwined with what *will be*; they are forever united (as "one and the same.")

So each moment of living involves that moment dying (i.e., ending) to transform into something else regarding living; it is a constant, harmonious, unbroken, holistic flow. The "something else," that a moment is transformed

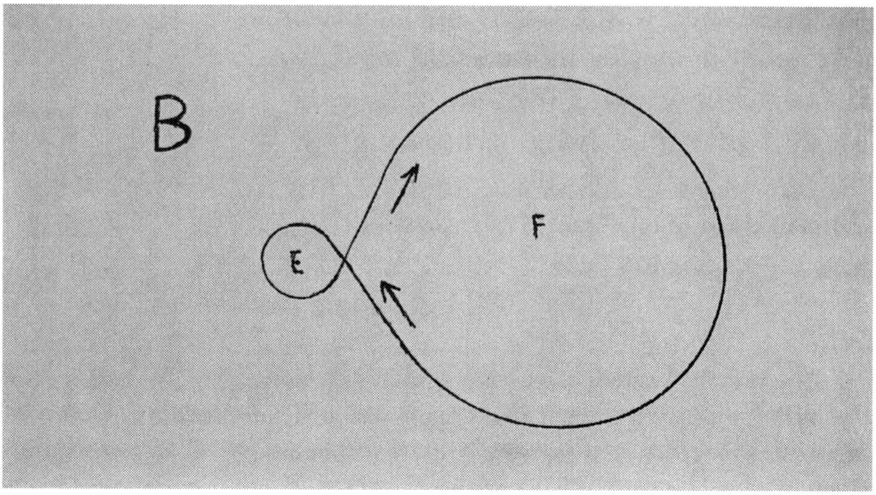

Diagram B

into, is not truly separate from the "previous moment"; they are forever bonded. An intelligent mind is, at times, one that is dying to the symbolic images and abstract representations that help formulate it. This dying may truly lead to a majestic and sacred *living*. *Dying*, psychologically, to rather dead, second-hand, mental symbols is, indeed, truly *living*.

Physical death, of course, is another thing, and nobody likes to physically end (at least no one who is sane), wherein one's sequential patterns are extinguished and annihilated. However, the psychological realm is different than the physical realm, and when one's prejudiced thoughts come to an end, it is a good way of dying. *Psychologically dying* to stagnant, prejudiced thoughts is *actual living*. Therefore, dying and living are not two separate things; they are indeed "one and the same."

Diagram "A", by the way, is much like the symbol for eternity that has existed, coincidentally, for quite some time. The *Lemniscate* (i.e., the infinity symbol) is a geometrical representation of the endless and eternal nature of energy. (It is remarkable about how it is so similar to my Diagram "A"!) Energy cannot be created or destroyed; it simply continues on forever in motion. This may also be applicable to the patterns that energy exists as. Properly regarding this symbol may help us to understand that the consequences of our thoughts and deeds may have effects that can indeed be infinite. John Wallis is credited with introducing the infinity symbol (∞) in 1655, in his *De Sectionibus Conicis*.

In the following poem, consider the center of Diagram "A" when you read about the *infinite states* on the *mid-line dividing*, at the *golden* (i.e., eternal treasure) *spot,* where the mid-line swells and yields to a supple, quivering, deep *inundation* (i.e., wave).

from Jean Le Roy, translated from the French by Wallace Stevens:

I feel an apparition, at my back, an ebon wrack,
Of more than man's condition,
That leans upon me there;
And then in back, one more; and then, still farther back,
Still other men aligned; and then, toujours plus grands,
immensities of night,
Who, less and less defined by light, stretch off in the black;

ancestors from the first days of the world.

Before me, I know more,
one smaller at the first, and then one smaller still,
and more and more, that are my son and then his sons.

They lie behind in dumb sleep,
Or bury themselves in the future.

And for the time, just one exists: I.
Just one exists and I am time, the whole of time,
I am the whole of light.
My flesh alone, for the moment, lives,
my heart alone gives, my eyes alone have sight.
I am emblazoned, the others, all, are black.
I am the whole of light!
And those behind and those before are only routineers of
rounding time.
In back, they lie perdu in the black: the breachless grime,
(just one exists and I am time) of an incalculable ether that
burns and stings.

My will alone commands me: I am time!
Behind they passed the point of man, before they are not embryo —
I, only, touch with prime. And that will last a long length of time,
Think what you will!

I am between two infinite states on the mid-line dividing,
Between the infinite that waits and the long-abiding,
At the golden spot, where the mid-line swells
and yields to a supple, quivering, deep inundation.

What do we count? All is for us that live!
Time, even time, and the day's strength and beam.
My fellows, you that live around me,
Are you not surprised to be supreme,
On the tense line, in this expanse of dual circumstance?
And are you not surprised to be the base
To know that, without you, the scale of lives
on which the eternal poising turns
would sing upon death's pitty under-place?
And are you not surprised to be the very poles?

Let us make signals in the air and cry aloud,
We must leave a wide noise tolling in the night;
And in the deep of time, set the wide wind rolling.

Apparently, it is easy to be apathetic, to drift through life unconcerned about others. One may care about one's immediate family, or about a certain friend or two. One may care about one's dog or cat. One may care about oneself. Is such very limited love... really love at all? If it is circumscribed and one is unmoved and indifferent about what lies beyond the circumference, is that love? It is easy to love what you were taught to love; anyone can do that.

A superlative mind, that is orderly, loves. Being in order, it does not easily get gloomy or feel dismal. A truly orderly mind loves the simple things in life. Such a mind is extremely appreciative of the natural beauty of trees, birds, flowers, insects, and so many miraculous things. To be aware of the beauty of every single moment is to learn beyond the mere limitations of categorization, labeling, and memorizing. A passionless mind may not even be open to actually look at things. A passionless mind is dead before it ever gets to the grave. Labeling and memorizing is important and necessary. Looking with a mind of silence, without merely labeling and memorizing, is equally necessary. (As we previously stated, true silence is not merely empty, as some would have us think; it is bubbling with life. Vast space is a majestic plenum bubbling with life.)

When i was very young (physically speaking), my upstairs bedroom was in the attic area. Behind the walls of my bedroom, there were spaces and passageways (because the attic-oriented, angled ceiling was too low, in certain sections, to accommodate room enough to walk upright). I remember that there were trap doors going into some of the passageways. I remember having found something rather mysterious and magical within one of those hidden passageways. I remember that, in one of the spaces or passageways, there was a very ornate, large porcelain vessel, full of images of people and animals, all depicted as moving in one direction (around the vessel). The vessel had beautiful trees. I remember that, upon the vessel, there were people with flutes, and fair maidens depicted in exquisite colors. They seemed to be fixed, in what they were partaking in, as if they were doing it forever. That is why the following poem by Keats, about a Grecian Urn, is very dear to me.

What if our lives, as we have lived them, were depicted (forever) upon that Grecian Urn? Would we be proud and honored by what we saw? It is never too late (before you die) to change what the Urn will depict about you and your life.

from John Keats:

Ode On A Grecian Urn

Thou still unravished bride of quietness,
    Thou foster child of silence and slow time,
Sylvan historian, who canst thus express
    A flowery tale more sweetly than our rhyme:
What leaf-fringed legend haunts about thy shape
    Of deities or mortals, or of both,
        In Tempe or the dales of Arcady?

What men or gods are these? What maidens loath?
  What mad pursuit? What struggle to escape?
    What pipes and timbrels? What wild ecstasy?

Heard melodies are sweet, but those unheard
  Are sweeter; therefore, ye soft pipes, play on;
Not to the sensual ear, but, more endeared,
  Pipe to the spirit dities of no tone.
Fair youth, beneath the trees, thou canst not leave
  Thy song, nor ever can those trees be bare;
    Bold Lover, never, never canst thou kiss,
Though winning near the goal—yet, do not grieve;
  She cannot fade, though thou hast not thy bliss
    Forever wilt thou love, and she be fair!

Ah, happy, happy boughs! that cannot shed
  Your leaves, nor ever bid the Spring adieu;
And, happy melodist, unweari-ed,
  Forever piping songs forever new;
More happy love! more happy, happy love!
  Forever warm and still to be enjoyed,
    Forever panting, and forever young;
All breathing human passion far above,
  That leaves a heart high-sorrowful and cloyed,
    A burning forehead, and a parching tongue.

Who are these coming to the sacrifice?
  To what green altar, O mysterious priest,
Lead'st thou that heifer lowing at the skies,
  And all her silken flanks with garlands dressed?
What little town by river or sea shore,
  Or mountain-built with peaceful citadel,
    Is emptied of this folk, this pious morn?
And, little town, thy streets for evermore
  Will silent be; and not a soul to tell

Why thou art desolate, can e'er return.

O Attic shape! Fair attitude! with brede
Of marble men and maidens overwrought,
With forest branches and the trodden weed;
Thou, silent form, dost tease us out of thought
As doth eternity. Cold Pastoral!
When old age shall this generation waste,
Thou shalt remain, in midst of other woe
Than ours, a friend to man, to whom thou say'st,
"Beauty is truth, truth beauty,"—that is all
Ye know on earth, and all ye need to know.

There has been a most magnificent, golden colored fox coming out around our house in the evenings. It has the most splendid black legs, and its ears are pert and fluffy with their wonderful golden and blackened tones. I have been giving it some leftover dog food now and then — due to the bitter-cold winter weather, as i am writing this — and it seems to be very appreciative of it. I really hope that it isn't hit by traffic. Animals, these days, have it so tough anymore. They are running out of room and hardly have any place left to go. Many animals, and even plants, have gone into extinction recently (or are about to); such extinction has been unprecedented since the last mass extinction event (of the dinosaurs), and it is due to human destruction, not natural causes. We human beings have overpopulated this planet far too much, and we want to explore other planets, so that we can go to them and, I suppose, ruin them as we are doing to this planet. What are we thinking? Let's stay here and clean up our act — get the population down to more like a half a billion or less — and forget all about "out there." If we change our ways, we can have heaven on earth. If we do not change, we will create a horrid hell for the whole of life. The winds are furious; the larger animals and smaller insects are quickly fading away; mother earth is dying, and things will get ugly if we do not change our ways very soon.

Population on this planet has run rampant. Human babies surely are cute and are so much fun to be around; but to keep having babies when this planet is *going under*, because of so much overpopulation, is heartless. We could have heaven on earth, with plenty of jobs and property for everyone, if we just turned in another direction concerning population numbers. If we remain with an extremely high earth population, people will be forced to vehemently fight over water and food sources. We additionally, as we have suggested before, need to do much more with regard to *green energy*.

Another thing that needs to be done, especially considering the possibility that our universe is cyclic, is to protect adults, and especially children, with implanted GPS devices. Small devices implanted within our arms or shoulders, for example, would enable abducted children to be quickly found, and criminals and murders to be quickly located. If a victim was attacked in a certain location, at a certain time, GPS computers could reveal who was with them or near them (when the attack was initiated). Computers could show, after a bank robbery, who the perpetrator was, fleeing from the bank at the exact time of the robbery; additionally, the same GPS devices could reveal exactly where he is hiding. GPS devices would go a long way in regard to curtailing a lot of serious crime.

The best way to prevent crime is to educate everyone properly, so that they see the true meaning of orderly living with true integrity. Right education truly comes when the number of students is small, when students are not merely indoctrinated with a lot of rigid ideas and dead systems. It comes when there is a cooperative, compassionate atmosphere, and when they are not pushed away from the joy of being what they are. Students must be cared for immensely. They should learn to realize how special, unique, and miraculous they are. A real student goes out and investigates (and builds things, like solar energy devices); he (or she) grows plants and friendships; he (or she) does not merely sit in a confined, isolated, stagnant room, stuck in some miserable, *highchair oriented, so-called desk.* A real student always learns, throughout his or her entire life, about investigating inwardly/outwardly, (and he or she does so without merely relying on limiting authorities and methodologies). A real student learns to teach himself/or herself. There need not be "teachers" ever, only "learning-assistants." "Learning-assistants" need to be always learning, themselves. Such learning is endless.

from Walt Whitman:

Excerpts from: To Think of Time

To think of time—of all that retrospection,
To think of to-day, and the ages continued henceforward.
Have you guess'd you yourself would not continue?
Have you dreaded these earth-beetles?

Have you fear'd the future would be nothing to you?
Is to-day nothing? is the beginningless past nothing?
If the future is nothing they are just as surely nothing.
To think that the sun rose in the east—that men and women were flexible, real, alive—that every thing was alive,
To think that you and I did not see, feel, think, nor bear our part,
To think that we are now here and bear our part.

What will be will be well, for what is is well,
To take interest is well, and not to take interest shall be well.
The domestic joys, the daily housework or business, the building of houses, are not phantasms, they have weight, form, location.
Farms, profits, crops, markets, wages, government, are none of them phantasms,
The difference between sin and goodness is no delusion,
The earth is not an echo, man and his life and all the things of his life are well-consider'd.
You are not thrown to the winds, you gather certainly and safely around yourself,
Yourself! yourself! yourself, for ever and ever!

It is not to diffuse you that you were born of your mother and father, it is to identify you,
It is not that you should be undecided, but that you should be decided,
Something long preparing and formless is arrived and form'd in you,
You are henceforth secure, whatever comes or goes.
The threads that were spun are gather'd, the wet crosses the warp, the pattern is systematic.
The preparations have every one been justified,
The orchestra have sufficiently tuned their instruments, the baton has given the signal.

The guest that was coming, he waited long, he is now housed,
He is one of those who are beautiful and happy, he is one of those that to look upon and be with is enough.
The law of the past cannot be eluded,
The law of the present and future cannot be eluded,
The law of the living cannot be eluded, it is eternal,
The law of promotion and transformation cannot be eluded,
The law of heroes and good-doers cannot be eluded,
The law of drunkards, informers, mean persons, not one iota thereof can be eluded.

Slow moving and black lines go ceaselessly over the earth,
Northerner goes carried and Southerner goes carried, and they on the
Atlantic side and they on the Pacific,
And they between, and all through the Mississippi country, and all over the earth.
The great masters and kosmos are well as they go, the heroes and good-doers are well,
The known leaders and inventors and the rich owners and pious and distinguish'd may be well,
But there is more account than that, there is strict account of all.
The interminable hordes of the ignorant and wicked are not nothing,
The barbarians of Africa and Asia are not nothing,
The perpetual successions of shallow people are not nothing as they go.
Of and in all these things,
I have dream'd that we are not to be changed so much, nor the law of us changed,
I have dream'd that heroes and good-doers shall be under the present and past law,
And that murderers, drunkards, liars, shall be under the present and past law,

For I have dream'd that the law they are under now is enough.
And I have dream'd that the purpose and essence of the known life, the transient,
Is to form and decide identity for the unknown life, the permanent.
If all came but to ashes of dung,
If maggots and rats ended us, then Alarum! for we are betray'd,
Then indeed suspicion of death.
Do you suspect death? if I were to suspect death I should die now,
Do you think I could walk pleasantly and well-suited toward annihilation?
Pleasantly and well-suited I walk,
Whither I walk I cannot define, but I know it is good,
The whole universe indicates that it is good,
The past and the present indicate that it is good.
How beautiful and perfect are the animals!
How perfect the earth, and the minutest thing upon it!
What is called good is perfect, and what is called bad is just as perfect,
The vegetables and minerals are all perfect, and the imponderable fluids perfect;
Slowly and surely they have pass'd on to this, and slowly and surely they yet pass on.

I swear I think now that every thing without exception has an eternal soul!
The trees have, rooted in the ground! the weeds of the sea have! the animals!
I swear I think there is nothing but immortality!
That the exquisite scheme is for it, and the nebulous float is for it, and the cohering is for it!
And all preparation is for it—and identity is for it—and life and materials are altogether for it!

I feel, as was suggested before, that plants, such as trees and flowers, are places where energy often flowers in amazing realms of bliss and profound rapture. Plants, having no pain receptors, can succumb to drought or consumption by animals, and yet feel no fear, suffering, or remorse. In a sense, plants exist in a timeless realm, where measurement of spans of occurrences never takes place. Yet plants may be where an abundance of life-renewing energy bubbles and flowers.

Unlike plants, animals do feel pain. I personally suffer from arthritic pain, in my old age; my wife often has to deal with physical pain; however, the mind can learn to go beyond the pain, leaving it, oftentimes, in the background. One can over-identify with pain, making it out to be more than it actually is. Moreover, there are those who heartlessly cause others to suffer, not feeling much empathy or compassion toward so-called others. Such entities are the mentally ill extruders of pain; they are the dark ones that are the cause of pain and agony of man.

Tonight, as i was writing this book, my wife mentioned that she heard, on her police scanner, that someone was driving on the wrong side of the road (on a highway very near to where we live) and was being apprehended for driving under the influence. Thank goodness, a family was not involved in a calamitous accident involving this. Some people are just heartless and thoughtless about themselves and about so-called others. Many depend on alcohol or other mind-altering drugs to achieve what they think is happiness. However, is true happiness something that can be taken by a pill (or by a beverage that is, in actuality, a depressant)? To destroy one's mind is not part of the pathway to true bliss and true joy. A brain that depends on mere substances is, in itself, a mere substance. To truly be of a blissful, uncorrupt, infinite energy, one must (as do plants) go beyond the confines of mere measurement, fear, plotting calculation, and detailed desire. We are not suggesting that one should vegetate in some kind of stagnation; we are saying that the true precision of life may exist beyond heartaches, despair, despondency, and dependence.

from Emily Dickinson:

I TASTE a liquor never brewed,
From tankards scooped in pearl;
Not all the vats upon the Rhine
Yield such an alcohol!

Inebriate of air am I,
And debauchee of dew,

Reeling, through endless summer days,
From inns of molten blue.

When landlords turn the drunken bee
Out of the foxglove's door,
When butterflies renounce their drams,
I shall but drink the more!

Till seraphs swing their snowy hats,
And saints to windows run,
To see the little tippler
Leaning against the sun!

If one lives in a universe that is part of a cyclical framework — that repeats everything that occurs within it, over and over, everlastingly — then how one lives one's life has tremendous significance. What is most important may not be the comforts that one can have in life, nor the quantity of the experiences that one can have… but, rather, in what way one can exist with tremendous order while benefiting the world. Merely to grope after one experience following another, in life, may mean that one is smitten with habitual and run-of-the-mill conditioning. Interestingly, a mind that is smitten in such a manner is not capable of the extraordinary insights that lead to the most profound order, bliss, and understanding. A mind that merely gropes and hunts for happiness is a mind that is intrinsically insufficient and deficient. What is broken and incomplete cannot be the holistic integrity that manifests as *true bliss* and *true harmony*. An unintelligent mind is likely to be heavily conditioned and, as such, will likely cause a great deal of suffering and needless destruction in the overall realm of life on earth. To function merely as a conditioned entity is to manifest as a dark cloud over what was thriving in the beneficent sunlight. To function merely as a conditioned entity is to mechanically unfold as the disastrous, calamitous, unpleasant *un-fortune* of man and life. Entities such as this are dispassionate, aloof, incurious, and uninvolved; they are, unfortunately, most assuredly "dead-from-the-neck-up." Many are "dead-from-the-heart-up." This is why embedded GPS devices must be employed, especially for children and for those that are young, to curtail as much unhealthy, cruel and unwholesome behavior as possible, which may occur against such youth and against what is truly alive. (Such GPS devices can be monitored in a very non-intrusive way, and would only be checked upon, by non-governmental groups, in very limited, specific areas where serious crimes were committed.)

We can stand together, as one. However, are we likely to stand together, as one, if we are an ongoing array of isolated thoughts that never end? If we are composed of ceaseless symbols, involving separative boundaries, limited conceptions of self, and circumscribed formulations involving mere self-gratification, mere opportunistic behavior, and mere egocentric manifestations, will we ever go beyond what is merely machine-like, puppet-like, and robotic?

from Wallace Stevens:

The Place of the Solitaires

Let the place of the solitaires
Be a place of perpetual undulation.

Whether it be in mid-sea
On the dark, green water-wheel,
Or on the beaches,
There must be no cessation
Of motion, or of the noise of motion,
The renewal of noise
And manifold continuation;

And, most, of the motion of thought
And its restless iteration,
In the place of the solitaires,
Which is to be a place of perpetual undulation.

If the cosmos is indeed one, and if parts of it are indeed cyclic, then had we better (directly and not abstractly) realize the seriousness of our actions and the unity of all that there is? Of course, those who inevitably insist that we are indeed separate, and not together as *one*, will likely be some of those who project a "separate heaven" in their minds. Their heaven, obviously, will be a heaven that is separate from what they can have now. A mind that perceives through a screen of separation will (naturally) look with ideas and conceptualizations constituted of separation. A mind riddled with separation will (naturally) cling to abstractions of a "separate heaven," a "distant heaven." A mind riddled with mere symbolic representations will (naturally) project a heaven of abstraction.

from Ralph Waldo Emerson:

If the red slayer think he slays,
Or if the slain think he is slain,
They know not well the subtle ways
I keep, and pass, and turn again.

Far or forgot to me is near;
Shadow and sunlight are the same;
The vanished gods to me appear;
And one to me are shame and fame.

They reckon ill who leave me out;
When me they fly, I am the wings;
I am the doubter and the doubt,
And I the hymn the Brahmin sings.

The strong gods pine for my abode,
And pine in vain the sacred Seven;
But thou, meek lover of the good!
Find me, and turn thy back on heaven.

In a portion of the cosmos, that happens to be cyclic, one is born (at what one may call the "beginning point"); let us call it point A. (See the following Diagram "C".) One lives one's life and then, at the so-called end, one dies; let us call it point Z. Point Z represents the time of physical death (of the individual). Since there is no recorded experience and memory, in a cyclic universe, between when one dies and when one is again born, there is no recollection of the experience of time between those two events. In a cyclic universe, since there is no experience of time, following point Z, to where and when point A begins again, no sequential activity is capable of being recognized. Therefore, in essence, psychologically, as soon as one dies, one is again born into the same, exact life sequence. After one dies, it may take many billions of years for the cycle to exist again in the exact, same way that one was born in before; nevertheless, the brain is not around (after death) to record time, so (in reality) consciousness and time (for the individual) begins immediately following the point of death. The end is the beginning. The beginning is the end. (Hopefully, if very young children happen to die prematurely, the "*timeless immensity*" may bless them with some additional dimension of bliss; it would be a dimension of harmony, beyond all the friction.)

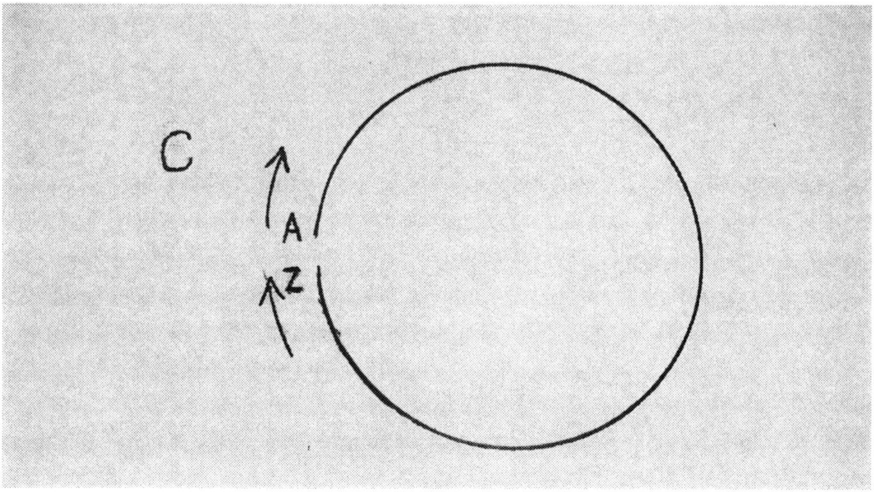

Diagram C

So, in a cyclic portion of the cosmos, everything is repeated. Each end is a beginning. Moreover, each beginning is not so very separate from what the end will be. If we are compassionate and orderly, we will be compassionate and orderly forever. If we are uncaring, cold, and indifferent, we will be disorderly and "dead-from-the-heart-up" forever. What goes around comes around.

All of the orthodox, manmade religions readily try to tell you what happens after death. What they give to you consists of empty, shadow-like abstractions and projections from what others have formulated. What they give you is not very tangible. What we are telling you is no manmade religion. Do not build organizations and temples around it, charging others to enter for a fee; do not make it into something separate from all that there is. What we are telling you may not merely be an abstraction. What we are telling you consists just partially (but not absolutely) of what abstractions consist of; you and eternity are constituted of more than mere abstractions. We are saying to look all around you at what actually *is*.

In a cyclic universe, it may be that the thing that happens after you die… is *you*. It may be you exactly as you were before. Do you want to actually see what happens after death? Go look into a mirror. That may give you something tangible to reflect on. (If you look in that mirror, and think that you are ugly, you are wrong; you are beautifully there as the whole.)

from Walt Whitman:

Who Learns My Lesson Complete?

Who learns my lesson complete?
Boss, journeyman, apprentice, churchman and atheist,
The stupid and the wise thinker, parents and offspring, mer-
chant, clerk, porter and customer,
Editor, author, artist, and schoolboy—draw nigh and com-
mence;
It is no lesson—it lets down the bars to a good lesson,
And that to another, and every one to another still.
The great laws take and effuse without argument,
I am of the same style, for I am their friend,
I love them quits and quits, I do not halt and make salaams.
I lie abstracted and hear beautiful tales of things and the reasons
of things,
They are so beautiful I nudge myself to listen.
I cannot say to any person what I hear—I cannot say it to
myself—it is very wonderful.
It is no small matter, this round and delicious globe moving so
exactly in its orbit for ever and ever, without one jolt or
the untruth of a single second,
I do not think it was made in six days, nor in ten thousand
years, nor ten billions of years,
Nor plann'd and built one thing after another as an architect
plans and builds a house.
I do not think seventy years is the time of a man or woman,
Nor that seventy millions of years is the time of a man or
woman,

Nor that years will ever stop the existence of me, or any one else.
Is it wonderful that I should be immortal? as every one is immortal;
I know it is wonderful, but my eyesight is equally wonderful, and
how I was conceived in my mother's womb is equally wonderful,
And pass'd from a babe in the creeping trance of a couple of summers and winters to articulate and walk—all this is equally wonderful.
And that my soul embraces you this hour, and we affect each other without ever seeing each other, and never perhaps to see each other, is every bit as wonderful.
And that I can think such thoughts as these is just as wonderful,
And that I can remind you, and you think them and know them to be true, is just as wonderful.
And that the moon spins round the earth and on with the earth, is equally wonderful,
And that they balance themselves with the sun and stars is equally wonderful.

Most all of us were taught about death. We were taught that death is an ending. We were spoon-fed by our authorities to believe that death was final. We were taught that death is the final end for us here on earth.

To truly live in the present is to have no learned knowledge about "death as an ending." To truly live in the present, there is no such learned thing as "the future apart from the past." There is no such thing as the past apart from the future.

from Archibald MacLeish:

An Eternity

There is no dusk to be,
There is no dawn that was,
Only there's now, and now,
And the wind in the grass.

Days I remember of
Now in my heart, are now;
Days that I dream will bloom
White the peach bough.

Dying shall never be
Now in the windy grass;
Now under shooken leaves
Death never was.

from John Keats:

Bright Star

Bright star, would I were steadfast as thou art—
  Not in lone splendor hung aloft the night,
And watching, with eternal lids apart,
  Like nature's patient, sleepless Eremite,
The moving waters at their priestlike task
  Of pure ablution round earth's human shores,
Or gazing on the new soft fallen mask
  Of snow upon the mountains and the moors—
No—yet still steadfast, still unchangeable,
  Pillowed upon my fair love's ripening breast,

To feel forever its soft fall and swell,
  Awake forever in a sweet unrest,
Still, still to hear her tender-taken breath,
And so live ever—or else swoon to death.

If there is no real separation between "the perceiver" and "the perceived," then what one looks at, as we have suggested, becomes what consciousness entails and actually *is*. Therefore, psychologically, one is not separate from *what the perceived is*. One's environment, then, is not so very separate from what one is. One's environment constitutes the perceptions that one has; one's environment constitutes the perceptions that one is.

This may also be applicable to animals, whether they realize it or not. In the following poem, it may be an animal that "slipped by the terrace, made a sudden leap, and seeing that it was a soft October night, curled once about the house, and fell asleep." Alternatively, of course, that part of the following poem, instead, may merely be an explanation about the movement of fog. You decide.

Furthermore, in the following poem, could it be that a cat is described when it is written that: "The afternoon, the evening, sleeps so peacefully… smoothed by long fingers, asleep… tired… or it malingers"? By the way, T. S. Eliot loved cats!

The following poem, by a sly fox in sheep's clothing, will be a slight bump in the road for you, as you travel through time. Ride it out, and do not let it bother you too much. As you are traveling, you can regard cats within your consciousness, in time. To mentally regard cats, within consciousness, takes time. All time may have significance. Merely groping, in time, for pleasure, may have very limited significance. What has more than limited significance, however, may be found in the simple process of rolling a ball. When a rolling ball moves, does it, in a way, repeat the same circular, cyclic-oriented movement over and over again, for a significant time?

From T. S. Eliot

Excerpt from The Love Song of J. Alfred Prufrock

S`io credesse che mia risposta fosse
A persona che mai tornasse al mondo,
Questa fiamma staria senza piu scosse.
Ma perciocchè giammai di questo fondo
Non tornò vivo alcun, s'i'odo il vero,
Senza tema d'infamia ti rispondo.

Let us go then, you and I,
When the evening is spread out against the sky
Like a patient etherized upon a table;
Let us go, through certain half-deserted streets,
The muttering retreats
Of restless nights in one-night cheap hotels
And sawdust restaurants with oyster-shells:
Streets that follow like a tedious argument
Of insidious intent
To lead you to an overwhelming question. . .
Oh, do not ask, "What is it?"
Let us go and make our visit.

In the room the women come and go
Talking of Michelangelo.

The yellow fog that rubs its back upon the window-panes
The yellow smoke that rubs its muzzle on the window-panes
Licked its tongue into the corners of the evening
Lingered upon the pools that stand in drains,
Let fall upon its back the soot that falls from chimneys,
Slipped by the terrace, made a sudden leap,

And seeing that it was a soft October night
Curled once about the house, and fell asleep.

And indeed there will be time
For the yellow smoke that slides along the street,
Rubbing its back upon the window-panes;
There will be time, there will be time
To prepare a face to meet the faces that you meet;
There will be time to murder and create,
And time for all the works and days of hands
That lift and drop a question on your plate;

Time for you and time for me,
And time yet for a hundred indecisions
And for a hundred visions and revisions
Before the taking of a toast and tea.

In the room the women come and go
Talking of Michelangelo.

And indeed there will be time
To wonder, "Do I dare?" and, "Do I dare?"
Time to turn back and descend the stair,
With a bald spot in the middle of my hair—
[They will say: "How his hair is growing thin!"]
My morning coat, my collar mounting firmly to the chin,
My necktie rich and modest, but asserted by a simple pin—
[They will say: "But how his arms and legs are thin!"]
Do I dare
Disturb the universe?
In a minute there is time
For decisions and revisions which a minute will reverse.

For I have known them all already, known them all;
Have known the evenings, mornings, afternoons,

I have measured out my life with coffee spoons;
I know the voices dying with a dying fall
Beneath the music from a farther room.
  So how should I presume?

  And I have known the eyes already, known them all—
The eyes that fix you in a formulated phrase,
And when I am formulated, sprawling on a pin,
When I am pinned and wriggling on the wall,
Then how should I begin
To spit out all the butt-ends of my days and ways?
  And how should I presume?

  And I have known the arms already, known them all—
Arms that are braceleted and white and bare
[But in the lamplight, downed with light brown hair!]
Is it perfume from a dress
That makes me so digress?
Arms that lie along a table, or wrap about a shawl.
  And should I then presume?
  And how should I begin?

. . . .

Shall I say, I have gone at dusk through narrow streets
And watched the smoke that rises from the pipes
Of lonely men in shirt-sleeves, leaning out of windows? . . .

I should have been a pair of ragged claws
Scuttling across the floors of silent seas.

. . . .

And the afternoon, the evening, sleeps so peacefully!
Smoothed by long fingers,
Asleep . . . tired . . . or it malingers,
Stretched on the floor, here beside you and me.

Should I, after tea and cakes and ices,
Have the strength to force the moment to its crisis?
But though I have wept and fasted, wept and prayed,
Though I have seen my head (grown slightly bald) brought in upon a platter,
I am no prophet–and here's no great matter;
I have seen the moment of my greatness flicker,
And I have seen the eternal Footman hold my coat, and snicker,
And in short, I was afraid.

And would it have been worth it, after all,
After the cups, the marmalade, the tea,
Among the porcelain, among some talk of you and me,
Would it have been worth while,
To have bitten off the matter with a smile,
To have squeezed the universe into a ball
To roll it toward some overwhelming question,
To say: "I am Lazarus, come from the dead,
Come back to tell you all, I shall tell you all" —

Many young people, while in their youth, have a deep, abiding sense of being immortal. As time goes by, most of them lose that precious, insightful feeling. Do not grow up. Do not let them take that away from you. Do not age, by becoming full of worn-out conclusions about "death" and "dying." What the elders spoon-feed to you — along with ideologies about their superior religious structures and high-and-mighty country — may be a lot of contaminated rot.

Stay young. Be immortal. Do not lose that feeling of immortality. This does not mean that one is endorsing doing risky and potentially hazardous things; it does mean that one can be what one truly is. What one truly is may not be what one can merely "purchase or acquire." What one truly is may be what one was when one was very young, when everything was a treasure within the *here* and *now*.

from Ralph Waldo Emerson:

Each and All

Little thinks, in the field, yon red-cloaked clown,
Of thee, from the hill-top looking down;
And the heifer, that lows in the upland farm,
Far-heard, lows not thine ear to charm;
The sexton tolling the bell at noon,
Dreams not that great Napoleon
Stops his horse, and lists with delight,
Whilst his files sweep round yon Alpine height;
Nor knowest thou what argument
Thy life to thy neighbor's creed has lent:
All are needed by each one,
Nothing is fair or good alone.

I thought the sparrow's note from heaven,
Singing at dawn on the alder bough;
I brought him home in his nest at even;—
He sings the song, but it pleases not now;
For I did not bring home the river and sky;
He sang to my ear; they sang to my eye.

The delicate shells lay on the shore;
The bubbles of the latest wave
Fresh pearls to their enamel gave;
And the bellowing of the savage sea
Greeted their safe escape to me;
I wiped away the weeds and foam,
And fetched my sea-born treasures home;
But the poor, unsightly, noisome things
Had left their beauty on the shore
With the sun, and the sand, and the wild uproar.

The lover watched his graceful maid
As 'mid the virgin train she strayed,
Nor knew her beauty's best attire
Was woven still by the snow-white quire;
At last she came to his hermitage,
Like the bird from the woodlands to the cage,—
The gay enchantment was undone,
A gentle wife, but fairy none.

Then I said, "I covet Truth;
Beauty is unripe childhood's cheat,—
I leave it behind with the games of youth."
As I spoke, beneath my feet
The ground-pine curled its pretty wreath,
Running over the club-moss burrs;
I inhaled the violet's breath;
Around me stood the oaks and firs;
Pine cones and acorns lay on the ground;
Above me soared the eternal sky,
Full of light and deity;
Again I saw, again I heard,
The rolling river, the morning bird;—
Beauty through my senses stole,
    I yielded myself to the perfect whole.

Do not look to the future (i.e., to some future heaven) for eternity, as the elders have taught you to. Much of what they taught you may be folly. What you feel, intrinsically, in your youth, may be what truly exists as the way things are. The elders look for their heaven (i.e., their eternity) to be at a distance, in the future. Young children do not look for their immortality into the future; the immortality exists where they are now. The elders are corrupted by their own screens of perception; these screens are imbued with false distance and erroneous separation. He or she, who is wise, does not look with that contaminated sense of separation. No wonder that so many of the elders are corrupt; distance and separation are the essence of their limited frameworks. They don't mind exploiting "others," from whom they are separated, at a distance. Separation is their "essence," which they have learned. Is your "eternity" at a distance — with separation — from where you actually are now?

from Emily Dickinson:

OUR lives are Swiss, —
So still, so cool,
Till, some odd afternoon,
The Alps neglect their curtains,
And we look farther on.
Italy stands the other side,
While, like a guard between,
The solemn Alps,
The siren Alps,
Forever intervene!

It would be prudent to have a mind that naturally comes into realms of silence, at times, throughout the day. Otherwise, that *benediction of sacredness* may not ever visit one. That *benediction* will not likely ever come to what is merely saturated with limited, symbolic representations. What is limited, circumscribed by self-centered perspectives, and is crippled by its own indifference, is not ever likely to be visited by what is unlimited, compassionate, and boundless. Deep and profound order is not likely to be in communion with a disorder that reacts in very superficial ways. Therefore, it would be prudent to have a mind of silence, at times, throughout the day (and night). This silence allows the mind to be open. The mind cannot be open if it is prejudiced and full of demarcations involving limitation. The mind cannot be open if it is endlessly chattering with mere representational patterns.

from Emily Dickinson:

THE soul should always stand ajar,
  That if the heaven inquire,
He will not be obliged to wait,
  Or shy of troubling her.

Depart, before the host has slid,
    The bolt upon the door,
To seek for the accomplished guest,—
    Her visitor no more.

Chapter 7

It benefits the mind, oftentimes throughout the day, to look at things simply and directly, without a lot of complicated desires and wants. A mind that is full of innumerable desires and wants is a crippled mind, a broken mind. Only a mind of fragmentation, with a great deal of desires at a distance, is in a state of "unfulfillment." A brain that is riddled with many desires is, indeed, full of distance and space, space between what it wants and what it actually is. Such a mind must, by natural law, be distorted; because what is teaming with limited space, involving deficient gratification, must be what is intrinsically unhappy and incomplete.

We are not saying that it is wrong to have desires about graduating from nursing school, for example, so that one can help those that suffer with disease. That goal is a necessary reality in a world that has disease, pain, and suffering. That goal is not one of many superficial desires. However, to have many desires about impressing other people for social-popularity purposes, for example, may indeed be superficial and rather absurd. A mind that functions to help other life forms may not be having superfluous, superficial desires in that regard. However, a mind that exclusively functions for concentric, limited pleasures… may be like an ignorant dog that perpetually chases its own tail. Though people who do serious crimes should be incarcerated (to protect the public), those who never get caught have not, in reality, gotten away with anything. The criminal is the crime. The "hurter" is the "hurt." Sick minds intentionally (or unintentionally) hurt. No intelligent mind would want to be a cause for what hurt is. There is enough suffering in the world.

One can help in complicated affairs, such as in the medical or veterinary field, or in conservation or environmental endeavors, and yet still oftentimes have a simple mind that sees directly and holistically. If one cannot afford to pay for going through school to be a veterinarian, for example, that is fine too; one can do something simpler and, nevertheless, help others significantly and joyfully. A garbage collector can undoubtedly be someone who significantly helps others. A youthful minded garbage collector can do his job with a smile on his face; he may even help with innovative recycling endeavors if he is very lucky. To be a simple mind without many unnecessary, complicated desires may be a key to existing in harmony and joy. Real joy need not look far to be the essence of what it really is; it is what it is. To go a long distance to find joy may be a false and arduous journey. This is because the secret is that: there is no distance to joy. There is no road to joy. Neither is there a road to what is *sacred* and *immeasurable*. You can travel along a path (to get to a place, like Jerusalem, as Jesus did), but there is no path to joy and integrity.

from Emily Dickinson:

HOW happy is the little stone
That rambles in the road alone,
And does n't care about careers,
And exigencies never fears;
Whose coat of elemental brown
A passing universe put on;
And independent as the sun,
Associates or glows alone,
Fulfilling absolute decree
In casual simplicity.

We are not saying that one should not go out and enjoy things and marvel at the wonders of the world. It is just that one need not go very far. There are vast miracles all around one, not too far away. Even in an overcrowded town, one can see the sky, the bustle of the crowd, and the façade that each building and person have. Seeing a little bird on the wing may be what beauty is in abundance. It is good to be appreciative of the beauty of life and to have integrity, because that is the essence of what we have. A holistic mind that is of deep integrity is beautiful. That beauty is shared by all human beings. Such a mind is of all of humanity. Such a mind belongs to man; it is not separate from mankind. Such a mind is of *all men.* True beauty shares itself with all. True beauty has no crude boundaries and delineations separating itself from the whole. It is one with the whole.

Beauty is all around us. Unfortunately, few of us are truly appreciative of it. A mind without boundaries perceives the beauty that is vast and immeasurable. Such a mind is beyond depression. Depression exists in what is limiting, confined, and circumscribed. Beauty is an explosion of integrity, wisdom, compassion, and deep perception.

from John Keats:

A thing of beauty is a joy for ever:
Its loveliness increases; it will never
Pass into nothingness; but still will keep
A bower quiet for us, and a sleep
Full of sweet dreams, and health, and quiet breathing.
Therefore, on every morrow, are we wreathing
A flowery band to bind us to the earth,
Spite of despondence, of the inhuman dearth
Of noble natures, of the gloomy days,
Of all the unhealthy and o'er-darkened ways
Made for our searching: yes, in spite of all,
Some shape of beauty moves away the pall
From our dark spirits. Such the sun, the moon,
Trees old, and young, sprouting a shady boon
For simple sheep; and such are daffodils
With the green world they live in; and clear rills
That for themselves a cooling covert make
'Gainst the hot season; the mid-forest brake,
Rich with a sprinkling of fair musk-rose blooms:
And such too is the grandeur of the dooms
We have imagined for the mighty dead;
All lovely tales that we have heard or read:
An endless fountain of immortal drink,
Pouring unto us from the heaven's brink.

Nor do we merely feel these essences
For one short hour; no, even as the trees

That whisper round a temple become soon
Dear as the temple's self, so does the moon,
The passion poesy, glories infinite,
Haunt us till they become a cheering light
Unto our souls, and bound to us so fast
That, whether there be shine or gloom o'ercast,
Thcy always must be with us, or we die.

Even small animals have a profound sense of self-preservation and love of existence. Some people say that animals were placed on this earth for man to eat. If they were placed here for such a reason, why do they desperately flee like the dickens when they are hunted and pursued? In an overpopulated world, it takes ten times as much land to produce food for an average meat consumer compared to someone engaging in a vegetarian lifestyle. Deforestation and overpopulation are ruining our planet. Mass extinction of wildlife is the norm at this time. If we just roll our eyes and indifferently look the other way, we will all go down the toilet-bowl in a handbag.

The small is the large. If we unhesitatingly harm the small, or conveniently pay someone else to do it for us, we harm the immensity. (Sometimes the truth may be hard to swallow.)

from Ralph Waldo Emerson:

Forbearance

Hast thou named all the birds without a gun?
Loved the wood-rose, and left it on its stalk?
At rich men's tables eaten bread and pulse?
Unarmed, faced danger with a heart of trust?
And loved so well a high behavior,
In man or maid, that thou from speech refrained,
Nobility more nobly to repay?
O, be my friend, and teach me to be thine!

If we think that eternity is not what is occurring *here* and *now*, will we be forever fooling ourselves? If we think that wisdom within the universe is not what is holy, sacred, and majestically miraculous in the current time and place, are we sadly mistaken?

from Emily Dickinson:

Forever – is composed of Nows –
'Tis not a different time –
Except for Infiniteness –
And Latitude of Home –

From this – experienced Here –
Remove the Dates – to These –
Let Months dissolve in further Months –
And Years – exhale in Years –

Without Debate – or Pause –
Or Celebrated Days –
No different Our Years would be
From Anno Domini's –

I strongly suspect that the above poem is indicative of the fact that Emily recognized her "nows" as being precious, eternal, and of an immense holiness. She was truly blessed. She was eternally blessed. Are you?

If parts of the cosmos are cyclic, then there is a chance that you will always be reading this sentence here as you are now. There is a good chance that you will be eternally going from left to right (and back to left again) as you are reading these sentences. One can be forever disagreeing with what was written within these sentences. Seeing conceptually is not the same thing as perceiving with fluid insight, and it, likewise, is not the same as understanding beyond reactions and limited mental frameworks. Merely reading this book conceptually has little value. Sequential functioning in time can come up with all kinds of ways to exploit others, due to merely having conceptualized what this book presents.

A mind that merely functions as sequential shapes and patterns may delight in notions about its own eternity. However, a mind that merely functions as sequential patterns has not learned profoundly enough.

If the patterns of the particular universe that we live in were not created at any *beginning point* but, instead, existed always, then one cannot directly thank or blame that *sacred benediction* for the components of the universe's existence. (This does not mean that the *sacred* does not support the manifestation of life as it is, by the way.) If it (i.e., our universe) existed always, and was never created, then nothing fabricated it or initiated it. Its natural laws may have been eternally present; interestingly, similar (parallel) universes can also exist that, though different, have the same laws, only sequenced in different patterns. It is largely a roll of the cosmic dice, so to speak, as to what happens within our particular universe; it is essentially a roll of the dice regarding what happens in each of the other different (but not separate) universes, within the multiplex of universes. Whatever happens, natural laws are likely seldom interfered with by divine intervention, for to do so would be unnatural and abnormal. Each existence in life is precious and to ask for favoritism in regard to exclusively benefiting one, particular existence invites limited, reserved exclusion.

Although what is *sacred* did not create this universe, *it* (i.e., the *sacred*) still can exist (as *it* always has). The *sacred,* through love of the whole, allows the patterns of the multiverses to exist as they do. Although the sacred did not create this universe, its supreme order and infinite energy has always been used (and exploited) for this universe to exist as it does. The immeasurably deep order of the *infinite presence* is always being used by the patterns of all that is; the patterns of the cosmos aren't necessarily "living," but the *infinite* presence is. The natural patterns borrow the flow of life and movement from the *infinite presence* and, in doing so, they "take on" or assimilate infinity. What "uses" or "borrows from" the *supremely orderly* and *infinite* must, by natural law, have substantial order and *infinity* within it. The cosmos, as it exists, has sprung, and will always spring, from that vast, supreme order and infinite energy. What springs from order must, by natural law (due to its leaving), have some disorder within it. (It did not leave the supreme order, entirely, because that is impossible, and that is why it retains a vast degree of perfect order overall.) Interestingly, the *sacred whole's* timeless existence may not merely be a sequential cause-effect phenomenon, caught in a space-time continuum. What is truly *sacred* exists beyond time, beyond space, beyond all sequential patterns, and beyond the limited field of the known.

From Alfred Lord Tennyson:

Nothing Will Die

When will the stream be aweary of flowing
Under my eye?
When will the wind be aweary of blowing
Over the sky?
When will the clouds be aweary of fleeting?

When will the heart be aweary of beating?
And nature die?
Never, oh! never, nothing will die;
The stream flows,
The wind blows,
The cloud fleets,
The heart beats,
Nothing will die.
Nothing will die;
All things will change
Thro' eternity.
'Tis the world's winter;
Autumn and summer
Are gone long ago;
Earth is dry to the centre,
But spring, a new comer,
A spring rich and strange,
Shall make the winds blow
Round and round,
Thro' and thro',
Here and there,
Till the air
And the ground
Shall be fill'd with life anew.
The world was never made;
It will change, but it will not fade.
So let the wind range;
For even and morn
Ever will be
Thro' eternity.
Nothing was born;
Nothing will die;
All things will change.

The great Japanese poet-sage Issa (1763-1827) once wrote, "Never forget: we walk on hell, gazing at flowers." He also wrote, "Treated shabbily by fleas, by flies, day quits." Additionally, he wrote, "A poor quarter: flies, fleas, mosquitoes live forever."

(Now for a little story): Once upon a time, in a golden age, many years ago, there lived a mouse. He was a typical mouse and believed in heaven, as all typical mice typically do. His notions of heaven were, of course, that it was a place that had plenty of cheese. Naturally, this wee, tiny mouse was not a human being, and it should not ever be directly compared or associated with what a human being is. However, after further contemplation about it, one realizes that it is true that mice can be associated with human beings in a very big way. There is a definite connection between the two. Where one is, the other (similarly) goes. Such are the lives of mice and men.

from Emily Dickinson: (Single Hound Version, public domain, less expensive to self-publish version that suffices…)

PAPA above!
Regard a Mouse
O'erpowered by the Cat;
Reserve within thy kingdom
A "mansion" for the Rat!

Snug in seraphic cupboards
To nibble all the day,
While unsuspecting cycles
Wheel pompously away.

In actuality, men are far more dynamic than mice will ever be. I doubt that any mouse ever experienced nirvana and became enlightened. I must admit, though, that i really like the taste of cheese!

The following is a poem about Walt Whitman. It was published in 1897. Walt Whitman was not as popular, back then, as he should have been. Furthermore, Walt Whitman currently is not as popular as he ought to be. Hopefully, that will change.

To realize that we are all a part of each other is significant and important. To realize that we are all a part of the *eternal whole* is significant and important. To realize that everything we do may be recorded in eternity (and is repeated an eternal number of times) is significant and important.

We can be eternally kind-hearted and alive; or we can be eternally cold-hearted and rather dead. There is a strong possibility that *whatever we do, we do eternally*.

from Edwin Arlington Robinson:

Walt Whitman (a poem about Walt Whitman)

The master-songs are ended, and the man
That sang them is a name. And so is God
A name; and so is love, and life, and death,
And everything. But we, who are too blind
To read what we have written, or what faith
Has written for us, do not understand:
We only blink, and wonder.

Last night it was the song that was the man,
But now it is the man that is the song.
We do not hear him very much to-day:
His piercing and eternal cadence rings
Too pure for us—too powerfully pure,
Too lovingly triumphant, and too large;
But there are some that hear him, and they know
That he shall sing to-morrow for all men,
And that all time shall listen.

The master-songs are ended? Rather say
No songs are ended that are ever sung,
And that no names are dead names. When we write
Men's letters on proud marble or on sand,
We write them there forever.

I don't know about you, but i am in the mood for a little of old Walt.

from Walt Whitman:

I swear I will have each quality of my race in myself,
(Talk as you like, he only suits these States whose manners favor the audacity and sublime turbulence of the States.)

Underneath the lessons of things, spirits, Nature, governments, ownerships, I swear I perceive other lessons,
Underneath all to me is myself, to you yourself, (the same monotonous old song.)

O I see flashing that this America is only you and me,
Its power, weapons, testimony, are you and me,
Its crimes, lies, thefts, defections, are you and me,
Its Congress is you and me, the officers, capitols, armies, ships, are you and me,
Its endless gestations of new States are you and me,
The war, (that war so bloody and grim, the war I will henceforth forget), was you and me,
Natural and artificial are you and me,
Freedom, language, poems, employments, are you and me,
Past, present, future, are you and me.

I dare not shirk any part of myself,
Not any part of America good or bad,
Not to build for that which builds for mankind,
Not to balance ranks, complexions, creeds, and the sexes,
Not to justify science nor the march of equality,
Nor to feed the arrogant blood of the brawn belov'd of time.

I am for those that have never been master'd,
For men and women whose tempers have never been master'd,
For those whom laws, theories, conventions, can never master.

I am for those who walk abreast with the whole earth,
Who inaugurate one to inaugurate all.

I will not be outfaced by irrational things,
I will penetrate what it is in them that is sarcastic upon me,
I will make cities and civilizations defer to me,
This is what I have learnt from America—it is the amount, and it I teach again.

(Democracy, while weapons were everywhere aim'd at your breast,
I saw you serenely give birth to immortal children, saw in dreams your dilating form,
Saw you with spreading mantle covering the world.)

Sometime, when you get a chance, read Kurt Vonnegut, Jr.'s novel entitled *"Slauterhouse-Five"* (concerning what is said about the aliens on the plant Tralfamadore); the following is a little of what is said: "The most important thing I learned on Tralfamadore was that when a person dies he only appears to die. He is still very much alive in the past, so it is very silly for people to cry at his funeral. All moments, past, present and future, always have existed, always will exist. The Tralfamadorians can look at all the different moments just that way we can look at a stretch of the Rocky Mountains, for instance."

If you do not measure time, in the ways in which you were taught or had learned via experience, then there is no psychological problem or deep worries about ending or about coming to a conclusion. We learn linear time from elders who, themselves, have learned from others. To be truly spontaneous and young, one may best be free of conclusions and stored knowledge concerning time. Youth feels immortality because that feeling rings true.

The Oxford American Dictionary defines "allegory" as 'A story or description in which the characters and events symbolize some deeper underlying meaning.'

from Samuel Taylor Coleridge:

Time, Real and Imaginary — An Allegory—

On the wide level of a mountain's head,
(I knew not where, but 'twas some faery place)
Their pinions, ostrich-like, for sails out-spread,
Two lovely children run an endless race,
    A sister and a brother!
    This far outstripp'd the other;
   Yet ever runs she with reverted face,
   And looks and listens for the boy behind:
    For he, alas! is blind!
O'er rough and smooth with even step he passed,
And knows not whether he be first or last.

Though Emily Dickinson wrote a lot about "heaven after death" (which may or may not occur for us, up above), was she, in reality, wise enough to understand that what occurs during our life on earth is, in itself, eternal? May it be that the eternity on earth, *here and now*, that one can actually see (within a cyclic universe), is superior to an "abstract, promised heaven up above" that one cannot see?

from Emily Dickinson:

Which is best? Heaven –
Or only Heaven to come
With that old Codicil of Doubt?
I cannot help esteem
The "Bird within the Hand"
Superior to the one
The "Bush" may yield me
Or may not
Too late to choose again.

Many considered the Native American Indians, back when they were being slaughtered, as being inferior. Rationalizations brought many to categorically label them as being crude "savages." Perhaps many of them had profound, deep understanding concerning the nature of reality and existence. Unsurprisingly, a people that spends a great deal of time outdoors, living with nature and appreciating nature's treasures, must have a very high probability of perceiving the nature of reality with keen insight and an abundance of profundity.

The pain that these people suffered is similar to what occurred to the Jews during World War II. Do you have any reservation about saying that it is beneficial to appreciate them for what they were? They were an insightful, infinitely wise, noble family. We should be eternally grateful for them, as they were.

from a Navajo Native American Indian Song:

Song of the Earth

All is beautiful,
All is beautiful...All is beautiful, indeed.
Now the Mother Earth, and the Father Sky... Meeting, joining one another,
Helpmates ever, they.
All is beautiful... All is beautiful... All is beautiful, indeed.
Sisnajinni, Tsodsichl,
Meeting, joining one another,
Helpmates ever, they.
All is beautiful... All is beautiful... All is beautiful, indeed.
Now Doko-oslid and Depenitsa... Meeting, joining one another,
Helpmates ever, they.
All is beautiful... All is beautiful... All is beautiful, indeed.

And the night of darkness… And the dawn of light… Meeting, joining one another… Helpmates ever, they.
All is beautiful…All is beautiful… All is beautiful, indeed.
Now Hastyeyalli and Hastyehogan… Meeting, joining one another,
Helpmates ever, they.
All is beautiful… All is beautiful… All is beautiful, indeed.
And the white corn and the yellow corn… Meeting, joining one another,
Helpmates ever, they.
All is beautiful… All is beautiful… All is beautiful, indeed.
And the corn-pollen and the Ripener… Meeting, joining one another,
Helpmates ever, they.
All is beautiful… All is beautiful… All is beautiful, indeed.
Life-that-never-passeth,
Happiness-of-all-things… Meeting, joining one another,
Helpmates ever, they.
All is beautiful… All is beautiful… All is beautiful, indeed.
Now all is beautiful,
All is beautiful,
All is beautiful, indeed.

At one time, in the distant past, while working on a book that never became published —(because all the submissions regarding it were rejected by publishers), but which contributed greatly to the writing of this "self-published book" — i was searching for more poems that would be appropriate to utilize, regarding conveying insights concerning eternity regarding the present life on earth. During that time, for a very brief period, i started eating fish again. What happened was that i had gotten some "skin-problem issues," around my upper legs/thighs toward the groin area, and i thought that i needed better protein; that is why i began eating fish for a while. A couple of days after starting to eat fish, i discovered the following poem.

I soon ended eating fish (after reading the following poem); my thighs healed fine without fish being in my diet. (If you eliminate fish from your diet, as i did, please ensure that you take an essential fatty acid supplement daily; there are many convenient vegetarian types available.)

Regarding the following poem (and similar works), perhaps sometimes that *immensity* may act in impassioned ways, through the creative works of gifted writers/poets. I sure took the *bait*, back then, regarding the following poem's "luring" title! Brother! (This thing about fish seems to be pursuing me forever!)

from Archibald MacLeish:

THE SNOWFLAKE WHICH IS NOW AND HENCE FOREVER

Will it last? He says.
Is it a masterpiece?
Will generation after generation
Turn with reverence to the page?

Birdseye scholar of the frozen fish,
What would he make of the sole, clean, clear
Leap of the salmon that has disappeared?

To *be*, yes! — whether they like it or not!
But not to last when leap and water are forgotten,
A plank of standard pinkness in the dish.

They also live
Who swerve and vanish in the river.

If the entire universe repeats what it was before, in a perfect cyclic fashion with supreme order, will we forever be pondering the implications of being within it? Will we reflect on these eternal implications, not only by reflecting upon ourselves in psychological mirrors, but also by being more orderly ourselves (by caring better for mother earth and all her creatures)? If it is true that the consciousness of each person on earth is constituted of all that is eternally around it (which it, as consciousness, perceives and feels), then had we better start taking ever much better care of our precious surroundings?

from Walt Whitman:

Will the whole come back then?
Can each see signs of the best by a look in the looking-glass?
is there nothing greater or more?
Does all sit there with you, with the mystic unseen soul?
Strange and hard that paradox true I give,
Objects gross and the unseen soul are one.

It is a privilege to get old. I deeply wish that everyone could get old. I do not mean *old* in the sense of having a brain that is full of old, stale, and rather dead thoughts; i do not mean *old* by way of having a brain that is burdened with the antiquated past. I am referring to *old* in the chronological sense, wherein one's age entails many, many years. One can be old chronologically, yet have a mind that is fresh, young, and uncontaminated. So many of us try to avoid looking old externally. Internally, most of us are incredibly old: so full of dead, worn-out memories and second-hand opinions. Our old ideas, ingrained within by others, will forever fight about religion, nations, politics, and systems; we all think that our particular system is the best, be it of religion, government, politics, or whatever. We are all too willing to fight over our systems. So internally, we are full of what is *old*. However, we look to be (and appear to be) fresh on the outside, with artificially dyed hair and tucked-in skin. However, most of us only *appear* to be young. Most of us are contaminated with old, shoddy, worn-out ideas, unfortunately. To look at life afresh, each day, moment to moment, is to be *young*. Unfortunately, most of us look through the jaded screens of the past, and what we see is usually worn-out and stale.

from E. E. Cummings:

but the other
day i was passing a certain
gate,   rain
fell(as it will

in spring)
ropes
of silver gliding from sunny
thunder into freshness

as if god's flowers were
pulling upon bells of
gold   i looked
up

and
thought to myself   Death
and will You with
elaborate fingers possibly touch

the pink hollyhock existence whose
pansy eyes look from morning till
night into the street
unchangingly   the always

old lady sitting in her
gentle window like
a reminiscence
partaken

softly   at whose gate smile
always the chosen
flowers of reminding

What we do may be eternally significant. As we have suggested repeatedly, if we live in a cyclic portion of the cosmos, then whatever we do may recur repeatedly. You can always disagree with this; but that might not be the wisest thing to do, considering the circumstances. I didn't create this universe. It is highly likely that nobody (i.e., not even a higher deity) created the universe as it is. It may well have existed always. As it is, I happen to live here, and figuring it out may be beneficial. Additionally, discovering that the truly *sacred* exists may be immeasurably beneficial and profound.

It is my sincere feeling that that profundity must, in some way, affect us and help us. It will help us if we learn to open our eyes and act, not merely react. We must learn to go beyond limitation. Conflict is limitation, isn't it? If we live in separative countries with separative religions that are at each other's throats, then we may never really go beyond crude limitation. If we do not change, we may eternally find ourselves in a corruption and in a death that is unending.

The night before last, my wife told me of someone, whom we know, whose husband had left her (for the third or fourth time, or whatever) for another, much younger woman. The woman whom we know happens to be extremely sweet and is broken by all this. She and her so-called husband may be getting a divorce (if he doesn't bamboozle her further); probably the Whitman poem of "I Sit and Look Out" would mean little to him. The so-called husband told her that God forgave him for what he had done. Not to be judgmental, but is that likely so? Can any of us really "know" what the sacred does, as long as we are limited, fragmented, self-centered, and self-interested? There is a poem, by Ralph Waldo Emerson, entitled "The Past." That pretty much sums it up.

from Ralf Waldo Emerson:

The Past

The debt is paid,
The verdict said,
The Furies laid,
The plague is stayed,
All fortunes made;
Turn the key and bolt the door,
Sweet is death forevermore.

Nor haughty hope, nor swart chagrin,
Nor murdering hate, can enter in.
All is now secure and fast;
Not the gods can shake the Past;
Flies-to the adamantine door
Bolted down forevermore.
None can reenter there, -
No thief so politic,
No Satan with a royal trick
Steal in by window, chink or hole,
To bind or unbind, add what lacked
Insert a leaf, or forge a name,
New-face or finish what is packed,
Alter or mend eternal Fact.

If we continue to fight, in wars, and then (as a group of people) die in a massive war, will our legacy be to immerse ourselves within eternal combat, eternal hatred, and eternal, unending conflict? We might think that God is on "our side" and think that peace is just over the horizon. However, does God take sides in conflict and killing? Is war a real path to peace? So many of us have been conditioned into so many conflicting ways; we are immersed in heavy conditioning, and we are bred to support and nourish conflict. Mortal conflict and deadly physical competition (both being the same thing) is embedded in so many of our bones.

The song entitled "***23/24/11***," by Jon Anderson, is indicative of what war is and of what it does; listen to it sometime, please, when you get a chance.

from Wallace Stevens:

We live in a camp....Stanzas of final peace
Lie in the heart's residuum....Amen.
But would it be amen, in choirs, if once
In total war we died and after death
Returned, unable to die again, fated
To endure thereafter every mortal wound,
Beyond a second death, as evil's end?

It is only that we are able to die, to escape
The wounds. Yet to lie buried in evil earth,
If evil never ends, is to return
To evil after death, unable to die
Again and fated to endure beyond
Any mortal end. The chants of final peace
Lie in the heart's residuum.

How can
We chant if we live in evil and afterward
Lie harshly buried there?

If earth dissolves
Its evil after death, it dissolves it while
We live. Thence come the final chants, the chants
Of the brooder seeking the acutest end
Of speech: to pierce the heart's residuum
And there to find music for a single line,
Equal to memory, one line in which
The vital music formulates the words.

Behold the men in helmets borne on steel,
Discolored, how they are going to defeat.

You did not think that i would leave out, from this book of mystery poems, the king of all writers himself, did you? I could not omit the best master-writer of all time! I could not leave out the illustrious, great bard himself!

Ralph Waldo Emerson wrote the following words about the master-king of writers, who is known as William Shakespeare (and i quote):

"What point of morals, of manners, of economy, of philosophy, of religion, of taste, of the conduct of life, has he not settled? What mystery has he not signified his knowledge of? What office, or function, or district of man's work, has he not remembered? What king has he not taught state, as Talma taught Napoleon? What maiden has not found him finer than her delicacy? What lover has he not out-loved? What sage has he not outseen? What gentleman has he not instructed in the rudeness of his behavior?"

Would the mysteries that this book unravels, via poetry, be complete without William Shakespeare? "Of course not!" would be an appropriate answer!

If our universe really is cyclic, then could it be that there is nothing (pattern-wise) truly new, in terms of what people normally experience within (and "as") time? Therefore, if one is trying to invent something, may it be that when one actually does invent it, he or she is really discovering something that one had already discovered innumerable times during previous cycles?

Moreover, if one could mystically decipher the many multitudinous *cause and effect* relationships within a specific environment fully enough, could one then determine (within an old book of antiquity) who or what would be alive (or exist) years into the future?

If you — exactly as you are now — have read this multitudinous times before, will you be reading this multitudinous times in the future?

from William Shakespeare:

Sonnet LIX

If there be nothing new, but that which is

Hath been before, how are our brains beguiled,
Which, labouring for invention, bear amiss
The second burden of a former child!
O, that record could with a backward look,
Even of five hundred courses of the sun,
Show me your image in some antique book,
Since mind at first in character was done!
That I might see what the old world could say
To this composed wonder of your frame;
Whether we are mended, or whether better they,
Or whether revolution be the same.
O sure I am the wits of former days,
To subjects worse have given admiring praise.

Was William Shakespeare ignorant enough to allow death's scythe to cut him down and finish him once and for all? What do you (eternally) think? We think that the great pyramids are rather permanent and enduring. We also have thought that our life on earth is not very permanent and lasting. Not enough of us have considered that we may be in a cyclic portion of the cosmos, wherein everything that "is"… essentially *exists forever,* as it *always has*.

from William Shakespeare:

Sonnet CXXIII

No, Time, thou shalt not boast that I do change:
Thy pyramids built up with newer might
To me are nothing novel, nothing strange;
They are but dressings of a former sight.
Our dates are brief, and therefore we admire
What thou dost foist upon us that is old,
And rather make them born to our desire
Than think that we before have heard them told.
Thy registers and thee I both defy,
Not wondering at the present nor the past,
For thy records and what we see doth lie,
Made more or less by thy continual haste.
This I do vow and this shall ever be;
I will be true, despite thy scythe and thee.

Most of us have thought that summer lasts only for a very limited time. Most of us have thought that life (on earth) lasts only for a very limited time. Most of us think that, when death comes (as when the season of fall, as an ending of life, comes to destroy the flowers and greenery of summer), the splendid, unique, and exquisite blossoming (that we have briefly seen) fades away. Many of the very elderly might think, as summer (and as their life on earth) ends, that they (in the "fall" of their lives) may never see such unique and miraculous arrangements of foliage ever again.

from William Shakespeare:

Sonnet XVIII

Shall I compare thee to a summer's day?
Thou art more lovely and more temperate:
Rough winds do shake the darling buds of May,
And summer's lease hath all too short a date:
Sometime too hot the eye of heaven shines,
And often is his gold complexion dimm'd;
And every fair from fair sometime declines,
By chance or nature's changing course untrimm'd;
But thy eternal summer shall not fade
Nor lose possession of that fair thou owest;
Nor shall Death brag thou wander'st in his shade,
When in eternal lines to time thou growest:
So long as men can breathe or eyes can see,
So long lives this and this gives life to thee.

Is it, as some say, that all we are is dust in the wind? Is man and the bounty of life upon this planet just some transient, separated, passing, shadow-like affair that fades away into obscurity? Are we just an interlude, a momentary flicker in a fleet burst of time? Is everything that we've ever done, written, or said: destined to be lost forever in the murky void of nothingness and vacancy? Alternatively, is anything that we've ever written or loved… being written and loved for eternity?

from William Shakespeare:

Sonnet CXVI

Let me not to the marriage of true minds
Admit impediments. Love is not love
Which alters when it alteration finds,

Or bends with the remover to remove:
O no! it is an ever-fixed mark
That looks on tempests and is never shaken;
It is the star to every wandering bark,
Whose worth's unknown, although his height be taken.
Love's not Time's fool, though rosy lips and cheeks
Within his bending sickle's compass come:
Love alters not with his brief hours and weeks,
But bears it out even to the edge of doom.
If this be error and upon me proved,
I never writ, nor no man ever loved.

When Shakespeare put his immortal hand to paper, did he realize that his poetry would live on forever? If Shakespeare was sagacious enough to realize that his poems were immortal, did he also realize that whoever would be reading his poems would also be immortal? Is it a good thing, sometimes, that the "observer" is "the observed"? Please be sure to note, within the following poem, how Shakespeare wisely suggests that war is wasteful; and please be sure to note how Shakespeare additionally suggests that whoever reads the poem will be working against "death" (death being that which seems to be a terrible, annihilating ending) and against enmity… (enmity being "the hostility between enemies.")

from William Shakespeare:

Sonnet LV

Not marble, nor the gilded monuments
Of princes, shall outlive this powerful rhyme;
But you shall shine more bright in these contents
Than unswept stone besmear'd with sluttish time.
When wasteful war shall statues overturn,
And broils root out the work of masonry,
Nor Mars his sword nor war's quick fire shall burn
The living record of your memory.

'Gainst death and all-oblivious enmity
Shall you pace forth; your praise shall still find room
Even in the eyes of all posterity
That wear this world out to the ending doom.
So, till the judgment that yourself arise,
You live in this, and dwell in lover's eyes.

In the following poem, is Shakespeare asking one to rejuvenate oneself into what transcends mere self-indulgence, lust, gluttony, and avarice? Is Shakespeare stating that one can be filling one's mind with a gluttonous and insatiable quest for limited desires (and for his mere symbolic words now), but that one should soon be finished with them and eternally live without exclusive dependence on them? Can one use the words that Shakespeare has provided, and then grow in a warm, eternal summer that exists beyond limited desires, finite symbols, and fleeting messages?

from William Shakespeare:

Sonnet LVI

Sweet love, renew thy force; be it not said
Thy edge should blunter be than appetite,
Which but to-day by feeding is allay'd,
To-morrow sharpen'd in his former might:
So, love, be thou; although to-day thou fill
Thy hungry eyes even till they wink with fullness,
To-morrow see again, and do not kill
The spirit of love with a perpetual dullness.
Let this sad interim like the ocean be
Which parts the shore, where two contracted new
Come daily to the banks, that, when they see
Return of love, more blest may be the view;
Else call it winter, which being full of care
Makes summer's welcome thrice more wish'd, more rare.

In the following poem, is Shakespeare's verse barren of "new pride" because, in a cyclic universe, things that are occurring have occurred innumerable times (before) in the past? In a cyclic universe, are "new-found methods" not truly new (because they have been discovered innumerable times in the past, during previous cycles)? In the following poem, is Shakespeare's verse "still telling what is told" because, in a cyclic cosmos, it was told (by him) innumerable times before? Is Shakespeare always writing about the person whom he admires because, in a cyclic universe, he (Shakespeare) is always going through the same (repetitive) patterns of behavior? Additionally, is it interesting that in older editions of *The World Book Encyclopedia*, such as the 1934 edition, adjacent to the section about Shakespeare, which has illustrations of his place of birth and where he and his family are interred, there exists an article about the noted weed called the Shamrock?

from William Shakespeare:

Sonnet LXXVI

Why is my verse so barren of new pride,
So far from variation or quick change?
Why with the time do I not glance aside
To new-found methods and to compounds strange?
Why write I still all one, ever the same,
And keep invention in a noted weed,
That every word doth almost tell my name,
Showing their birth and where they did proceed?
O, know, sweet love, I always write of you,
And you and love are still my argument;
So all my best is dressing old words new,
Spending again what is already spent:
For as the sun is daily new and old,
So is my love still telling what is told.

In the following poem, by Stephen Crane, the "eternal clown" may actually be the *naked woman.* The "eternal clown" may be the *naked woman* because the "*observer*" is "*the observed*" (i.e., you are the images of what you see), and because, even though the comical dwarf is dead, she will (in a cyclic universe) be looking at his antics forever.

from Stephen Crane:

A naked woman and a dead dwarf;
Wealth and indifference.
Poor dwarf!
Reigning with foolish kings
And dying mid bells and wine
Ending with a desperate comic palaver
While before thee and after thee
Endures the eternal clown—
—The eternal clown—
A naked woman.

Interestingly, we all employ various tests throughout life. Interestingly, one definition of the word "test" is 'A means of determining the presence, quality, or truth of something.'

from Walt Whitman:

Tests

All submit to them where they sit, inner, secure, unapproachable to analysis in the soul,
Not traditions, not the outer authorities are the judges,
They are the judges of outer authorities and of all traditions,
They corroborate as they go only whatever corroborates themselves, and touches themselves;
For all that, they have it forever in themselves to corroborate far and near without one exception.

The following is a little premonition of the future, for all of you Once-lers who think that this book is a waste of time.

from Archibald MacLeish:

Excerpt from the poem "Seeing", entitled:

At the Saturday Club

Harlow: Our generation discovered the universe.

Robert: That's why we're lost.

Harlow: Men before us
thought in beginnings and ends, all of them.
Nobody knew that time is a circle,
that space is a circle, that space-time
closes the circle.

Robert: They weren't lost.

Harlow: They didn't know they were lost but they were:
they were wrong.

Robert: And we're right and we're lost.

Harlow: When you're right
you can't be lost: you know where you are.

Robert: You know where you are when you're lost.

Harlow: Where?

Robert: Lost.

From the Bible (Ecclesiastes 1:9-11):

The thing that hath been, it is that which shall be… and there is
no new thing under the sun. Is there anything whereof it may be said, "See,
this is new?" It hath been already of old time, which was before us. There is
no remembrance of former things.

from Walt Whitman:

Continuities

Nothing is ever really lost, or can be lost,
No birth, identity, form—no object of the world.
Nor life, nor force, nor any visible thing;
Appearance must not foil, nor shifted sphere confuse thy brain.
Ample are time and space—ample the fields of Nature.
The body, sluggish, aged, cold—the embers left from earlier fires,
The light in the eye grown dim, shall duly flame again;
The sun now low in the west rises for mornings and for noons continual;
To frozen clods ever the spring's invisible law returns,
With grass and flowers and summer fruits and corn.

Not long after the death of Jesus, there were many bibles and bible stories flourishing. During this time, different people had different bibles as their favorites. At first, during the time of Jesus, there was no such thing as organized "Christianity"; Jesus would praise those most who stood alone. Two major groups eventually formed: those who felt that God and Jesus could be found directly, without intermediaries, and those who believed that priests, temple leaders, and religious authorities were needed to guide them. (The second type of group was similar to what had existed before the time of Jesus.) At around the middle of the fourth century, the New Testament scriptures, as people know them at the time of this writing, began to be defined and collated. Around 367 AD, Bishop Athanasius of Alexandria assimilated a selection of writings — of what he considered the true contents of the bible to be — that were eventually approved by the Council of Hippo (393AD) and then by the Council of Carthage (397 AD). It (as can be seen) was the so-called religious *authorities* (i.e., priests and temple leaders) who did this "selecting" and, naturally, they would not choose gospels that advocated self-reliance and staying away from official, religious authoritarians. A lot of power, control, and money happened to be involved in the decision-making. These councils, with their bishops and their hierarchy, rejected and banned a good number of Jesus-oriented bibles. Those groups that held bibles that were different from the "selected bibles" were persecuted, banned, and terminated; also, their books were burned and destroyed. For centuries, these "selected bibles" were further "edited and adulterated," and many important and significant passages – presumably those which the Church saw as possibly undermining its authority or likely to cause dissension – were excluded or altered. (It should also be noted here that Jesus was crucified by the high priests, the leaders of organized religion in his home area, and by the leaders of Rome and their soldiers; he was not executed and spat upon because he highly endorsed their orthodox systems involving religious hierarchy and their traditional militaristic institutions.)

There were Greek fragments of *The Gospel of Thomas* found at Oxyrhynchus, Egypt, in ancient dump heaps; however, they were merely fragments, not a complete text of the gospel. The temple high priests, their cronies, and their submissive, orthodox followers, did a very thorough job of eradicating the "unapproved" bibles along with the "independent" people who appreciated them. Then, in 1945, while looking for fertilizer near the town of Nag Hammadi, an Egyptian farmer found a large collection of ancient, leather bound codices within a sealed, buried, earthenware jug; the earthenware jug, which was discovered in 1945, had a more complete version of *The Gospel of Thomas* within it. Currently, the Greek fragments and the Nag Hammadi Coptic translation are the only surviving exemplars of *The Gospel of Thomas*. There is a growing consensus among top biblical scholars that *The Gospel of Thomas* dates to the very beginnings of the Jesus era and may well have taken first form before any of the four traditional, canonical Gospels. Indeed, there is much evidence that some of the traditional gospels may have borrowed sayings from *The Gospel of Thomas* and then elaborated upon them, as they did with the Jesus sayings source called "Q" (i.e., Quelle, which means "source" in German). (Recent scholarly writings also suggest that *The Gospel of John* is largely an attempt at rebuttal against *The Gospel of Thomas.*) The sayings in *The Gospel of Thomas* allegedly consist of secret sayings, given to the disciples in private; these sayings were written from direct statements to them by Jesus (Yeshu'a). (*Yeshu'a* is the actual, original Aramaic name for Jesus; *Yeshu'a's* native language was Aramaic; but we'll, nevertheless, mostly write "Jesus" from now on for ease of understanding.)

Note the following passage from *The Gospel of Matthew*. Please be sure to note how Jesus (i.e., *Yeshu'a*) is telling the disciples that he has been telling them the hidden secrets of truth directly, but to the public, he talks in (ambiguous) parables (because they, at the time, are incapable of perceiving and understanding much of anything anyway). So to the disciples, in private, the secrets were told directly, but not to the disorderly, indifferent masses.

from Jesus:

Gospel of Matthew (13:10), Open English Bible

10Afterwards his disciples came to him, and said: "Why do
you speak to them in parables?"
11 "To you," answered Jesus, "the knowledge of the hidden truths
of the kingdom of heaven has been imparted, but not to
those. **12** For, to all who have, more will be given, and they will
have in abundance; but, from all who have nothing, even what
they have will be taken away. **13** That is why I speak to them in
parables, because, though they have eyes, they do not see, and
though they have ears, they do not hear or understand. **14** In them
is being fulfilled that prophecy of Isaiah which says —

'You will hear with your ears without ever understanding,
and, though you have eyes, you will see without ever perceiving,

15 for the mind of this nation has grown dense,
and their ears are dull of hearing, their eyes also have they closed;
Otherwise some day they might perceive with their eyes,
and with their ears they might hear,
and in their mind they might understand, and might turn — and I might heal them.'
16 But blessed are your eyes, for they see, and your ears, for
they hear; 17 for I tell you that many prophets and good people have longed for the sight of the things which you are seeing, yet never saw them, and to hear the things which you are hearing, yet never heard them.

Therefore, as you can see, Jesus is saying that he will provide "hidden" (secret) truths to the disciples, but not to the psychologically blind and callous masses of that time. (After Jesus's death, the majority of these "masses of people", by the way, primarily ended up following orthodox temple leaders, just as they have always done.) Perhaps the essence of those secrets, that Jesus told, lies hidden from people up until they are more fully revealed, such as in this particular book. Unlike those ignorant masses of people, during the time of Jesus, will your eyes be open (rather than closed)? *The Gospel of Thomas* was written from sayings of Jesus; Thomas (the twin) wrote the Gospel from what Jesus said. Though some of what we get from *The Gospel of Thomas* was probably distorted and altered over time, there is enough of the ripened crop of intelligence there to distinguish it from the false and twisted weeds that were planted there by others.

The Jesus of *The Gospel of Thomas* was fond of wisdom sayings; he stated things simply and directly. The Jesus of this gospel was not fond of blindly following orthodox, leader-oriented intermediaries; nor was he interested in a heaven apart from the "here" and "now."

from *The Gospel of Thomas*:

These are the secret sayings that the living Jesus spoke and Didymos Judas Thomas recorded.

1. And he said, "Whoever discovers the interpretation of these sayings will not taste death."

2. Jesus said, "Those who seek should not stop seeking until they find. When they find, they will be disturbed. When they are disturbed, they will marvel, and will rule over all."

3. Jesus said, "If your leaders say to you, 'Look, the (Father's) imperial rule (i.e., heaven) **is in the sky,' then the birds of the sky will precede you. If they say to you, 'It is in the sea,' then the fish will precede you. Rather, the (Father's) imperial rule is inside you and outside you. When you know yourselves, then you will be known, and you will understand that you are children of the living Father. But if you do not know yourselves, then you live in poverty, and you are the poverty."**

4. Jesus said, "The person old in days won't hesitate to ask a little child seven days old about the place of life, and that person will live. For many of the first will be last, and will become a single one."

5. Jesus said, "Know what is in front of your face, and what is hidden from you will be disclosed to you. For there is nothing hidden that won't be revealed."

In the preceding section, is Jesus saying that (after we die, we will become little children again, as we were in the past)? Will the last become first and, then, become a single phenomenon, as the preceding *Saying 4* alludes to? If we truly realize that we are the children of the "living Father," then are we eternally youthful? Did Jesus say that he would reveal something that few, if any, have ever considered before?

17. Jesus said, "I will give you what no eye has seen, what no ear has heard, what no hand has touched, what has not arisen in the human heart." (Per some translations, Jesus ends this saying with: **"I will give you… what has never occurred to the human mind.")**

In the following excerpts of the *The Gospel of Thomas,* is Jesus saying that the end and the beginning are "one and the same," just as the Diagram "C", within this book, presents the end and the beginning as being "one and the same"? Furthermore, concerning Diagram "C", is not Jesus alleged to have said that he is the alpha and the omega (i.e., the beginning and the end)? [Alpha (Α) and omega (Ω) are, respectively, the first and last letters of the classical Greek alphabet. Together, they are one.] If you are at the very end of your life, and if you truly realize that it is the beginning (as it was before), then you actually are at the beginning; then, the end and the beginning are "one and the same." As *Saying 19* alludes to: If, in a cyclic universe, you come into being in a life that you existed in multitudinous times before, and you realize that with keen insight, then you should be congratulated.

18. The disciples said to Jesus, "Tell us, how will our end come?"

Jesus said, "Have you found the beginning, then, that you are looking for the end? You see, the end will be where the beginning is. Congratulations to the one who stands at the beginning: that one will know the end and will not taste death."

19. Jesus said, "Congratulations to the one who came into being before coming into being. If you become my disciples and pay attention to my sayings, these stones will serve you (i.e., these stones will minister to you)**. For there are five trees in Paradise for you; they do not change, summer or winter, and their leaves do not fall. Whoever knows them will not taste death."**

It may be that five evergreen trees — in a cyclic, orderly universe — are ever green (and, therefore, forever green). In addition, in regard to the above *Saying #19*, if Jesus was around stones while preaching to the disciples — and if it is true that the "observer" is "the observed" — then does that explain why stones are "serving and ministering to the disciples"? (Incidentally, in *Saying #48,* of *The Gospel of Thomas,* similar to Stephen Crane's poem about the "perceiver" being "the perceived," with "marching mountains" occurring, Jesus states that the very wise will perceive "mountains moving.")

Did the youthful Jesus realize that being simple oftentimes, like newborns that do not fret and worry about innumerable things, may be a key to living in eternal bliss? Additionally, did Jesus perceive the unity of all life, such that each thing is a part of everything else? If you see that you are *one with everyone else*, will you put eyes in place of an eye, a hand in place of a hand, a foot in place of a foot and put empathy in place of a selfish, central, little "I"?

22. Jesus saw some babies nursing. He said to his disciples, "These nursing babies are like those who enter the (Father's) domain."

They said to him, "Then shall we enter the (Father's) domain as babies?"

Jesus said to them, "When you make the two into one, and when you make the inner like the outer and the outer like the inner, and the upper like the lower, and when you make male and female into a single one, so that the male will not be male nor the female be female, when you make eyes in place of an eye, a hand in place of a hand, a foot in place of a foot, an image in place of an image, then you will enter [the (Father's) domain]."

Ponder again about Diagram "A", within this book. The cyclic nature of the universe, depicted by Diagram "A", moves (and, at the same time, does not move). It moves, yet it remains at rest; consider this attentively when you read *Saying 50*. However, it is a fact that very young people feel the eternity within their essence without needing to refer to diagrams and explanatory examples.

Additionally, please ponder the fact that Jesus, in *Saying 49*, congratulates those who stand alone. Those who remain in groups, as those who belong to gangs, armies, organized religions, fancy political establishments, dictatorships, and similar separative, illusory institutions, he does not congratulate.

49. Jesus said, "Congratulations to those who are alone and chosen, for you will find the (Father's) domain. For you have come from it, and you will return there again."

50. Jesus said, "If they say to you, 'Where have you come from?' say to them, 'We have come from the light, from the place where the light came into being by itself, established [itself], and appeared in (i.e., to) **their image.' If they say to you, 'Is it you?' say, 'We are its children** (i.e., its youth), **and we are the chosen of the living Father.' If they ask you, 'What is the evidence of your Father in you?' say to them, 'It is motion and rest.'"**

51. His disciples said to him, "When will the rest for the dead take place, and when will the new world come?"

He said to them, "What you are looking forward to has come, but you don't know it." (Per some translations of Thomas, Jesus says, **"What you are looking forward to has come, but you do not recognize it.")**

Does Jesus, in the act of endorsing being like children (i.e., like youth) while also endorsing being of a movement that doesn't move (such as what Diagram "A" depicts), fit in with all of what we have been suggesting? Waiting until one dies to perceive God may be a big mistake if the only way to come upon God is while you are living. In a cyclic universe, if you wait until you are physically dead to find God, it may be too late.

59. Jesus said, "Look to the living one as long as you live, otherwise you might die and then try to see the living one, and you will be unable to see."

Why, currently, do so many people think that drinking alcohol is some kind of blessing?

28. Jesus said, "I took my stand in the midst of the world, and in flesh I appeared to them. I found them all drunk, and I did not find any of them thirsty. My soul ached for the children of humanity, because they are blind in their hearts and do not see, for they came into the world empty, and they also seek to depart from the world empty. But meanwhile they are drunk. When they shake off their wine, then they will change their ways."

Is the Jesus of *The Gospel of Thomas* a man of isolated parts, of separation, and of fragmentation, or is he a wise, holistic entity that perceives without mere separation and division?

61. Jesus said, "Two will recline on a couch; one will die, one will live."

Salome said, "Who are you mister? You have climbed onto my couch and eaten from my table as if you are from someone."

Jesus said to her, "I am the one who comes from what is whole. I was granted from the things of my Father."

"I am your disciple."

"For this reason I say, if one is (whole), one will be filled with light, but if one is divided, one will be filled with darkness."

62. Jesus said, "I disclose my mysteries to those [who are worthy] of [my] mysteries. Do not let your left hand know what your right hand is doing."

72. A [person said] to him, "Tell my brothers to divide my father's possessions with me."

He said to the person, "Mister, who made me a divider?"

He turned to his disciples and said to them, "I'm not a divider, am I?"

73. Jesus said, "The crop is huge but the workers are few, so beg the harvest boss to dispatch workers to the fields."

Did the clairvoyant Jesus realize that *The Gospel of Thomas* would be rejected before it ever actually was rejected? Did the same Jesus know that Peter would deny him three times?

66. Jesus said, "Show me the stone that the builders rejected: that is the keystone."

How could Jesus have known that he would be crucified and that Peter would deny him three times (before it ever happened) except for the fact that the universe is cyclic, and things that will happen are enfolded within what is always coming (and going to happen)? Could it be that Jesus was deeply in tune with what was omnipotent and omnipresent? Though most all of the patterns that our universe takes existed forever, would they not occur again for all of us if not for the living essence (i.e., life giving breath) of the *divine source/divine mind*?

77. Jesus said, "I am the light that is over all things. I am all: from me all came forth, and to me all attained. Split a piece of wood; I am there. Lift up the stone, and you will find me there."

(The slightly different Robert Grant and David Noel Freedman translation of Sayings # 77 is: Jesus said, "I am the light which is over everything. I am the All; from me the All has gone forth, and to me the All has returned. Split wood: I am there. Lift up the stone, and you will find me there.")

True bliss occurs when the brain is not merely measuring via the process of thought and thinking, as the following may indicate.

7. Jesus said, "The [Father's] imperial rule (i.e., heaven) **is like a woman who was carrying a [jar] full of meal. While she was walking along [a] distant road, the handle of the jar broke and the meal spilled behind her [along] the road. She didn't know it; she hadn't noticed a problem.** (i.e., She wasn't measuring things via the thought process… via the "stored known.") **When she reached her house, she put the jar down and discovered that it was empty."**

If the "perceiver" is "the perceived," and if a man thrusts his sword into a wall, destroying that wall, then is he, at that very precise moment, destroying himself?

98. Jesus said, "The Father's imperial rule is like a person who wanted to kill (i.e., destroy) **someone powerful. While still at home he drew his sword and thrust it into the wall to find out whether his hand would go in. Then he killed** (i.e., destroyed) **the powerful one."**

My slightly different translation of # 98 fits better with the aforementioned comment about the fact that the "perceiver" is "the perceived"; for when a man, who realizes that the "perceiver" is "the perceived," destroys a *limiting wall*, he destroys the limitation that "he is."

My translation:

98. Jesus said, "The Father's imperial rule is like a person who wanted to dismantle the powerful. While still at home he drew his sword and thrust it into the wall to find out whether his hand would go in. Then he dismantled (i.e., destroyed) **the powerful one."**

The "key" to understanding *Saying 98* lies in the phrase "While still at home" and the word "Then." "Then" can mean "at that exact time."

Did the clairvoyant Jesus perceive that, one day, the world would be dreadfully overpopulated? Did he realize that the women — at that time in the future — who did not bear children would be the wise ones and, therefore, the lucky ones?

79. A woman in the crowd said to him, "Lucky are the womb that bore you and the breasts that fed you."

He said to [her], "Lucky are those who have heard the word of the Father and have truly kept it. For there will be days when you will say, 'Lucky are the womb that has not conceived and the breasts that have not given milk.'"

Did the living Jesus realize that letting one's elders or one's old-fashioned "authorities" dictate what the truth is: may be a path leading to deception and deceit? Is it interesting that, during the time of Jesus, the strict, orthodox, temple-attending, so-called "normal," religious people — being ultra-conservative, religious fundamentalists with a pathological devotion to obeying hosts of manmade traditions, (while obeying authoritarian-high-priest-leaders) — were known as "Pharisees"? Even though the historical, youthful Jesus was a man of wholeness and unity, away from division, did he, nevertheless, not endorse the embracing of old falsities (and orthodox, intermediary leaders who propagated illusory methodologies) concerning what can be discovered as truth?

101. "Whoever does not hate [father] and mother as I do cannot be my [disciple], and whoever does [not] love [father and] mother as I do cannot be my [disciple]. For my mother [...], but my true [mother] gave me life."

102. Jesus said, "Damn the Pharisees! They are like a dog sleeping in the cattle manger *(such as in the feeding trough)*: **the dog neither eats nor [lets] the cattle eat."**

In *Saying #78,* which is not provided here, Yeshu'a asks his listeners why they have come out to the countryside (i.e., away from the large towns and their temples) to see him. He, around that point, asks them if they have come out to the countryside to see a weed shaken by the wind, to see a man dressed in soft clothes (just as their rulers and powerful bureaucrats are dressed). Then he goes on to say that they (the rulers and powerful ones) are dressed in soft (i.e., fancy) clothes, but they cannot understand the truth. In *Saying #108,* also not provided here, Yeshu'a states that whoever drinks from his mouth will become like him, and that the secret things will be revealed to that person. (If the cosmos is "all one," not really composed of separate parts, then, when you drink from a cup, your lips are Yeshu'a's lips; this does not, of course, mean that you can go around creating miracles like some kind of sunlight. It does, however, mean that you are a miracle, and that it would be prudent to function with less dark reaction and, instead, act with more dignity and brilliant, passionate order.)

Was Thomas, who deeply understood the limitation and mediocrity of thoughts and words, utterly intoxicated by the eternal fountain of youth that Jesus (*Yeshu'a*) lovingly provided?

13. (Excerpt) Thomas said to him, "Teacher, my mouth is utterly unable to say what you are like."

Jesus said, "I am not your teacher. Because you have drunk, you have become intoxicated from the bubbling spring that I have tended."

Each of us is tremendously important regarding changing things for the better on this planet. Even if you do not believe any of the cyclic oriented propositions within this book, at least (please) agree that what we do on earth is of profound significance. Some of us may fall; some of us may succumb to misfortune and not reach their goals. However, if we, as humanity, walk together, we will attain true order and true bliss as one family. Then, all of us attain those goals, as one, global family. That all-encompassing family includes (not excludes) all of nature. That is why we must end wars and become the true protectors of mother earth.

There is a possibility that whatever path you have taken to get here, to the reading of this book, was exactly the same path that you have taken repeatedly (in each cycle). That path, though involved in a larger, more encompassing order, most likely was a smaller path involving illusory distortion and an illusory lack of order. We, together, can change the path that we are upon; we, as a global family, can make it more of a fully orderly path and not a path involving a lot of destruction. To make that path more orderly, please do not merely sit around praying for things to get better. Get up, roll up your sleeves, and do something.

from T. S. Eliot:

Excerpt from Little Gidding, from the Four Quartets:

If you came this way,
Taking any route, starting from anywhere,
At any time or at any season,
It would always be the same: you would have to put off
Sense and notion. You are not here to verify,
Instruct yourself, or inform curiosity
Or carry report. You are here to kneel
Where prayer has been valid. And prayer is more
Than an order of words, the conscious occupation
Of the praying mind, or the sound of the voice praying.
And what the dead had no speech for, when living,
They can tell you, being dead: the communication
Of the dead is tongued with fire beyond the language of the living.
Here, the intersection of the timeless moment
Is England and nowhere. Never and always.

So, are you still horsing around as a mere mortal? Will you merely educate your children to become like the childish, fragmented, adulterated entities that run the world now, such as the bourgeois and upper class bureaucrats? Will you, if you are the ordinary mother of your child, easily disregard what this book propounds and easily continue to be thinking that you are indeed separate from the run-of-the-mill, indifferent, bourgeois authorities and stale, upper class bureaucrats that fabricated your thoughts over time?

from Wallace Stevens:

Questions are Remarks

In the weed of summer comes this green sprout why.
The sun aches and ails and then returns halloo
Upon the horizon amid adult enfantillages.

Its fire fails to pierce the vision that beholds it,
Fails to destroy the antique acceptances,
Except that the grandson sees it as it is,

Peter the voyant, who says, "Mother, what is that" –
The object that rises with so much rhetoric,
But not for him. His question is complete.

It is the question of what he is capable.
It is the extreme, the expert aetat. 2.
He will never ride the red horse she describes.

His question is complete because it contains
His utmost statement. It is his own array,
His own pageant and procession and display,

As far as nothingness permits… Hear him.
He does not say, "Mother, my mother, who are
you,"
The way the drowsy, infant, old men do.

I have always been a big fan of the rock group *Yes*, even way back in my college days, before i cared anything about wholeness, wisdom, sobriety, and truth. (Incidentally, I never communicated with *Yes's* lead singer Jon Anderson, except for applying for permission to use some of his lyrics; and that permission was requested to him and granted from him indirectly, via his Publicity Agent, Billy, at Glass Onyon PR. Thank you much, Billy!) I've always had an affinity for Jon's singing, and rightfully so. He is a man who can pull out true mystic lyrics from his hat as easily as most people pull out rather meaningless lyrics from theirs. I strongly suspect that Jon is a man of true peace with love for the whole of life. The following lyrics are from the song entitled *Open,* which Jon Anderson sings very youthfully, despite his elderly, physical-chronological age. Listen to the song sometime, when you get a chance; it is very beautiful. I discovered the following song lyrics while i was far into completing the last half of this book; the lyrics seem to fit in (here) rather nicely.

from Jon Anderson (rock singer):

OPEN

Forever taken to the place of understanding…
In reaching forward standing higher than the stars
Within without the framework of that simple meeting
To watch in wonderment, the meeting of all life...

Remember first to know you're spoken forever
As wisdom shines within your heart within your soul
Attracting everything around each for a reason
Forever taken to the place of understanding…

Sun is calling, sun it sings you
Sun is calling, sun it shines forever ever, ever, to be with you
Sun is calling, sun it sings you
Sun it shines, forever to be singing as it echoes you

Sound is the sound of the sky ever opening first to remember this

Dancing in the light forever firmament of realizing everything
Talk, talk forever to chase all forgiving to open releasing
Echo in the rhythm of the circle of the sign of how you're standing here

Touching forever the sky in your eyes… Love stay open closer now
To be standing *forever* to see the truth… Seeking outward opening
To be offering all that you are, you are, you are, you are

Please to remember *new words* offer *peace and light*
Be the *caretakers and guardians* of *mother earth*
Faster, true companion, faster than the eagle light

Please to remember that first and important song
Deep in your love of forever forgiven sing
Words are for forever… Opening my very soul
Reach fast told song… Talking out clear sound
Deeper for a reason… seeking asking, listening for the stories,
Reaching for the first song ever to be sung

Reach fast told song… (Over the stories of time)
Talking out clear sound… Deeper for a reason… (Over the stories of time)
Seeking, asking, listening for the stories, (reaching for light)
reaching for the first song…(Listening for) destiny calling.

Music is freedom forever receiving it, all that you are
Dancing in the light forever firmament of realizing everything
Sing to the sign of the earth, sing to the glory of life, sing to the sound of all time
Chasing the story to open the way… Sound out reason singing true

It will offer you all you are, you are… Sound out reason singing true
It will offer you all you are, you are

The seasons forever caressing
The seasons forever cascading

Make me to make me to know to remember that hope is for all,
that hope is for truth
Here in this world, *in this lifetime, forever is*
Open doors will open hearts
Open hearts will *always* open doors
Given this gift for the given for living
The life that you love, you'll love the life you live
Here in this place to remember forever
There is light!… There is light!

(Open doors)… Open doors will *always* open hearts
(Open hearts)… Open hearts will *always* open doors
(Open hearts)… Open hearts will *always* open doors,
Who better than who better than… Who better than love?
Who better than love?... Who better than love?… Who better than love?

Sun it shines… forever to be singing as it echoes you, as it echoes you
Sun is calling, sun it sings you
Sun it shines… forever to be singing as it echoes you

God given right to know… God given right to begin the chase forever found
This freedom hits your heart
This freedom to begin forever strong… forever take you to eternity

Knowing is "all is standing there"… Brighter than the sky you are
Quick to receive, quick to receive; In the rhythm, in the rhythm of the given chase
In the rhythm of the given chase, light enough to see
Be the morning bright… Be the gift of song

Be the everlasting song of life
In the presence of the presence of the given light… Take it out take it in

Be there the will to *be* so *free*… It is the only reason to live
It is the only reason for life… Shouting out this very reasoning
Sunlight evermore… (Dancing)… Dancing out all our lives to be clear
(Dancing)… Dancing out all our lives to be clear
(Dancing)… Better let your mind be *ever sure*
Better let your heart be *ever sure*… Be there the will to *be* so *free*

Knowing *all* is *love*… Knowing *all* is *love*…
Knowing *all* is your *true love*… (Know that- know that- know that)
Knowing that in truth our freedom sings
Knowing that in truth our freedom really sings
This God given right to know our wisdom… This God given right to sing of freedom… God given right….To sing of freedom
God given right… To sing of freedom
Sing of freedom's light… Sing of freedom's light
To sing the presence of the light…
Sun is calling to sing the *presence for forever*

There were song lyrics from many years ago, by *Yes*, which also would have been excellent here, (like the song, from the *Union* album, entitled

Shock to the System, or the song, from the *Close to the Edge* album, entitled *And You And I*). Additionally, song lyrics such as from *Pink Floyd's A Momentary Lapse of Reason* album, or from the second half of *Jethro Tull's Aqualung* album, or lyrics from *Living in the Past,* or *Thick as a Brick* would have been nice. Certain songs from some of *Rush's* albums, such as *Ceiling Unlimited* and *Out of the Cradle,* from the *Vapor Trails* album, and *Vital Signs,* from the *Moving Pictures* album, as well as various other lyrics (from a number of other well-known musicians) would have been nice. For example, in *Pink Floyd's A Momentary Lapse of Reason* album, within the instrumental entitled *Terminal Frost*, after about 4 minutes and 25 seconds into the piece, i clearly hear a man's voice saying, "One thing... one thing will bring me here, ever and ever again, ever again, ever again." The *Pink Floyd* songs, within *A Momentary Lapse of Reason*, entitled *A New Machine-Part 1* and *A New Machine-Part 2* ("I will always be you here"), are additionally relevant, as is the most important song entitled *On the Turning Away.* However, there is not enough space to include all these lyrics, by various musicians, here. Additionally, paying for publication permission for lyrics would be difficult (as it definitely has been for this retiree, regarding paying for permission for those poems not within the public domain). More lyrics would be too costly, most likely. (Jon did not charge for his! Thank you!) (By the way, this book is initially being released only in the U.S., because paying for worldwide permission for copyrighted poems is problematic for a retiree.)

The following song, by Jon Anderson, was pivotal for me, regarding completing the second half of my book (concerning "eternity") the way that i wanted to. I wrote my book halfway through and (then) was not sure if i should go on; i shelved the book for quite some time. I thought that the profundity of the book might be too much. I thought that maybe the world was not ready for such disclosures yet. I waited for some kind of sign or indication, from that *higher intelligence* (or from some orderly source), regarding whether or not i should finish the book (with all the understanding and all the miraculous poetry about eternity that i knew about). *The Living Tree* music album, including the song entitled *Morning Star,* within it, helped me to decide to go on with the completion of the book. Serendipity can be a beautiful thing. One day, previous to retiring from my job, while driving to work in the morning, (after hearing, in the news, about a young boy, Jamey R., a 14-year-old from Williamsville, NY, who committed suicide because of other kids teasing him too much about being gay), i thought of the following song. I thought about the song while looking at our sun (i.e, our morning star); then i decided to complete the book, going all the way. I cried a lot on the way to work that morning for Jamey, wishing i could have been there for him. Crap!

from Jon Anderson (rock singer):

Morning Star

Speak to feel the breath of ever life.

Where were you this morning, star… when I needed you the most?
Where's the answer?... through the door
Where are you "my future days," breaking all the rules of life?

Where are you "let truth be told,"… when I'm needing you the most?
(Come on the) "breaking all the rules"!

Stop that game of youth zooming out the door.
Sick and tired of this… Stop this getting old…

Where are you that "mystic voice," when I need the strength of truth?
There, the signs are getting strong…
What are we waiting for?… What are we waiting for?…

Catch that deeper spell… full of hope and life…
Stop them breeding hate… Let them see the light…

So all remember how the perfect day was ready… How millions changed the greeting of that perfect day… For all, the calling out, the steady dream implanted,
On days remembered, yet the path, it still remains…The path, it still remains…

Speak to feel the breath of ever life… ever life… ever life…
Ever life of love, too too, too… Ever life of love, too, too, too…Ever life of love too, too, too… Ever life of love …

And *the more we see* the *world* as *one*, *not fractured, but regained…*
(To the *question*, there's the *answer…* There is hope in every day.)
Be "the beacon to eternal youth"… be "the voice of all you see"…
Be "the answer to the question"… knowing this eternally:
We are tuned into the heavens… We the song and we the truth…
As the more resounding point of love is centered around you.
"The more," "the echo," "every song" is centered around you.

There you are, my "morning star"
When I needed you the most; there's the answer on the door
Here we are: "*our future selves*."
Take this space of truth in every life.
Take this space of truth in every life.

When i first heard the preceding song, i had a lot of pictures of dinosaurs on the door of my computer room, as well as a single picture of J. Krishnamurti upon it. Additionally, Krishnamurti's last book, *The Future is Now,* comes to mind; in the book, he briefly hints: "The future, the past, is *now.*" Let me briefly here, before we go on further, say a few things about J. Krishnamurti. Reading his books was, i feel, instrumental for me concerning attaining the enlightenment/nirvana experience that i had partaken in. His early works (from the late 1920s/early 1930s) mention a lot about "*the eternal Now*," but some of his later books make statements about there being no permanency; in actuality, all his works may be equally correct; things may recur eternally, but it isn't necessarily the same entity who lives through them each time. Actually, the living essence of each of us is different and truly "new" from moment to moment, in a most significant way, even though things happen repeatedly in exactly the same patterns. (If you wisely often live beyond mere patterns and experiences, you are eternally "*new*," which is an excellent way to be.) I still am fond of the wording of his early (1930s) talks, however, wherein he seemed more positive and youthful. (By the way, i did not read his earlier works, from the late 1920s and the early 1930s, nor that last book of his last talks, until i was much older, after i well understood all about the cyclic nature of existence.) As we previously hinted about, the book of his last talks, entitled *The Future is Now,* alludes to the cyclic nature of time; however, a number of his other books mostly do not do so (except for those earlier works, such as during the late 1920s and early 1930s, wherein he sometimes mentions "*the eternal Now.*")

The rose, for an infinitely long time, has stood for purity and beauty. With regard to Tarot Cards, the rose is a remarkable, poignant representation of the beauty that can blossom as affection within each of our hearts; it is additionally indicative of the beauty that we can be eternally appreciative of all around us. In regard to beauty, John Keats would, i feel, maintain that the *infinite reason* is the *Bright Star* that you can have or not have; it is up to you. The *Bright Star* is the beautiful reasoning that you can have or not have; it is up to you. Limited reasoning may be what you can darkly have; it may not be something that is up to you, as you are forever looking coldly down.

"I'll deck tradition's buttonhole, and give the rose to you."

from Archibald MacLeish:

The Infinite Reason

(1)
Rilke thought it was the human part
To translate planet into angel —
Bacteria of mortal heart

Fermenting, into something rich and strange,
The orchard at home, the sky above Toledo:
Sight into soul was what we lived to change.

The key, he told us, was the angel's need,
Not our necessity — and yet
No angel answered for *his* heart to feed.

(2)
The truth is nearer to the true than that.
The truth is, the necessity is ours.
Man is creature to whom meaning matters.

Until we read these faces, figures, flowers,
These shapes averted from us that all vanish,
Everything vanishes — a swarm of hours

Swirling about a bonfire that began
When? Why? To end where? And for what?

(3)
Miser of meanings in the stars, O man

Who finds the poem moonlight has forgotten!
Eternity is what our wanderers gather,
Image by image, out of time — the cut

Branch that flowers in the bowl. Our father,
Thou who ever shalt be, the poor body
Dying at every ditch hath borne Thee, Father.

(4)
Our human part is to redeem the god
Drowned in this time of space, this space
That time encloses.

From the Tyrrhenian flood

The floated marble, the cold human face!

from Emily Dickinson:

I keep my pledge.
I was not called —
Death did not notice me.
I bring my Rose.
I plight again,
By every sainted Bee —

By Daisy called from hillside —
by Bobolink from lane.
Blossom and I —
Her oath, and mine —
Will surely come again.

from T. S. Eliot:

Excerpt from Little Gidding, from the Four Quartets:

We shall not cease from exploration
And the end of all our exploring
Will be to arrive where we started
And know the place for the first time.
Through the unknown, remembered gate
When the last of earth left to discover
Is that which was the beginning;
At the source of the longest river
The voice of the hidden waterfall
And the children in the apple-tree
Not known, because not looked for
But heard, half-heard, in the stillness
Between two waves of the sea.
Quick now, here, now, always—
A condition of complete simplicity
(Costing not less than everything)
And all shall be well and
All manner of thing shall be well
When the tongues of flame are in-folded
Into the crowned knot of fire
And the fire and the rose are one.

At the time of the writing of this book, we think that we are modern and that we are advanced. Homo sapiens is only around 200,000 years old; we are just at the beginning. However, it is soon going to be an ending, if we do not "get our act together." Some texts maintain that man had reached behavioral modernity around 50,000 years ago. With all our separative, isolated, linear-oriented, small, self-oriented, limited minds, i do not feel we've reached behavioral modernity yet. We are still in the "crudely barbaric" stage. We need to change. Unfortunately, those that are psychologically old and stuck in their ways are not going to want to change. Cement too is inflexible and readily engulfs, dominates and destroys life, coincidentally.

We are, whether we like it or not, related to each other and connected (all humans, animals, and plants included). The left hand is not so very separate from the right hand, even though it may hate, despise, or think little of the right hand. We can go beyond superficial perspectives and superficial conflicts. This movement (i.e., myself) does not think that it has an independent soul, apart from the whole of life on earth. Only a psychologically isolated, cold, conditioned entity would think that it has a special, separate soul (apart from all others). We, all of us, have a universal soul. (That is why the lyrics to the song entitled *On the Turning Away* are so immensely important and significant; listen to these lyrics; they are crucial.) No one who is truly intelligent, young, and fresh ever thinks that they are separate from the dinosaurs, separate from the mammals, separate from the invertebrates, separate from the plants, or separate from the whole of life. Our blessing is that we can grow beyond what is merely a series of reactions. However, we can only do that if we remove the mask that separates and divides us from others. That mask is constituted of what we have learned. That mask is what was spoon-fed into us. Many of us wear it unhesitatingly. It is old, and it is shabby. No one who is young and fresh ever desires to lick the boots of old codgers who want us to fight against those whom they consider to be "separate, at a distance." (We can exchange our armies from country to country and then dissolve them forever, unless you want more spitting and crucifying.)

The eternal sacredness, that *true timelessness,* is not what thought or thinking can ever be. That *timelessness, the eternal sacredness,* only comes directly to those who are of true goodness and true silence. It comes to those that are truly still. True stillness, though, acts; it doesn't just carelessly sit around doing nothing. You can change. Be truly orderly, and sometime (in the future or whatever) the *timeless* may visit you. (Do not, however, just live for the future.)

We can go through life fearful, disturbed, unsure, confused, confined, broken, militaristic, subservient, and unceasingly greedy. Alternatively, we can live simply, with affection and heartfelt wisdom. We can sing and be the song; additionally, we can also be much more than the song. True religion may be beyond some concocted, structured rituals within some man-made, limited enclosure, with stone and mental fabrications forged by old middlemen. Moreover, if you would like to drink from that bubbling spring of eternal life, any good cup and healthy, quenching beverage (preferably non-alcoholic) will do. In the Gospel of Thomas, Jesus says something about coming to him because his yoke is easy and his lordship is gentle. (That is for sure!) Is it very possible — unlike what ordinary, traditional establishments have said — that the historical Jesus told us that the eternal is "now, in the present (with all things immeasurably as one)"? Did Jesus additionally tell us to be forever young and innocent, to go beyond crippling institutions and old-fashioned authorities, and to be whole and not fragmented?

from E. E. Cummings:

what freedom's not some under's mere above
but breathing yes which fear will never no?
measureless our pure living complete love
whose doom is beauty and its fate to grow

shall hate confound the wise?doubt blind the brave?
does mask wear face?have singings gone to say?
here youngest selves yet younger selves conceive
here's music's music and the day of day

are worlds collapsing?any was a glove
but i'm and you are actual either hand
is when for sale?forever is to give
and on forever's very now we stand

nor a first rose explodes but shall increase
whole truthful infinite immediate us

The End

****

—Addendum —

(The following are additional suggestions for further possible research regarding the contents of this book.)

1. The online music album, entitled *Open,* by *Jon Anderson; available at www.jonanderson.com*
2. The music album, entitled *The Living Tree* by *Jon Anderson*; available at amazon.com
3. Songs from the album entitled *A Momentary Lapse of Reason,* by *Pink Floyd.* [Especially the songs: *On the Turning Away, A New Machine (Part 1), Terminal Frost,* and *A New Machine (Part 2).*]
4. Certain songs from the rock group *Rush*, such as *Ceiling Unlimited* and *Out of the Cradle,* in the *Vapor Trails* album, and *Vital Signs,* in the *Moving Pictures* album.
5. Poems by Robert Graves, such as *Counting the Beats* and *Serpent's Tail*
6. The poem entitled *The Eternal Return,* by Robert Hillyer
7. The works by J. Krishnamurti (i.e., books and videos). Works from the early 1930's are more open about "the eternal Now." His last book of talks/discussions also alludes to it quite nicely; that book is entitled *The Future is Now;* in the book, K states that "All time is contained in *now,* at this second;" K further states, in it: "The future, the past, is *now.*"
8. *Leaves of Grass* by Walt Whitman. A great book to uplift one's spirit! (If you are a Muslim brother, please read *A Persian Lesson*, within *Leaves of Grass.* If you are a Christian brother, please read *To Him That Was Crucified.* If you are a brother from South America, please read *A Christmas Greeting,* and have a blessed holiday season each time it comes around! If you are from anywhere else in the world, read *Leaves;* it's about you!)
9. The book entitled *Knots,* by R.D. Laing
10. The later art work of M. C. Escher
11. The poem *We Have Been Here Before,* by Morris Bishop

12. Certain songs by the rock group *Yes*, such as *Shock to the System* (within the *Union* album), as well as *And You and I* (within the *Close to the Edge* album)
13. The novel *Slaughterhouse-Five,* by Kurt Vonnegut, Jr.
14. *Thus Spoke Zarathustra,* by Friedrich Nietzsche
15. *K-Pax*, the movie
16. *The Story of the Three Little Pigs* (wherein at least one of them lives happily ever after)
17. Poetry of Rumi, by Coleman Barks
18. *T. S. Eliot, The Complete Poems and Plays 1909-1950*
19. *E. E. Cummings Complete Poems 1904-1962*
20. *The Complete Poems of Emily Dickinson*
21. *The Collected Poems of Wallace Stevens* and *Wallace Stevens Opus Posthumous* (But do not read the poem entitled *Add This To Rhetoric* from the *Collected Poems* edition.)
22. *The Complete Poems of Stephen Crane*
23. *Archibald MacLeish Collected Poems 1917-1982*
24. *The Gospel of Thomas (Westar Institute, Polebridge Press)* and, additionally, the so-called regular *Bible*
25. The *Sonnets* of William Shakespeare
26. The music albums, entitled *Aqualung, Thick as a Brick,* and *Living in the Past,* by the rock group *Jethro Tull.* (The song *Wond'ring Again,* in the *Living in the Past* album, may be indicative of what will occur if we do not change our ways on this small planet.)
27. Any other poems/songs/lyrics that are relevant to this line of understanding or non-.
28. Different translations of the *Tao Te Ching* by Lao Tzu
29. The poem entitled *What are Years?* By Marianne Moore
30. The poem entitled *Sudden Light* by Dante Gabriel Rossetti
31. The poems entitled *Subject, Object, Sentence* and *One More New Botched Beginning* by Stephen Spender
32. Lyrics to the *Walt Disney* song entitled *Beauty and the Beast* from the *Disney* movie classic; (i.e., "Ever just the same… Ever a surprise… Ever as before… Ever just as sure… as the sun will rise…")
33. "Wholeness and the Implicate Order" by David Bohm.
34. *The Thunder, Perfect Mind,* from *The Nag Hammadi Library;* (substitute the word "messagers" for the word "angels" when you read it, however; and never stop respecting "the small", for it is "the large," as part of the living whole.)
35. *Plato's Republic* (*The Republic by Plato*)
36. Stanley Kubrick's movie entitled *A Clockwork Orange;* and *Music from the Soundtrack: Stanley Kubrick's "A Clockwork Orange"*

Therein: *"Find in cycle, wind in air, cast in our lures, wind in truth, love adventure, follow truth, and our lives are to feel you."*

37. The various translations of Issa's poetry.
38. *The Logical Song*, by *Supertramp*
39. (Oh, no! Not that rotten number 39 again! Well, forget the number; anyway, sometimes words, or numbers, can have two meanings.) *Stairway to Heaven* by *Led Zeppelin* (Gold is the eternal treasure… just as we have learned in the previous poem of Jean Le Roy.)
40. Please reconsider Shakespeare's Sonnet 94, where it may be explained that what blossoms in cool goodness remains best when it is steadfast and perpetually unchanging without a false mask of heeding to others while succumbing to their mediocrity. Also consider Sonnet 77, for how it may advise about perceiving without memory in order to enhance one's book.
41. The movie *Hugo.*

—Acknowledgements — and Highly Recommended Sources —

(Very Special Thanks to the following…)

For currently copyrighted T.S. Eliot poems: Excerpt from "Burnt Norton" Part I and V in FOUR QUARTETS by T.S. Eliot, copyright © 1936 by Harcourt, Inc. and renewed 1964 by T.S. Eliot, reprinted by permission of Houghton Mifflin Harcourt Publishing Company.
Excerpt from "Little Gidding" Part I and V in FOUR QUARTETS, copyright © 1942 by T.S. Eliot and renewed 1970 by Esme Valerie Eliot, reprinted by permission of Houghton Mifflin Harcourt Publishing Company.***

For currently copyrighted Wallace Stevens poems: "Extracts from Addresses to the Academy of Fine Ideas," Questions Are Remarks," Human Arrangement," from THE COLLECTED POEMS OF WALLACE STEVENS, by Wallace Stevens, copyright © 1954 by Wallace Stevens and renewed 1982 by Holly Stevens. Used by permission of Alfred A. Knopf, a division of Random House, Inc. For on-line information about other Random House, Inc. books and authors, see the Internet web site at http://www.randomhouse.com***

For currently copyrighted Emily Dickinson Poems: Reprinted by permission of the publishers and the Trustees of Amherst College from THE POEMS OF EMILY DICKINSON, Thomas H. Johnson, ed., Cambridge, Mass.: The Belknap Press of Harvard University Press, Copyright © 1951, 1955,1979, 1983 by the President and Fellows of Harvard College.***

For currently copyrighted Archibald MacLeish poems: "Eternity" "Lines for a Prologue" "The Snowflake which is Now and hence Forever" "The Infinite Reason" and "At the Saturday Club" from COLLECTED POEMS, 1917-1982 by Archibald MacLeish. Copyright © 1985 by the Estate of Archibald MacLeish. Used by permission of Houghton Mifflin Harcourt

Walt Whitman by Edwin Arlington Robinson; from: *The Children of the Night,* published in 1897 (source: poetry.poetryx.com/poems/9090/).***

Song of the Earth— Navajo Native American Indian Song; from *The Path on the Rainbow, an Anthology of Songs and Chants from the Indians of North America;* edited by George W. Cronyn; New York: Boni and Liveright, Inc. 1918.***

Shakespeare's Sonnets; from shakespeare.mit.edu/Poetry/. Thank you!***

For public domain poems of Emily Dickinson, Stephen Crane, and Wallace Stevens, E. E. Cummings, et al: books.google.com; www.fullbooks.com; en.wikisource.org; poemhunter.com; www.poetry-archive.com; www.archive.org; Libri Vox Recordings of the complete Public Domain Poems of Wallace Stevens at www.archive.org/details/poems-of-wallace-stevens-volume-1-add-librivox. Thank you!***

CPSIA information can be obtained at www.ICGtesting.com
Printed in the USA
LVOW052108270912

300665LV00001B/10/P